The Seduction of Christianity

BOOKS BY JILL SHANNON

A Prophetic Calendar: The Feasts of Israel

AVAILABLE FROM DESTINY IMAGE PUBLISHERS

The Seduction of Christianity

OVERCOMING THE
LUKEWARM SPIRIT OF THE CHURCH

Jill Shannon

DESTINY IMAGE® PUBLISHERS, INC.

P.O. Box 310, Shippensburg, PA 17257-0310

"Speaking to the Purposes of God for This Generation and for the Generations to Come."

This book and all other Destiny Image, Revival Press, MercyPlace, Fresh Bread, Destiny Image Fiction, and Treasure House books are available at Christian bookstores and distributors worldwide.

For a U.S. bookstore nearest you, call **1-800-722-6774.**

For more information on foreign distributors, call **717-532-3040.**

Reach us on the Internet: **www.destinyimage.com.**

Trade Paper ISBN 13: 978-0-7684-3259-6

Hardcover ISBN 978-0-7684-3462-0

Large Print ISBN 978-0-7684-3463-7

E-book ISBN 978-0-7684-9108-1

For Worldwide Distribution, Printed in the U.S.A.

1 2 3 4 5 6 7 8 9 10 11 / 13 12 11 10

Acknowledgments

I love my Abba in Heaven, the Lord Yeshua, and His Holy Spirit for pouring such treasures into me that they had to spill out onto these pages. Thank You, Lord, for staying close to me every day, until it was written. Your faithfulness blows my mind.

I thank my darling family for their love and constant generosity with my time: Dear Dror, my brother Larry, Raviv and Amber, Keren and Ariela. How blessed I am to have a family such as this!

I thank my dear sister, Cathy, for your tireless work in transcribing my teachings, editing this book so lovingly, and for supporting me in continual prayer and encouragement. You are the most loyal and generous person I know.

My thanks to Pastors John and Sandra Shantz, and Pastors Curt and Anita Malizzi: you have loved me unconditionally and have opened doors of utterance to me, without which this book would not have come to birth. You have been a safe haven for me during crushing times in my life. I love you all so much!

I thank my awesome sister Ronda Ranalli, who graciously opened a completely new path to me, which I could never have hoped or imagined.

You have released an ever-expanding cycle of blessings in my life, which continues to amaze me.

To my publishing family at Destiny Image: I cannot imagine the world of Christian publishing without your courage, vision, and integrity. I am so honored to be a part of you.

I bless Brian, Kathy, and Jeff Banashak and Kerry Dierking at Gazelle Press, for your friendship and professional support since *Coffee Talks* until today. You gave me a priceless beginning as a writer, and you continue to bless my ministry. May the Lord greatly increase your territory!

My profound thanks to my anointed brother, David Michael: I cannot express all that you have imparted to me, as well as being a personal blessing to me. I am particularly indebted to you for your tremendous revelations and insights that fueled the chapter on sexual brokenness. It would not exist without your broken heart of love and justice. I am honored to call you my friend.

I wish to thank the following teachers and ministries, who have brought me closer to the Lord's heart: Sadhu Sundar Selvaraj, Neville Johnson, Paul Keith Davis, Sid Roth, Steven Shelley, Steven Brooks, Mike Bickle, Nita Johnson, Lance Lambert, Choo Thomas, Dr. Bill Hamon, Robert Stearns, Rick Joyner, and Carol Levergood.

I honor the memory and Jewish heritage of my parents, Irv and Mitzi Sher, who gave me their very best.

Thank you, Lyn, for telling me about the Savior. I always wondered who He was, but you were the one who led me into His kingdom. May the Lord lavishly bless you and your family.

How can I thank my precious Yeshua? I am lovesick beyond words for this dearest, most beautiful Man, who has done more for me than could ever be written. I love You with all my heart, Lord! Thank You!

Endorsements

God has placed within Jill's heart a capacity to feel the Lord's passion and jealousy for His Bride. The cry for holiness and sanctification has never been more needed, and Jill's uncompromising message rings true to the core. Unmasking seductive trends in the Church, Jill's prophetic pen flows sharp and to the point, leaving the reader with fresh clarity and a true understanding of the value of a surrendered life. I heartily recommend this book as a spiritual catalyst for ministers, and as essential reading for all saints who thirst for truth.

—Steven Brooks
Moravian Falls, North Carolina

We are entering the final hours of this age, and our eyes will see all the end-time prophecies fulfilled in this generation. But the Bride of Yeshua has not made herself ready. Jill's book is a comprehensive biblical and prophetic equipping manual for the battle-ready company who will overcome!

—Sid Roth
Host, It's Supernatural! TV

Jill Shannon has written an eye-opening book to the true Church. She gives us a biblical view of what Jesus intended for His Church to be, but the majority of the Church has fallen below that standard. Read and discover how to ascend to the place you are to occupy as a member of Christ's own beloved Church. The truths found within are an extension of the heart of God to His Church. Everyone should read this book and be restored to his or her rightful place in Christ Jesus.

—Dr. Bill Hamon
Bishop of Christian International Ministries Network (CIMN)
Author of *Day of the Saints*, and many other major books

The Seduction of Christianity is the compressed and urgent "sound-the-alarm" training manual for the churched and the unchurched alike. Jill is even more vulnerable for the sake of God's flock in this, her third eye-opening book. As you read, the precious oil of preparedness will fill your lamp, and you will be ignited with the fire of holiness and intimacy with Yeshua needed to face your personal giants and the giants that are organizing on the horizon, as we see biblical prophecy being fulfilled. Keep your Bible close, and read this book again to find fresh revelation revealed to you in new ways!

—Cathy Minnick

Contents

Foreword

SINCE reading Jill Shannon's previous book *A Prophetic Calendar: The Feasts of Israel*, I clearly recognized in her a depth of understanding, intellectual foundation, and prophetic insight that is vital for the end-of-the-age Bride of Christ and the harvest of the ages. Once again Jill has incorporated all of these virtues in her latest book, *The Seduction of Christianity*, and has provided a valuable tool essential in this generation's preparation for its great confrontation with the armies of darkness.

This powerful and timely book formulates an introduction to one of the most important end-time mandates: the development and emergence of the Lord's Bride and mature sons and daughters of the Kingdom who become the habitation of God. If that is your desire, then this book will be like a biblical adventure to uncover vital secrets in God and a journey to discover depths of revelation that will satisfy your hungry heart.

The Bible is clear that there will be a victorious, overcoming army of God's people in this last generation, who exhibit the full appropriation of the Lord's provision of grace and favor purchased through His blood. They will be a company of saints who possess the Lord's nature and ability and have experienced the grace to overcome the spirit of this age and all opposition, in order to enter this place in God.

The book that you hold in your hand is like an equipping manual to help facilitate this reality. The admonition to overcome is more than just an encouragement; it is a command given to God's people, that they might share in the fruit and benefits promised to those who aspire to this reality and learn to appropriate this grace to our generation. Even so, few people have adequately articulated the practical means by which this can be accomplished through biblical directives and Spirit initiatives—until now. This book functions as a clarion call to awaken our generation to its place in destiny and the provisions set apart for us in this mandate. It also identifies counterfeit anointings, false revivals, and spiritual tares that function as stumbling blocks to our highest calling, and practical ways of dealing with them.

The evidence is abundant pointing to this as the end-time generation. Israel is in her homeland, and Jerusalem is back in the hands of the Jewish people. Political upheavals, military confrontations, and signs in the heavens all announce a decisive spiritual crossroad. Authentic prophetic voices like Jill's are emerging with messages of preparation and expectancy for the Lord's empowering presence. It is as though water is being poured upon spiritual seeds of destiny in order to make us a fruitful vine and true ambassadors of the Lord's Kingdom. Clearly all of Heaven is attentive to this present hour in human history. The Bible emphasizes that prior champions and overcomers of previous ages surround us and are awaiting our appropriation of God's promises so that they will be made perfect (see Heb. 11:39-40). This book provides crucial insights to help make that a reality.

History itself has so worked as to bring us to this place in God's plan, but unfortunately very few recognize it. Nevertheless, Jill Shannon highlights important Kingdom principles in this book that unravel the mystery of bridal intimacy and awaken the sleeping Bride to mobilize her into a place of power and authority. Jill's contributions in this book to help make us ready for the coming Bridegroom King are invaluable. Even so, Lord Jesus, come quickly.

Paul Keith Davis
Founder, WhiteDove Ministries

Part 1

Wisdom and Revelation

Chapter 1

Equipping the Overcoming Bride

Since completing *Coffee Talks With Messiah* in late 2006, I have filled many bottles of tears in Heaven. When they are finally poured out on the earth, I suppose they will water an orchard of late-ripening fruit.

Some of these tears flowed from my own weakness, pain, exhaustion, and fear of the future. Some were for the bloody atrocities committed by a nation that was founded on Judeo-Christian values, although these values were not held deeply enough to arouse our consciences. Some of my tears were for family members, who are in pain.

And a great number of these tears flowed simply because I am lovesick for my Lord Yeshua (Jesus). Although the Lord constantly makes Himself vulnerable and available to us by His sweet Spirit, I miss Him and need much more of Him than I have. I am so grateful for how much of Himself the Lord has allowed me to touch, and yet I am unsatisfied.

In this first chapter, I'm encapsulating the streams of truth presented in this book. In my spirit are related strands of teaching and revelation, which are interwoven to form a *manual of intense spiritual preparation*. This manifold exhortation will equip the true Church to overcome the rigorous hardships, battles, deceptions, and seductions that will assail her as we face the final hours of this age.

If the early apostles (that great cloud of witnesses) are looking down at many of our church services today, I fear they are cut to the heart to see the condition of the Church that they gave their lives to establish. What their eyes see is often an unrecognizable organization, devoid of the intense, daily expressions of brotherly love, sacrifices, and disciplines that they had practiced so fervently. In continual prayer, worship, fasting, humility, holiness, and preparing for persecution, they were living in a fundamentally different mind-set than that exhibited by much of the Western church today. There are exceptions to this generalization, which I note with love and gratitude. My observations are not judgmental, and they pertain to me as well; but sadly, they are accurate.

Although the Lord spoke these words to the first-century Church, I believe this loving warning is truer today than ever before:

> Remember the height from which you have fallen! Repent, and do the things you did at first. If you do not repent, I will come to you and remove your lampstand from its place (Revelation 2:5 NIV).

THE BIRTH PAINS HAVE BEGUN!

The Lord's people are not prepared for what is coming, nor are we prepared for *who* is coming. There are events foretold in the Word of God that will come upon the generation that sees the Lord's return. These warnings are often ignored, as if they have no bearing on our earthly day-to-day realities. We are spiritually unprepared for the prophesied earthly and governmental events that are even now upon us. Additionally, the Bible reveals to us some cataclysmic events in the heavens that will cause the earth to reel under their weightiness.

Although the Lord's warnings about these birth pains are clearly laid out, we often live in a state of spiritual hibernation. We survive the difficulties and pressures of daily life, and we start our rat race over again each day. I also know what this rat race feels like.

We need the bigger picture, which will help us to know how to prepare spiritually. Otherwise, we will be swept away with the enormity of it all. I'm not talking about storing food in the basement, although that can be helpful in certain situations. *I'm talking about the preparations of our spirits* so that our dim lamps will not flicker out when we find ourselves enveloped in gross darkness.

The changes that will usher in the end of this age are already upon us, and they will force us to confront such upheavals in our lives that it will stagger the mind of man. The Lord Yeshua gave us two signs of the end, which He connected to two signs from the old:

> *As it was in the days of Noah, so it will be at the coming of the Son of Man* (Matthew 24:37 NIV).

> *It was the same in the days of Lot....Remember Lot's wife! Whoever tries to keep his life will lose it, and whoever loses his life will preserve it* (Luke 17:28a, 32-33 NIV).

We would do well to study the conditions on the earth in the days of Noah and in the days of Lot. Since the Lord deliberately pointed out the parallels between their generations and the last generation that will see the coming of the Son of Man, we must understand the evil that reigned in their generations. Otherwise, the evil that overcame them and brought destruction from the Most High will overcome our generation as well. If we learn from what destroyed their generations, we will be warned, sober, and vigilant. And if so, *"this day will not overtake us as a thief"* (see 1 Thess. 5:4-5).

FALLEN!

Before the days of man on the earth, there was a high-ranking angelic being who fell from his lofty place, due to pride, rebellion, and self-exaltation. As a spirit being, his fall was comprehensive and permanent. There is no blood sacrifice available for spirit beings, and so when they fall, it is irrevocable (see Luke 10:18; Isa. 14:12).

After the Lord God created mankind in His beautiful image, this fallen angel devised a scheme to lure these innocent creatures into joining him in his rebellious and doomed condition. He wanted to hurt the Lord by legally separating Him from the children He had made for fellowship with Himself.

Before the enemy enticed them, Adam and Eve were walking in intimate communion with their Creator in the garden, enjoying childlike wonder and walking in implicit obedience. But the tempter's snare was too subtle and deceptive, and our first parents fell from such a height of purity. Within one generation, hatred and depravity had entered the earth, and innocent blood was already shed.

After the flood, Noah's children were given the chance to start over on a newly washed earth. They were blessed with the privilege of repopulating the earth with the seed of God-fearing obedience, which was exemplified in Enoch and perpetuated through his great-grandson Noah. But within a few generations, pride, violence, and depravity had again overrun the earth. Man had fallen from such a height, from the promise of a new beginning, once again.

When the fullness of time had come, the Lord sent His only Son whom He loved, to come to the earth and live a perfect life. He came as a humble Jewish man and showed us that it is absolutely possible to live in obedience to the Father. Then, although He had done no wrong, He was hated and put to death in an atrocious manner, nailed to a tree.

But His enemies did not understand that His perfect obedience granted Him authority to shed His blood on behalf of all the sins ever committed on the earth, both before and after His arrival into human history (see 1 Cor. 2:8). And so, through His voluntary death and His resurrection from the dead, redemption and atonement were accomplished. We were given a new start on the earth, which was freshly washed in the blood of the sacrificed Lamb of God.

The Holy Spirit was deposited in all who would receive this perfect Savior, and *a new spiritual seed was created, with which to repopulate the earth: the Seed of the Son of God* (see John 12:24; 1 John 3:1-2a; 9-10; Isa. 53:10b; Rom. 8:21). As seeds always reproduce their own kind, we were appointed to be transformed into the image of this righteous Son of Man, from one level of glory to the next (see 2 Cor. 3:18). He suffered and died to purchase for God a pure and spotless Bridal company.

But we too have fallen from our first love, our first zeal, from such a height of imputed innocence and righteousness! We have not walked as He walked or loved sacrificially as He loved. We have not consecrated ourselves, nor are we circumcised of heart and lips.

We say that we are crucified with Christ, but our daily choices and private thoughts do not conform to this theology. We have asserted our own rights and our own wills above the will of the Father. In many churches, we have received a weekly vaccine of predictable, undemanding, and passionless Christianity, devoid of fervent prayer, tears, repentance, holiness, and urgent warnings of what the Lord expects to find us doing when He comes. Thus, we are inoculated against radical commitment, preparation, and extreme humility, which are the mark of the disciple and the martyr for Messiah. We have polluted the temples of our bodies and souls with the filth of this world, and with the subtle lies of that hateful fallen angel.

Yet again, we have fallen from such a height. The Lord is calling His Bride to repent, lest He come and remove our lampstand from its place.

THE PRINCE OF MY DREAMS

The Lord Yeshua is a beautiful, creative, and faithful Man. He is more real and alive than anyone you could meet on this earth. Although He seems quite invisible, I have been astonished at how many ways He has proven to me that He is very real, more real than what I see. There is no one who will ever come close to His excellence of character, truthfulness, wisdom, patience, power, and authority over the affairs of the universe, and *most of all, His humble and respectful love for each one of us.*

If you have ever wished there was someone who could love you as you are, someone who would not find fault and condemn you, someone you are allowed to love with abandon and whom you can trust with the most vulnerable and wretched recesses of your heart: *this is the Man!* He is the One you have always dreamed of, since you were a hurting and lonely child.

You always wished there could be someone like Him, but for many of us, there didn't seem to be. Even if you were raised in church, you might not have been aware of His nearness or affection. And how you suffered privately.

And yet, He was there all along, but most of us didn't know it. I wish I could have known someone as kind and loving as Jesus when I was a confused, lonely child, surrounded by many of the comforts of life and yet filled with a sadness and shame I could never understand. No earthly parent, no husband or wife, no boyfriend or girlfriend, no lover or casual hookup could ever remotely bring you the fulfillment you will find in an intimate relationship with this Man. Everything in your life that is truly good is from Him. Everything in your life that is confused, addictive, stressful, or abusive is not from Him, but He wants to *become* the solution to all that plagues your life.

He is generous to a fault, lavish in His gestures of affection to us. I want to write about the wonders of the Lord's favor and how to receive it, His wisdom and the things that delight His heart. I can also testify to the endless streams of comfort with which He has comforted my chronically broken and lost heart. The Lord's compassions flow like a never-failing river and are renewed every morning. His streams of love never dry up, but you must recognize your thirst and drink from Him. I want to pour out treasures of Yeshua's wisdom and truth as fast as I can distribute them into your hands, dear reader—into your hearts, into your laps and measuring cups, into your breadbaskets where you derive spiritual nourishment. *And I am required to warn you of how little time we have to get ready.*

The reason that there are so many strands of truth I must weave together is because of the manifold wisdom of God. I have always wondered what this word *manifold* meant. Paul writes to the Ephesians,

> *To me, who am less than the least of all the saints, this grace was given, that I should preach among the Gentiles the unsearchable riches of Christ...to the intent **that now the manifold wisdom of God might be made known by the church to the principalities and powers in the heavenly places*** (Ephesians 3:8-10).

The riches of Messiah are unsearchable; His wisdom is manifold. The dictionary defines *manifold* as "many and various, branching into several openings, diverse, varied and multiple."[1] Here are some of the attributes that will help us to mature into the fullness of Messiah's stature:

+ Consecration, transparency, and purity of motives;

+ Humility and meekness;

+ Willingness to allow the Lord to uproot soulish strongholds from our hearts;

+ The ability to overcome in our suffering;

+ Discerning what is true worship, which pleases the Father;

+ Discerning what the Lord considers to be "strange fire," that which is unacceptable worship to Him;

- Compassion for the lost and disenfranchised people groups;

- Preparation to resist the onslaught of seduction which will come upon the Lord's devoted servants;

- Distinguishing the marks of true and false revival;

- Agreeing with the righteous judgments of the Lord, which we must not dread;

- Embracing and reciprocating the Lord's jealous love for you personally.

A HIGH PRIEST WHO SYMPATHIZES

The issue of human suffering and the Lord's response to it is so critical that it will be covered in its own chapter. The Father and the Lord Yeshua feel pain when His people suffer. He cares deeply when people abuse us and when the pressures of this world overwhelm us with sorrow, fear, and stress. He watches with empathy when our painful and chronic illnesses and infirmities are not healed, and He patiently endures our agonized query: *"Couldn't You just heal me?"*

> *For we do not have a High Priest who cannot sympathize with our weaknesses, but was in all points tempted as we are, yet without sin. Let us therefore come boldly to the throne of grace, that we may obtain mercy and find grace to help in time of need* (Hebrews 4:15-16).

As a person with a long history of health problems, I have wrestled mightily with this issue. I wasted untold years imagining the Lord to be cold and indifferent to my suffering. (Though in reality, I suffered only light afflictions.)

"Since the Lord can do anything He wants," I reasoned, "He could have healed me by now if He cared about how hard it is for me to function, feeling this way."

I have finally learned late in life, that there were reasons for my lack of healing. I do not know all the reasons why I was not healed, but some problems were of my own making. *Many* were the enemy's incitement against me, and I did not know how to contend for my healing. Other problems were permitted by God to remain for His own purposes in preparing me for my destiny. I can now testify that I am generally in better health now than I was in young adulthood. The Lord has healed the vast majority of my physical afflictions as He has progressively healed my heart. I still have a few thorns in my flesh, and I will continue to petition the Lord to heal me.

I owe a debt of gratitude to one of the great cloud of witnesses, our brother Job, who suffered such extreme affliction that he despaired of life and could have wished he had never been born. This godly man had not seen behind the scenes, where the vile accuser of the brethren incited Job's loving Father to permit a torrent of torment to be unleashed on his unsuspecting soul. I weep each time I read Job's arguments with his Maker, as I can so relate to his questions and reasoning. We will deeply pursue this painful topic more thoroughly in our third chapter.

A JEALOUS GOD

One of the biblical characteristics of God that is difficult for many Christians to fathom, let alone embrace, is the Lord's jealousy. I have heard people say that they could never serve a God who was so controlling that He would exhibit the ugly trait of jealousy. In making this statement, they are revealing that they don't understand this trait accurately, as it exists in the Lord's heart. They have likely experienced the twisted, demonic version of jealousy in a spouse or friend who was angry or even violent, distrustful, controlling, and a frightening person to endure.

But when this attribute is seen accurately in the heart of the Creator, it becomes something intimate and sacred between an adoring husband and his beloved wife. The jealousy of God has become to me one of the most precious aspects of my relationship with Him. It makes me feel the secret delight of one who is fiercely desired and passionately loved by the kindest and most worthy of men.

> *Do not worship any other god, for the Lord, whose name is Jealous, is a jealous God. For the Lord your God is a consuming fire, a jealous God* (Exodus 34:14, Deuteronomy 4:24 NIV).

What should it mean to us that our Lord is a jealous Husband, a burning flame of jealous love toward His people? There is One who made us, and *we were designed for love* and to be loved. We were created for the express purpose of being united with our Lord in an intimate relationship, which He likens to a husband and wife.

Therefore, our Lover feels grieved and rejected when His Bride prostitutes herself with the world and its counterfeit pleasures and idolatrous systems. We see throughout the Bible that the Lord suffers terrible rejection at the hands of His own people, both Israel and the Church, as they have provoked Him to jealousy by their unfaithfulness (see Ezek. 16:15-19; James 4:4-5; 1 Cor. 10:22).

It is natural that those who are not in a covenant relationship with God will run after other beliefs and other objects of affection. But from His own covenant people, *the Lord has every right to demand wholehearted and unadulterated devotion.* I wouldn't want to be married to a God who didn't care if I flirted with other demonic religions or sacrificed my time, money, or affection to the idols of this evil and corrupted world.

We Are Not Prepared

One of the predominant themes in the Bible is the need for people to repent of their sins and to be reconciled to God before the great and terrible Day of the Lord. The prophets of the Old Testament cried out incessantly for repentance from the hearts of Israel. They prophesied that in the fullness of time, God would send a Jewish redeemer to the earth, who would offer forgiveness and atonement to Israel, as well as to the gentile nations (see Isa. 53:4-6; 9:6-7; Mic. 5:2; Zech. 12:10; Job 19:25).

A descendant of King David of the tribe of Judah, the Lord Jesus was born in Bethlehem of a virgin, having been sent from Heaven by His Father to grow to maturity as a sinless man. He would then voluntarily offer His life as a ransom for many. For the full plan of salvation, see the final section, "Receiving Eternal Salvation."

The Lord's death on the cross purchased eternal life for all people who have ever lived, for those who receive His sacrifice and yield to His complete Lordship over their lives (see Matt. 20:28; Heb. 9:11-15). The Lord expects His covenant people to be found walking in purity and obedience when He returns for His Bride (see Rev. 19:7-8; Matt. 7:22-23). He warned us,

> *Be ready, for the Son of Man is coming at an hour you do not expect....Blessed is that servant whom his master will find so doing when he comes* (Luke 12:40,43).

Because salvation is an undeserved free gift, many believers assume that they are automatically prepared for that moment when the Lord will descend from Heaven to receive His Bride from the earth. Paul tells us,

> *For the Lord Himself will descend from heaven with a shout, with the voice of an archangel, and with the trumpet of God. And the dead in Christ will rise first. Then we who are alive and remain shall be caught up together with them in the clouds*

to meet the Lord in the air. And thus we shall always be with the Lord (1 Thessalonians 4:16-17).

Some also assume that this great catching up will offer an early escape from the earthly upheavals and persecutions which will occur during the *"birth pains"* leading up to the Lord's return (see Matt. 24:7-13).

These two assumptions can lull professing Christians into complacency and can leave us unprepared for what the Bible calls *"the great and terrible Day of the Lord."* The Bible teaches that it is not only the unbelievers who need to repent before the Lord. The Lord warns us that His Church must repent to become the pure Bride who has *"made herself ready"* for her Bridegroom's soon return (see Rev. 2:5,16, 20-21; 3:3,19; James 4:2-4;8-10; Dan. 9:3-19).

Throughout this book, we will examine the Lord's high standards and requirements for His overcoming Bride, so that none of us will be unprepared. The small bit of time we have left is a precious gift to us. It means we can be roused from our stupor and stir our hearts to pray and prepare ourselves, so that this day will not close upon us like a trap (see Matt. 24:9-31; 25:1-13; Luke 21:25-28;34-36).

Our Lord is a man of infinite grace and compassion. His heart overflows with mercy toward all who appropriate His atoning work on the cross, through repentance and faith. Because He is forgiving and patient with our failings, *many assume that when they face this same Jesus on His throne of judgment, they will experience the same gracious forbearance they have come to expect from Him.*

I fear this will not be the case, my brothers and sisters. Some Christians have casually presumed upon His grace, and have continued to live a compromised or sinful lifestyle. Because of the Lord's patience and goodness, they have assumed that He approved of their lives. But there will come a terrible and irrevocable moment when the Lord Yeshua will be manifested as the Righteous Judge. And this Judge will do what His Father requires of

Him: to render judgment upon the lives, words, and hearts of all men, and to determine the eternal status of each soul who has ever lived (see Matt. 16:27).

Beloved, I sense that our gentle Savior dreads that terrible day. He knows that on that day, He will be compelled by the Spirit of Righteous Judgment to utter the most indelible words to those He loves with an undying love. The Lord Jesus knows that He will pronounce these eternal, bottomless words to an untold number of beloved people for whom He suffered and died in abandonment and humiliation. Many of those who hear these terrifying words will be professing Christians, who are caught ignorant and unaware of their own hypocrisy. On that day it will be too late to change the way they lived their lives on earth. But we can still examine our hearts now!

One of the Lord's most urgent purposes for the writing of this book is to bluntly warn the reader of how high and how exacting His standards will be for His Church on that day.

The Door of My Bride

Behold, I stand at the door and knock. If anyone hears My voice and opens the door, I will come in to him and dine with him, and he with Me (Revelation 3:20).

When the Lord says that He is knocking on the door, many assume this refers to the hearts of unbelievers needing salvation. However, the Lord spoke this word not to the unsaved, but to His Church. We find these words in the seventh letter to the seventh church, which was the Laodicean church. On one level, all seven letters in Revelation pertain to all believers throughout the ages. However, on the prophetic level, these seven letters can also be viewed as messages from the Lord to seven consecutive church ages, which have occurred from the day of Pentecost until the present generation.

THE SEDUCTION OF CHRISTIANITY

It is interesting to note that the commendations and warnings in each of the seven letters have particular relevance to each period in church history to which some scholars believe they are referring.[2]

Of particular interest to our generation, this seventh letter was written to the Laodicean church, whose description closely matches the final church age we are currently experiencing. The Lord Yeshua is addressing a lukewarm, blind, wretched, naked church, which He will spit out of His mouth if she remains in her present condition (see Rev. 3:16-17).

It is to this church that the Lord says, *"I stand at the door and knock. If anyone hears My voice and opens the door, I will come in to him and dine with him, and he with Me"* (Rev. 3:20). In making this statement, the Lord may actually be referring to the ancient Jewish customs of betrothal and marriage.[3] I will summarize this elaborate marriage protocol, as it relates to the Lord's desire to take a pure and spotless Bride for Himself.

When a young Israelite couple wished to become engaged, their fathers would make an appointment for a formal meeting of the two families at the house of the prospective bride. This meeting was a legal ceremony that included a sumptuous meal and the drinking of four ceremonial cups of wine. Each cup symbolized a particular stage of commitment and intimacy, leading up to the completion of their union at the time of the wedding. Part of this meal included the signing of a formal covenant.

On the day of the meeting, the groom and his father would arrive at the house of the bride's family and would knock on the door and announce their presence. If the bride recognized the voice of the groom and wished to accept this betrothal, she would open the door so that he could come in and dine with her. Opening the door was the language of saying "yes" to the engagement. If she or her parents had changed their minds and did not wish to enter into this betrothal process, she would simply not answer his knock on the door. Once they came in and began drinking the first three cups of wine, the commitment became more and more binding. Therefore, if she had changed her mind, it was better not to receive them into this formal meal.

After a reasonable period, the groom and his father would realize that this girl no longer wished to become engaged, or to enter into the covenants of this ceremony. Sadly, they would depart from her house.

When the Lord tells His last-days' Church that He is standing at the door and knocking, He is showing Himself to be a Bridegroom in love, desiring to enter the intense covenants of betrothal. His Father is with Him, waiting to enter the house of His prospective Bride. He stands outside of a complacent Church who is not passionately committed to this betrothal and who has not opened the door of intimacy to this Man. She thinks she is rich and well-clothed, and has need of nothing. She feels content and satisfied, and does not realize she is blind and naked and needy.

The Lord Jesus, who loved and died for this Bride with all His heart, soul, and strength, cannot marry someone in this self-satisfied and passionless state. He deserves a Bride who will drink with Him all four stages of the covenant: Servanthood, Friendship, Inheritance, and finally, Union.

If she opened the door, after the formal betrothal ceremony, the bridegroom would depart to his father's house for many months to build an addition or apartment for his new bride to live with him. It could take up to a year to complete this preparation.

When the work on the home was finished, he would ask his father to inspect the premises. The father would then determine that his son had built a worthy and pleasant home for his new bride to dwell, and he would declare that his son was ready to travel to his bride's hometown or country and bring her back in marriage. It is the Father who determines when the Son should return for His Bride.

When the marriage was consummated, the bride and groom would smash the empty glass under their feet. To this day, a Jewish bride and groom perform the glass-breaking ceremony as soon as they are declared man and wife. This glass was the fourth cup of wine, the cup of union and consummation. No one could ever drink from that cup again, for it was theirs and theirs alone. Remember that at the Last Supper, the Lord said that He would not drink from this cup (the final, fourth cup in the Passover ceremony) until He would drink it anew with His Bride in His Kingdom. He is waiting for that cup until the joyful consummation, which He eagerly desires to share with us at the wedding supper of the Lamb.

Our Bridegroom is offering to come in to dine with His beloved, but we must recognize His voice and open the door. We must drink the cup of covenant and radical, lovesick commitment. If we will not open the door, He will not come in and dine with us and will suffer rejection by His own Church. Is it possible that the Lord's Church has closed her door to the "real Him"? Is it possible that churches are conducting their spiritual business according to their own routines and programs, and have left the real Lord Yeshua on the outside, knocking? It is more than possible. It is a grievous reality.

The Lord's house should be a house of prayer and intimate worship. In the beauty of holiness, the Bridegroom sets foot in His Church with the thick train of His glory filling the house. The unified and lovesick Bride, barely able to breathe for the weight of the glory, pours out her costly perfume on His feet. She sings songs from her heart, and weeps tears of repentance and gratitude. She has been living a consecrated lifestyle since the last church meeting took place. She is not distracted by human chatter, activities, or announcements, because she has dove's eyes and can only gaze at her Beloved. This may sound exclusively feminine, but it is equally vital for male and female believers to be the lovesick Bride. In the same way, female believers are also called *"the sons of the kingdom"* (see Matt. 13:38; Rom. 8:14,19; Gal. 3:26). This is not about gender; it is about Union.

PASTORS, IS YOUR DOOR OPEN TO THE BELOVED?

If you are a church leader reading these words, please do not assume that you could not have left the Lord outside the door of your church. You might be so caught up with the administration of a smoothly-flowing church service that you don't realize that the Lord has been left out. I understand that God is omnipresent and is therefore present in all church services, even in all places on the earth. However, we see in the Bible that *His omnipresence is not the same as His manifest presence,* which fills the house with the thick and weighty cloud of His glory (see 2 Chron. 7:1-3).

Even if you love the Lord and would never deliberately leave Him outside, the truth is that we can do this without realizing it. Who has created the church's agenda—man or God? Earnestly ask the Lord if He feels welcome to come in as the Apostle, the Prophet, the Teacher, the Pastor, the Evangelist, the Healer, and the Priest of His own church. *If you are a leader, set aside quiet time, where the Lord can show you what He really sees and feels in your church services.* Just so there is no misunderstanding, I am in no way suggesting that a church should not have godly leaders functioning in the fivefold ministry offices. We know that God appoints and blesses human leadership to guide and exhort His flock. Even so, sometimes human leaders can promote their own ideas and programs, which were not birthed of the Holy Spirit.

Dining with the Lord speaks of spending time in the Lord's presence as individuals and as a corporate body. He has prepared fresh spiritual food for us each day, like new manna from Heaven. Not only has the Lord prepared food for us, but when the Lord says, *"I will come in to him, and dine with him"* (Rev. 3:20), He is also expecting that *we* have prepared a meal for our King. You may recall that the Lord told His disciples,

> *My food is to do the will of Him who sent Me and to finish His work....He who has My commandments and keeps them, it is he who loves Me* (John 4:34; 14:21a).

I learned from a revelation given to Pastor Steven Shelley that the meal which the King most desires His people to prepare for Him is the "meat of obedience."[4] Unquestioning obedience shows the Lord that we love Him, and is more valuable to Him than sacrifice (see 1 Sam. 15:22). Believers sometimes fail to obey something the Lord has told them to do, but try to do sacrificial acts within their churches or ministries. They think this compensates for their lack of obedience, but it does not. These sacrifices do not please the Lord if we have not obeyed what He has told us.

"WAS THAT REALLY YOU, LORD?"

Sometimes, I think the Lord might be asking me to do something, but I am not sure if I have heard His voice accurately. This is confusing to me, and probably to other people as well. When this happens, I kneel down and ask Him, "Did You actually tell me to do such-and-such, or did I just make that up in my head?"

Sometimes, I will hear a confirming answer in my mind, but often, I don't get a clear answer to this inquiry. In these cases of confusion, I say this: "Lord, I am willing to do this if I know it is really You. Please send me a dream, a vision, a word, or some other confirmation that this is really from You. Then I will do it."

I then continue to ask the Lord every night for a dream, vision, or confirming word until I know for sure that He wants me to do it. If no confirmation comes after a reasonable time period, I conclude that it was not from the Lord. If it is from Him, sooner or later He makes it clear to me. Then I do it without further hesitation.

Once I felt the Lord was asking me to do a large, sacrificial act toward a particular ministry. I wasn't sure I had heard Him correctly, so I started asking Him to confirm it, night after night. About a week later, I had three dreams in a row; all were about my giving to this ministry. I felt fairly certain that these dreams were the Lord's confirmation, but I still had some doubts.

The next morning, while having a coffee talk with the Lord in my rocking chair, I asked Him for one more sign that this was His will. You may or may not believe this, but I looked up from my rocking chair, and there was the man who leads this ministry, sitting opposite me on my bed. He looked as real and solid as if he was truly sitting there. He was just smiling at me with a big, sweet smile. After three or four seconds, the vision disappeared. As you can guess, I obeyed the Lord immediately.

Later, I wondered if I had merely seen a vision, or if this man's spirit was actually taken to my room, just to visit me for a moment (for biblical examples of spirit travel, see Acts 8:39-40; 2 Cor. 12:2-4; Ezek. 8:3;11:24; 1 Kings 18:12). If that was the case, then *he had seen me just as surely as I had seen him!* I had never met this man in person, nor had I given to his ministry before.

Many months later, I had an opportunity to travel to a conference where he was speaking. I got in the prayer line and when I reached the front, I nervously told him that I had seen him in my room while I was having a coffee talk, and asked him if I looked familiar to him. He smiled and said, "I was wondering why you looked so familiar."

To Him Who Overcomes

To be an overcomer is not one of the gifts of the Holy Spirit listed in the Bible. Rather, it is the acquired military rank of someone who has pressed through a difficult battle, or series of battles, and been victorious. When the Lord Yeshua refused to turn a stone into bread, despite being famished, He *overcame* His flesh, despite pain, weakness, and near-collapse. When the Lord allowed them to arrest Him and nail Him to the cross, even though He could have summoned thousands of angels to rescue Him, He *overcame* the anguish and sorrow of how much He would have to suffer. He did not desire to suffer any more than you or I would desire to suffer.

When the Pharisees demanded a miraculous sign, the Lord could have easily provided a sign that would have proven that He was Messiah. For Yeshua not to give them a sign was to *overcome the natural human desire to be vindicated* before those who insulted and demeaned Him.

When the pressure to receive the antichrist's mark becomes unbearable, even to the point of death, it will not be easy to win the *overcomer's crown*. It will take preparation and inward strength. It will require that we know our God well enough to trust that Heaven and hell are real places, and that the Lord is worth it all.

If we dine with the Lord in His Word, in implicit obedience and in transparent humility with Him, we will grow up into the full stature of Messiah's wisdom and maturity (see Eph. 4:13). This is the only way we will *overcome* the onslaughts that are being unleashed against the Lord's soldiers, His lovers, and His mighty men of valor in these last-days' battles.

In the parable of the wheat and the tares, we see that the sons of the evil one are permitted to grow to maturity, alongside the sons of the Kingdom. The Lord tells us that only after both have matured at the end of the age, will the harvesting angels separate the good crop from the bad crop (see Matt. 13:24-30;37-43). The Father will still cause His sun to rise upon the good and the evil. He will still send His rain on the just and unjust (see Matt. 5:45). Both wheat and weeds drink in the refreshing rains that fall on the earth (see Heb. 6:7). Even liars and hypocrites can prophesy, but you will know which seed is good or bad from its fruits. The angels will separate them at the end of the age, but will not uproot them early. The Father would wait and give all a chance to repent and be saved.

The good crop will grow to maturity, but so will the thorns and thistles. Since evil will be allowed to mature to its climax, we must expect a hellish onslaught as never before. Therefore, as the Lord told author and speaker Paul Keith Davis, *"The sons of the kingdom must respond in kind."*[5] In other words, the good crop must attain to the full measure of Messiah's authority and maturity, or we don't stand a chance against the enemy's mature sons.

No matter how busy your life is, make the time to sit with the Lord and dine with Him every day, even if it costs you sleep. He is always there, waiting for you at the table of His presence in your heart. There is always fresh food, and there is always more of Him to know. There are more treasures of wisdom and blueprints of your personal destiny, which He wants to reveal to you. There is more union and intimacy with Jesus to be had.

There is more food at His table than we have yet eaten, and we will need to eat all of it, for *the journey is too much for us* (see 1 Kings 19:7). The hardest part of our race is yet to be run. And yet, the overcoming grace needed to run this most difficult race was provided and set aside for us before the foundation of the world, precious reader.

> *To him who overcomes I will grant to sit with Me on My throne,*
> *as I also overcame and sat down with My Father on His throne*
> (Revelation 3:21).

To overcome means that there are real and dangerous battles to be fought. No one would go into battle unprepared for the enemy's cruel and devious tactics. We need this wisdom and revelation in order to prepare for battle. Ready or not, it is upon us, Church!

> *Therefore, as the elect of God, holy and beloved, put on tender mercies, kindness, humility, meekness, longsuffering; bearing with one another, and forgiving one another, if anyone has a complaint against another; even as Christ forgave you, so you also must do. **But above all these things put on love, which is the bond of perfection.** And let the peace of God rule in your hearts* (Colossians 3:12-15a).

Amen!

ENDNOTES

1. *The Oxford Desk Dictionary and Thesaurus*, American Edition (New York, NY: Oxford University Press, 1997).

2. For more teaching on the biblical interpretation pertaining to the seven church ages, go to: www.williambranhamhomepage.org.

3. This amazing teaching and insight was shared by Randy Demain at the Shekinah Worship Center in Lancaster, CA, August 2009.

4. The incredible teachings, visions, and revelations given to Pastor Shelley can be found at www.revival.org.

5. The teachings and books of Paul Keith Davis can be found at www. whitedoveministries.org.

Chapter 2

He Beckoned Me

Iɴ the fall of 2006, I completed *Coffee Talks With Messiah*. I have always been a "non-procrastinator." When I was in school, I always completed my assignments ahead of time, since I hated the feeling of having work hanging over my head.

Knowing that the Lord had initiated the writing of this first book, I was just like a girl back in school with a homework assignment. I wrote diligently for almost three months and finished in early October. However, within a week, I began to sink into a depression, which had been previously masked by the huge mental effort of writing the book. I was already suffering from illness and insomnia for an extended period, and for most of the following month, I usually couldn't feel the Lord's presence. Even so, I must testify that there were times the Lord made Himself known in various ways. Nevertheless, the combination of feeling alone, depressed, ill, and without sleep left me crying through most of our coffee talks.

I had just written a revelatory book, which was full of the glories of intimacy with the Lord, full of loving encouragements for His children to find His presence in an intimate way. Why was I suddenly unable to find the Lord's presence or hear His voice?

Maybe it was a natural letdown after the climactic birth of a new book, a type of *postpartum* depression. Maybe the Lord was teaching me that the awesome feelings of His presence, which I had just written about so enthusiastically, would not always be there for me to feel. Obviously, we walk by faith and not by sight, nor by feelings. In my mind I know this, and have taught about it countless times. But my faith was failing, and I couldn't tell whether the problem was my lack of physical strength or faith, or if it was the Lord's deliberate, strategic withdrawal to test my faith after having taught such faith-building testimonies for others.

Finally, I decided to go away for four days to a mountain retreat, desperate to get away from the normal responsibilities of life, hoping to find the Lord again. Rather than being an intimate retreat with the Lord, this turned out to be a huge emotional battle. I felt alone in an empty cabin. I tried so hard to perform all the disciplines I had practiced during my first "three days," which had yielded such extraordinary results. But now, it didn't matter whether I worshiped, played the guitar, sat with coffee at the little kitchen table, or tried to talk to the Lord. I just felt completely alone.

To make things worse, I couldn't sleep, due to some physical problems I was having. So the nights felt endless, and the days were a long series of attempts to get the Lord to respond to me. I cried from time to time when it grew too painful not to feel His presence. However, I kept up a healthy set of routines, including walks in the woods, morning worship, coffee talks every morning, and eating my semi-fasting meals with Him. The first sleepless night was nothing but grief and physical discomfort.

THE LORD IS STILL THERE

The second day was pleasant and peaceful. I worshiped and had breakfast, keeping a deliberate choice in my mind to imagine that He was with me in each activity. I walked in the late morning, and read many chapters in my Bible in the afternoon. A lengthy thunderstorm in the afternoon made me glad I had gotten outside that morning. I sang about the Lord's blood, took communion, showered, and decided to read a book while I ate my supper, consisting of a tangerine and a few grapes. I got my plate of fruit, and sat on the couch with my book. I had no sooner picked up my book, when I clearly heard, *"Is this your evening meal, My daughter?"*

Then I realized I had shut the Lord out of my heart because I wasn't hearing from Him. I normally would never have eaten my meal alone on the couch, but would have sat at the little kitchen table and "imagined" that Yeshua and I were dining together. But I had withdrawn from my rigorous efforts to commune with the Lord without realizing it.

The moment I heard these convicting words, I cringed with sorrow and said, "I'm sorry, Lord; of course You would want me to eat with You." I either hadn't realized that the Lord was truly there, or that He desired to dine with me. By asking this one little question, the Lord was teaching me that His previous and continued silence did *not* mean He was not present, nor did it mean that He did not desire my company and conversation.

This lesson spoke volumes to me about the Lord's emotions and desires, even when He seems so conspicuously absent. I then moved my fruit to the table, not bringing my book with me, and proceeded to tell the Lord all about my day and how I had enjoyed it. I also shared more with Him about my physical problems, asking for help and healing.

After dinner, I tried sitting on the couch and imagining that the Lord and I were resting together, but it was no use. I felt utterly alone on the couch and had no ability to pretend otherwise. I cried hysterically for a while. I was dreading the long night ahead, knowing both my grief and inability to sleep. Finally, still hysterical, I made a desperate attempt to place a demand on the Lord's help. My loud cry echoed in the empty cabin: "You can't leave me like this to go crazy all night!" I paused to see if this plea would bring a response. I then added, shouting at the top of my lungs, "I know You hear me!!"

That did it. The very moment I spoke these words, my crying instantly stopped, and a spirit of peace filled me for the rest of the night. My body still bore its discomforts, but my grief and loneliness did not return. I know beyond any doubt that the Lord sent His Spirit to comfort me. Even in my grief and anger at Him, I had declared the truth, which was that He was there. He had heard me perfectly well, and He was too good to leave me in that bereft emotional state for the long night.

THE BLANKET MAN

As I lay sleepless for this second night, I was determined to keep believing in the goodness of God and His love for me. He had sent me His peace, and that gave me more faith to stay cheerful into the night. As a deliberate decision, I spent many hours in worshipful thoughts and declarations.

At 2:00 A.M., the oddest thing happened. As I lay there, tossing and turning, I saw a very elderly man walk right into the bedroom of the cabin. I had no fear, and I somehow knew that he was only there on assignment to see if I had enough blankets. He was gentle and kindly and said nothing. He walked near to my bed, surveyed my bedding, and being satisfied that I didn't need another blanket, he turned and walked out or seemed to disappear.

I knew this was not a natural visit from a kindly old stranger, wandering through a deserted retreat center at two in the morning, entering a random, locked cabin. I felt that it must have been an angel or one of our elder brothers from among the great cloud of witnesses, come to check on the Lord's child in an isolated place. Since I didn't actually need another blanket (although I had suffered from chills the previous night), the visit may have been granted more for my emotional comfort than my physical needs. This brief visit gave me a little boost of encouragement that the Lord was mindful of my plight.

THE SEASONS OF THE TREES

On the third day, after two nearly sleepless nights, the first spent in despair, the second spent in faith, I took a mid-morning walk in the cold mountain air. It felt good to get out of that cabin. I complained to the Lord as

I walked, telling Him how I hated that He wasn't answering me during our days of seclusion, or letting me feel His presence. I said it was unfair that one person should have to do all the talking. Silence reigned.

I spotted a wooden bench up the hill, and sat down. I looked around at all the bare trees on the heavily wooded mountainside. I usually visited this breathtaking property in autumn's splendor, and this stark winter scene was less than glorious.

After waiting for the Lord on the bench and not hearing anything, I cried again and continued my walk, complaining to Him again that this was not OK. Then I went back to the same bench, for some reason, and waited a second time. This time, the Lord spoke to me the following word:

"There are seasons. Are there not seasons?"

"Yes, Lord, You made the seasons."

"Look at the trees. They look like dead, ugly, dry sticks. Did the trees sin or do anything to cause them to be ugly, dry sticks?"

"No, Lord, this is their season. They will live again in the spring. They are not dead. They just look dead and dry, for this is their season."

"Do I not love the trees when I cause all of their leaves to be blown off? Am I angry with them, or am I punishing them?"

"No, it is part of their cycle of life."

"Do they feel sad when this happens?"

"No, they know they will live again."

Then He showed me the eagles, as Sadhu Sundar Selvaraj had taught about them, concerning their molting cycles.[1]

"When the eagle goes to a high mountain and all of his feathers fall out, he is an ugly, weak, helpless bird. All he can do is stare at the sun. If other eagles do not feed him during this time, he will die, because he cannot get his own food. If other eagles feed him, his strength will be renewed, and he will be renewed and will grow

back more feathers and live again. This is your season, when your strength is gone, your leaves have blown off, your feathers have been removed. You are weak and helpless, and you look and feel like a dead, dry stick. You did not sin to cause this condition, but you are in a different season than you were in the spring. You wrote a book full of revelation and two-way communication with Me. All of those things really happened. But this is a different season. Can you accept that?"

"Yes, Lord, I must accept it. I have no choice."

"Do not exhaust yourself with sorrow or pleading with Me. You must accept My times and seasons in your life. They are for your training and your good. Everything I do to you is for your good.

"This is the time for you to press in and press on. I will do many great things for you and continue to bless you, just as you received the call from Sid to encourage you. I sent you this encouragement right before these three days, so you would know that I AM with you, even if I am not answering you in the way you would like."

LAUGHTER AFTER TEARS

My third and final night in the cabin was a Friday night, which was the beginning of our Shabbat (Sabbath), a special day of mutual love and affection. I lit the candles and trusted more peacefully that my Lord was with me and was enjoying our time together, no matter what I felt or didn't feel. That night, I was granted a full night's sleep, which was miraculous and wonderful to me.

The next morning, I sensed that the Lord was releasing me to leave the cabin earlier than I had planned. He knew that it wasn't the honeymoon I was hoping for, and I was quite ready to go back home.

Over breakfast that Shabbat morning, I was joking with the Lord about a fruit salad I had set at His "place" at the table. As you can guess, this invisible savior was not eating His fruit, but I had given Him a bowl of fruit anyway. Then I acted like a Jewish mother, trying to make Him feel guilty for not eating His fruit, which I had slaved over. I sighed deeply like a martyr, like Golda from *Fiddler on the Roof* and lamented, "Never mind! I'll just eat all this fruit by myself!"

I was hoping the Lord was enjoying my attempt at humor. I thought I was being pretty funny! Then the Lord answered me and said, "*You can't guilt Me. I have no sin!*"

This struck me as surprisingly funny, and I laughed hysterically. Over the course of breakfast, the Lord made two other jokes with me that caused me to go into paroxysms of laughter for a long time. Yeshua has a great sense of humor, and I must have needed that laughter desperately. I knew He wanted me to laugh after all of my days of tears. It was wonderfully therapeutic to laugh, and I left the cabin a very peaceful and happy child of God. All of my feelings of abandonment, self-pity, and other Jill-style miseries were completely erased from my heart.

Coffee Meltdowns

Over the next few months, I pressed on with my early morning "coffee talk" appointments with the Lord three times a week. On the other days of the week, I would still spend time with the Lord in other ways. I might worship to a CD, pray, or prepare a Bible study. But during these more intimate face-to-face encounters over coffee, I experienced an extreme range of emotions and perceptions of the Lord's reality. Before I share these diverse emotions, I need to explain the physical arrangement of my coffee talks, which will make the testimonies that follow easier to describe.

These appointments include a *tallit*—a Jewish prayer shawl—which I spread lengthwise on the side of the bed representing the Lord's seat of honor. Opposite the bed is my rocking chair, where I sit, talk to the Lord, and read my Bible. These sessions always end with a resting period of time where I get up from the chair and come over to lay on my side under the Lord's *tallit*.

Perhaps you remember in the Book of Ruth where she uncovers Boaz's feet, lies down next to him, and says, *"Spread the corner of your garment over me, for you are my kinsman redeemer"* (see Ruth 3:9). This is the perfect description of what I do with my Lord at the end of a coffee talk. I gently lift up the corner of the outspread *tallit;* I lay on that same strip down the side of the bed and cover myself with the *tallit.* He is my kinsman redeemer. In my heart, I am resting with Yeshua. I believe the Lord honors my faith and makes this a reality in His own generous heart.

The range of emotions and perceptions I experienced during coffee talks were these: there were times of intense communication, vulnerability, affection, and intimacy flowing in both directions. There were other times where I was ill and exhausted, but despite feeling like a lump of clay who had very little to offer the Lord, I always made an effort to stay focused and receptive. It was at these times of illness that the Lord would kindly invite me to move from my rocking chair to lie down under His *tallit* earlier in the session than was our custom, in order to combine fellowship with rest for my body.

There were periods of my life, often lasting many months, when I was suffering from extreme sleep-deprivation and minor health problems. Having been up so much during the nights, it was hard for me to get up early to meet with the Lord. When I did sit before Him, I was without strength or any motivation to communicate with Him. Nevertheless, I would press through these sessions, and when coffee talks were over, I would work hard every day, no matter how I felt.

It was during one of these long periods of exhaustion that I had a dream. In this dream, I was cleaning up many piles of "mess," which some large dog had left on the carpets in my home. By the way, I don't currently have a dog, but I grew up with large dogs, which sometimes left piles in various places. And so, my brain must still retain a strong memory of cleaning up piles on the rugs!

In the dream, I was cleaning up endless piles. Just when I thought I had picked up the last mess, I would walk to another room and find more piles.

My attitude in the dream was one of tired resolve. I just felt that it was my job to keep doing this disgusting job until the rugs were finally clean. In the middle of clutching one more mess in a flimsy piece of toilet paper, a man appeared to me in the room. He looked ancient; he wore a long white robe and had long white hair and a white beard that went down below his chest. He looked more like an Old Testament saint than God Himself. He looked at me with sad, stern brown eyes. The man said, "*You said that you are too tired to meet with Me. You don't want to meet with Me.*" I sensed that he was sad about this, but that he would respect my wishes.

I woke up and cried, realizing that I had hurt the Lord's feelings. I was treating my special early morning talks with Him as if they were one more tiresome chore that wore me out. I was plodding through them as something to "get through," rather than looking at these as times of intimate communion with the Lord.

I told the Lord that it was true that I was very tired, but that I was sorry that I treated Him like a chore. I asked Him to give me another chance. I desperately did not want to lose these meeting times with the Lord, as I still believe they are actually the source of strength and motivation for all the work I do for His Kingdom. After this dream, my attitude improved, even when my physical strength did not.

Worse than my physical weaknesses were the times when I felt totally alone in my chair, as if I was insecurely and awkwardly talking to an empty room. The Lord just didn't seem to be there in any sense of the word. On these days, I would often have a meltdown on my face, on the floor between my rocking chair and my bed. On February 16, 2007, I came the closest I have ever come to giving up completely. After having what seemed like a real internal dialogue with the Lord about my difficulty believing that He was really with me, my faith melted beneath me, and I just couldn't keep it up anymore. I broke down, looked up at Him and said, "I can't do this, Papa." (I don't normally call Him "Papa," but at this particular moment of vulnerability, this was the child-like name that popped out.)

He said, "*Come over here and kneel.*"

I knelt at the side of the bed. He asked me if I believed in His creation of the earth, the heavens, planets, moons, and rotations. I told Him I did believe.

He said, "*Despite all this, do you believe that I am near you all the time, 'by your side and in your heart'?*" (In using this phrase, the Lord was quoting our intimate love song, which He had recently inspired me to write, "A Part of Me.")

"Yes, I do."

The Lord then reassured me that despite weakness in my body and soul, my spirit and faith are strong. I was greatly comforted. Then He asked me to rest with Him, and I was well again, leaning against "His breast of ceaseless love."

The Three Rabbis

During this "faith-stretching" period of time, the Lord made the way for my first book to be published. However, it took an unusual dream and two weeks of prayer for this door to open.

I had finished writing *Coffee Talks With Messiah* in the fall of 2006, and the Lord promised me that He would help me get it published. I didn't have any contacts in the world of publishing, and I didn't know any "important" people who might endorse the book. Nevertheless, I knew the Lord had commissioned me to write the book, and so I trusted that somehow, it would work out. He told me which people to contact, both for endorsements and for publishing, and I gradually saw His favor overshadow my lack of connections. The Lord does not show favoritism, but He does show favor to anyone who will walk humbly and obediently before Him.

However, during the first months of 2007, I had not yet received an offer of publication, and I wondered how it would work out. I had an unusual dream during that period. I saw three stern and ancient rabbis standing before me. Each one had a long prayer shawl draped over his head, and they wore long, flowing robes. Although they looked like "triplets," quite identical in face and clothing, one man was standing in the center, just in front of the other two. One was at his right, slightly behind him, and the other was at his left, also set back. I was earnestly petitioning them for something I needed badly. I don't know what I was asking them for, but I somehow knew that they had all authority to grant me this petition, and in fact, I felt that they were somehow "God."

As I petitioned the one front and center, he looked at me with an unyielding and very stern face. I was a little afraid of his position of authority and the unfriendly look on his face, but I kept asking anyway. Finally, he spoke to me and said, "*We cannot grant what you are asking, because our names are not written in your address book.*"

I woke up, pondering what this meant. I thought about my life, and realized that the main thing I might have needed from the Lord at that time was to have my first book published. I wondered what He meant by, "*Our names are not written in your address book.*"

What is an address book? It is a way to contact someone, and it provides an address and phone number to reach that person. I thought about the contents of *Coffee Talks With Messiah*. Was there anything in the book that spoke about the Father, the Son, and the Holy Spirit, or how an unbeliever could "get in touch with them?" I realized that I had written a lot about the Lord Yeshua as a personal friend, but had not explained the fullness of the Godhead to the reader.

After praying about the interpretation for two weeks, I could not think of any other meaning but that the three rabbis were the Father, Son, and Holy Spirit. They all had the same face, because they are One, and the front and center Person was the Father, who is preeminent. I immediately wrote a section at the end of the book called, "Receiving Eternal Salvation." In it, I tried to explain the three distinct identities of the Godhead; even so, they still comprise one true God. I also wrote out the plan of salvation, trying to use original phrases, so as not to sound too "packaged." Soon after writing that section, I received an offer for publication from a wonderful company, which published my book within a few months of this dream. Praise the Lord's faithfulness!

POWER DREAMS

I think that many, if not most, believers have experienced a faith crisis at some point, when a promise that they believe the Lord gave to them does not come to pass. For me, there was an unfulfilled promise, which was one of the unresolved issues that likely contributed to my faith meltdowns during late 2006 and early 2007.

To explain this promise and how I viewed it, let me go back in time to exactly one year before the terrible faith meltdown described in the previous section. In the early months of 2006, I had a number of very significant experiences with the Lord, some occurring during dreams, and quite a few while awake.

Looking back on it, I now realize that the intensity and frequency of these glory encounters were happening during the two months that preceded my original "three days," as recorded in *Coffee Talks With Messiah*. Those three days, April 1-4, 2006, changed my life forever. It was here I learned of my martyrdom, and experienced the Lord Yeshua as a tangible and present friend, with whom I could converse normally, for three set-apart days in my room. And though I did not know it yet, it was from the revelations learned during these three days that my first book would be commissioned and written within months. However, I had not yet received the prophetic word to schedule these three days until March 24, shortly before these days of seclusion occurred.

Therefore, during February and most of March, I had no idea that the Lord was planning this life-changing encounter. But the Lord knew what would happen to me in early April just before Passover, and He sent me the following three experiences to prepare me for my acceleration into intimacy with Him, and for a difficult destiny that loomed in the near future.

In my first book, I described a special category of dream, which I call a "Power Dream." This means that the tangible presence of the Lord is so strong over me in the dream that I am not fully sleeping and not fully awake. His presence is intense to the point of frightening, and I feel myself breathing rapidly. Sometimes in the course of these dreams, the Lord does something that sends a jolt into my body, like an electric shock wave. This jolt wakes me up and keeps me up, as I remain in His strong presence long afterward.

The first of these dreams occurred on February 13. I encountered the Lord as a great figure in white robes, surrounded by much swirling angelic activity in a vast, heavenly setting. I saw Him with sword uplifted in one hand, and He told me to kneel before Him. As tired as I felt, I got out of bed to kneel, although it turned out that my body never actually got out of bed, only my spirit. But it seemed exactly as if I had truly obeyed Him and gotten out of bed. The moment my spirit knelt down, His power and presence exploded upon me in my bed, and I was jolted awake. As I lay in this power for some time, I could still see myself kneeling before the Lord; He then placed a crown on my head. I remained in this presence for a long time. I was not told what the crown represented.

On March 1, I had a visitation while awake. I woke up at 1:00 A.M., and sensing that the Lord wanted to meet with me, I turned onto my right side. I felt His strong presence and trembled. Then a much stronger power overshadowed my body, and I felt pressure in my womb. I somehow knew that I was entering a pregnancy at this moment. For the first few seconds, I worried about this, because I knew my husband was out of town on business that week, so how could I conceive a child that very night? I know that I wasn't thinking clearly or logically about this strange revelation, because I was momentarily worried that people would judge me for this pregnancy, which occurred while my husband was away.

Soon after this revelation, the presence departed. As I pondered it, I realized it must be a "spiritual pregnancy," as the physical would not have been possible. But I had no idea what I was pregnant with.

I lay awake for several more hours thinking about the Lord, and finally drifted back to sleep close to 4:00 A.M. As I slept, I was immediately aware of "someone" in my face, smothering and holding my face still, and kissing me passionately. It was more than a dream, because there was something real happening to me. My mind struggled to wake up and tried to assess what was happening. It felt human, and yet I was alone in the room. My eyes were still closed. Who was on top of me? I felt confused and afraid. I started to wake myself up and wondered if a demon could possibly be allowed to do such a thing. I started to rebuke it, but my mouth seemed to be smothered with its mouth, and yet I decided to try to speak some words anyway.

Sometimes we can experience a sensation that seems to be impacting our physical body, but later, it turns out to have been a spiritual event. It felt like I wouldn't be able to speak, but when I made an effort, it turned out that I was free to speak, although I was under the illusion of being smothered. I now know that I was free to speak because my physical body was untouched, but my spirit body was being assaulted. The problem is that the spirit realm feels as real as the physical, and it can be confusing. Paul expressed this in Second Corinthians 12:2-3, when he said, "*whether in the body or out of the body, I do not know.*" Paul could not distinguish between his spirit body and his physical body. Additionally, when Peter was physically taken out of prison by an angel, he thought it was only happening in the spirit (see Acts 12:9).

I began to command it to go in Jesus' name. I got louder and more forceful in my words, and said, "Go! Go!" At that moment I saw hideous, spindly hands loosen their grip on my arms and recede. I hadn't been aware of my arms before that moment. But still it covered my face and mouth. Then I said, "*The Lord rebuke you, satan! Go!*" It receded instantly and was fully gone.

I thanked the Lord for sending it away. I then wrote in my journal: "Is it a coincidence that this thing happened only a few hours after the Lord overshadowed me by His Spirit and impregnated me this day with a holy spiritual birth to come, a high and set-apart destiny?" It is often the case that soon after a revelatory encounter, the enemy will attempt to steal what we have just received from the Lord (see Matt. 16:16-23).

"I Will Come to You"

For the next two weeks, I experienced a number of powerful anointings from the Lord's Spirit. He seemed to be with me constantly in a very strong and tangible way during this period. I waited on Him in my chair regularly, after worship and prayer, and experienced His glory a number of times. The following promise came during one of these glory visitations, on March 17, 2006.

It was midmorning, and I had been in my chair for quite some time, overcome with weakness from the level of the Lord's glory. I knew I had a ministry-related lunch appointment coming up, and I was concerned that I needed to get ready. However, I had to lie down instead, because I was in no condition to just get up and begin my chores, in preparation for this lunch meeting. The Lord told me to wait, saying that I was still in His strong presence and should not attempt any normal activity. He was absolutely right, so I just waited. While waiting, I wondered, "I wonder what I'm pregnant with."

His Spirit answered, *"I will come to you before the end of the year."*

I was very happy to hear this, but was immediately doubtful that I heard correctly. I did not want to base my hopes on a false promise that the Lord did not actually promise me. I knew it would be devastating to wait and hope for the rest of the year, but never receive the desired visitation.

I said, "Lord, how can I know for sure that this is from You, so I don't get my hopes up and then be disappointed later if it wasn't You?"

In Genesis 15:1-7, the Lord made a very great promise to Abraham. In verse 6 we see that Abraham believed God. And yet in verse 8, Abraham asks, "*O Sovereign Lord, how can I know that I will gain possession of it?*"

The Lord was not upset with Abraham for asking how he could know for sure, and He gave him a great sign of the covenant to prove it. It was comforting to me to know that although I believed God's promise, it was not wrong to ask, "How can I know that this is true?"

The Lord answered me, "*You will not be able to move for five minutes.*"

I waited a few seconds, and then tried moving my fingers and hands, which I was still able to do. I thought that maybe I had heard wrongly.

Then I felt a slight pain and pressure applied to one precise spot on my middle spine. From the level of the spinal column that I perceived this touch, I wondered if the Lord was "paralyzing" my legs. I tried to move my legs…I couldn't move them! Fear and panic swept over me momentarily. I tried moving them again, and they felt like cement and could not budge.

Then I felt happy, because I felt this was my assurance that the Lord would come to me before the end of the year.

I watched the clock with some slight trepidation that the paralysis was permanent, and as soon as the five minutes had elapsed, I said, "Lord, my five minutes are up. I want to move my legs in Jesus' name." Then I tried moving them; my knees unlocked, and I was able to move them again.

Three weeks later, I would experience the wonder of the Lord Yeshua as a personal friend during my three days. I wondered if this was the fulfillment of the promise that He would come to me. The Lord had indeed come to me during those three days, but not in an open vision where my eyes could behold Him. I hoped very much that my three days were not the fulfillment of this promise, but that it was yet to take place.

The year passed with much awesome activity taking place in my life and ministry. Nine months after the original pregnancy word from March 1, I found that I had just completed my first book. Perhaps this had been the birth He was referring to, and yet the Lord had promised me something else...

As the end of the year approached, I grew nervous. What if it didn't happen? What does a person do with that? Obviously, the Lord cannot lie. Did I hear wrongly? But my legs, I couldn't move my legs. That had been my sign! Was it a psychological paralysis?

December came and went, with no obvious visitation. I tried to think of some other interpretation by which it might still be fulfilled. When we are trusting and yet doubting, we try to find a way to believe that the prophecy will yet be fulfilled. As December waned, my friend Katya gave me a word she felt was from the Lord. It said (approximately), "The Lord doesn't necessarily mean our normal calendar year."

Then I thought, "Maybe the Lord meant a full year from the date that He promised me. That would be March 17, 2007." So I waited in diminishing hopes for that date to come. But it too, came and went. At that point, my faith in my ability to hear wavered. Could I have made it up? It made me wonder if I had ever gotten anything right that I heard from the Lord. That is what is so devastating about unfulfilled promises. They can really damage a believer's faith. But beloved, things are not always as they seem.

He Beckoned Me!

Six days later, on March 23, I sat down for my coffee talk. According to later calculations, this was my 118th official coffee talk with the Lord, from the end of my three days until that moment. It was a day like any other. I discussed with the Lord my worries about the coming Passover Seders and all my compressed responsibilities. Then I talked to Him about some difficulties I was having with a particular personal relationship in my life. As often would occur after a time of discussion, journaling, or Bible reading, I lay on my face before the Lord, just worshiping Him and pouring love on Him.

Up until this particular day, I would happily stay on the floor until I would sense the Holy Spirit "inviting" me to come up for our closing resting time under the *tallit* on the bed. However, I noticed He wasn't inviting me, and I began to wonder how long I should stay down there. I felt the Lord nudging me to return to my rocking chair. I did so, but with some insecurity. I sensed that the Lord would not initiate the invitation, but rather, that He wanted me to ask Him if I could come over now.

I felt too insecure to ask. I thought, "What if I ask and He doesn't answer me? And I'm just sitting there...that would be the most awful, uncertain feeling." Silence reigned as I looked down into my lap. Finally, I knew I was supposed to ask. So, still looking down, I mustered my courage and said, "Lord, could I come over and lie with You?"

I looked up, expecting to see my usual empty air space over the bed. Instead, I saw the Lord Jesus Christ, opposite me in the same space where I always picture Him to be. I will share with you all the impressions I can recall from this brain-freezing moment of my life.

I saw a Man who was tall and relatively large, although not supernaturally large. He was not at all transparent, or spirit-like. He appeared as solid and real as we are. He was clothed in elegant, yet understated white garments, seemingly composed of at least three layers. The whiteness of this garment was not glowing or dazzlingly white, as some have been granted to see, but it was simply white. I had the impression that there were some other colors involved in this clothing, but I didn't have time to assess this. I sensed from His almost "normal" appearance, that the Lord had not come to me in His heavenly bright splendor, but had come humbly in such a way as not to dazzle or impress, but to reassure. It struck me that He was utterly unselfconscious. He was not trying to come across in any particular way, but He was there simply to answer my question with a visual response, rather than a verbal one.

His hair was neither black nor white. It seemed to be either brown or chestnut, yet possibly streaked with lighter strands, possibly white streaks.

The Lord had a gentle beard that was not overly long, but seemed rather neat. I would estimate that His beard was the same color as His hair, but had no time to judge all these artistic matters. I could not discern the color of His eyes, because of His head position.

This Man, who I knew beyond a doubt to be my very own Yeshua the Messiah, was looking slightly down at me, and He was using two different body gestures, one right after the other, to beckon me over to our resting place. The first gesture I saw was His head tipped slightly back, as one would signal someone to come forward by an upward motion of the head, with their eyes looking down at you from a slightly elevated position. Immediately following that, the Lord lifted His left hand and using only a quick motion of His fingers, beckoned me to come. Both gestures used the minimal movement needed to convey His meaning.

The expression on the Lord's face was quite serious, almost stern. Although He did not speak to me, the message I felt His expression carried was, "*Just come, just come. Why are you hesitating, why should you be insecure? Just come already.*" I could have even thought there was some impatience in His gesture, as if to say, "*I shouldn't have to do this. You should know that I want you.*" However, I can't be sure these were His exact feelings.

As soon as He was certain I had seen and understood the invitation, He seemed to rise to take His leave. As the Lord rose, I started to notice more about His garment. It went down to the floor, and was composed of hundreds of perfectly folded ripples of material, such as the finest drapery, only infinitely finer in its detailed and multitudinous foldings. As He stood, I saw an elegant swirling motion of the fabric near the floor. Like poetry in motion was the bottom of His garment. I noticed that there was a thicker layer of fabric on His shoulders, seemingly laid over His main garment. It seemed to jut out beyond the breadth of His shoulders with a square edge. Later, after much pondering, I realized that many Jewish men fold up their prayer shawls back over their shoulders in such a way as to create a flat, rectangular extension of their shoulders. I believe this may have been what I saw across Yeshua's shoulders, although I didn't see a recognizable prayer shawl.

And then He simply wasn't there anymore. The whole thing may have lasted four or five seconds. In stunned and perplexed reassurance, I quickly obeyed this personal invitation, and as I had always done, I lifted up the corner of His tallit and quietly and gently lay down with my beloved. This tiny visit, this inspiring yet fleeting encounter, so awed me that it gave birth to new songs and poetry, which soon afterward would become my second CD, appropriately titled, "Beckon Me."

When designing the cover for this CD, I made a great effort to duplicate the Lord's appearance and clothing as much as possible. The Lord pointed out to me a brother at my church, while we were sitting in Sunday school, and said clearly, "That's the face I want." The Lord chose this man to model for that cover; I would have never known where to find a model.

After praying about this offer with his family, my friend agreed. Then I went to the fabric store with a dear friend who is a talented seamstress, and we labored to find the materials which most closely matched my vision. Needless to say, there is no fabric anywhere that looks like the elegant drapery of Yeshua's kingly garments. But my friend Linda found the best we could find, and she sewed such a wonderful garment that I have now used it on two projects.

At a Shabbat worship service, the day before our model would be trying on the garments, the Lord granted Linda a vision of her Bridegroom dancing with her, wearing these very garments. This happened while she was dancing to a new song I had written, which was one of great intimacy. The King wanted to wear these robes before any man would wear them. I can hardly think of a greater gesture of appreciation from the Lord for her stellar work. The Lord must have liked the effort we put into duplicating His appearance, although He is a tough act to follow!

He Kept His Promise!

It would be over a year before I finally realized that the Lord had kept His promise about coming to me before the end of the year. How can this be?

> *Now the Lord spoke to Moses and Aaron in the land of Egypt, saying, "This month shall be your beginning of months; it shall be the first month of the year to you* (Exodus 12:1-2).

I had not considered that although Rosh HaShannah is the traditional Jewish new year, the biblical year actually begins with the month of Nisan, the month of Passover. If you are wondering how the author of *A Prophetic Calendar: The Feasts of Israel* could forget that the biblical year begins at Nisan, I can only say that the Lord loves to keep us humble.

As for the day itself, according to the rabbinic calendar, the day of my visitation would have fallen 12 days before Passover that year. Technically, this would be two days later than the first of Nisan, and the Lord's visit would still appear to be two days too late. However, it fell 12 days before Passover itself (on the 14th of Nisan), which the Lord may indeed consider the beginning of Israel's spiritual calendar.

Additionally, since the Lord has brought my faith this far, I am choosing to believe that He knows the precise date for each new moon that has ever appeared in the sky since the fourth day of creation. If there have been any human miscalculations in the lunar/solar cycles over the past 6,000 years, the Lord Yeshua could still have perfectly fulfilled His promise to me, without missing a single day. Since Jewish scholars have asserted that the calendar of Rabbi Akiva (the founder of the modern rabbinic calendar in A.D. second century) could be off by about 200 years, two days should not cause us to stumble.

THE ETERNAL POSTURE

What is the most important lesson for the Lord's people, concerning my visitation where He beckoned me? After the Lord's resurrection, He showed Himself to the apostles and many other people over a period of 40 days, but was He continually visible to them during that period? We know that the Lord would appear and greet His disciples, teach them, or eat with them. Then He would disappear, and reappear in another location at another time. And yet the Lord had promised them, *"I am with you always, even to the end of the age"* (see Matt. 28:20).

Yeshua the Messiah is the same, yesterday, today, and forever (see Heb. 13:8). So this same Yeshua is always with us, whether He is visible or invisible. I sat in my rocking chair for 117 coffee talks before this day that He appeared to me. Like all my brothers and sisters in the Lord, I had fixed my gaze on the One I could not see, looking with the eyes of faith. I believed (most of the time) that the Lord was there, teaching me, loving me, and even inviting me to come unto Him, hide under the wing of His garment, and rest in His arms of love.

I only *saw* the Lord beckon me once. But how many times has He really beckoned me, beckoned you, and beckoned His precious lambs from one end of the earth to the other, from creation till the Wedding Supper? *What my eyes saw that day was an eternal posture of invitation.* He is extending this at all times to all people, and at a few special moments, we are privileged to see Him in action.

When He spread out His arms on the cross, it was an eternal posture. No, our Lamb of God is not still nailed to that tree, but His arms are eternally stretched out in the same posture of embrace, humility, invitation, and vulnerability as the posture He displayed while being tortured and humiliated.

The words that Yeshua spoke were eternal words. They are as fresh and alive today as if He spoke them today, because from Heaven's perspective, He did speak them today. Every day is today for One who lives in eternity. May we join Him there, while we are yet on this earth.

Blessed are those who have not seen and yet believe. I am glad that He granted me 34 years to believe without seeing, for this brings a blessing. But since I saw the Lord, there is almost no day that goes by that I do not remember what my eyes saw. Every time I picture that scene, I am filled with awe and joy. I constantly try to recall every detail of the Lord's manifestation, so I won't forget.

My testimony has changed because my eyes have seen the One I love, and I must testify of what my eyes have seen.

> *That which we have seen and heard we declare to you, that you also may have fellowship with us; and truly our fellowship is with the Father and with His Son Jesus Christ* (1 John 1:3).

Walking on Water

Peter saw the impossible. He saw the Lord walking on the surface of the lake in the middle of the night. Could this really be their beloved Teacher? He said, *"If it is really you, Lord, bid me come to You across the water"* (see Matthew 14:28).

Peter knew that if the real Lord Jesus beckoned him to come, he could walk to Him without sinking. Only the real Yeshua could beckon someone to step out into the impossible without sinking. *Without gazing at the Lord, we are incapable of walking into the destiny He has planned for us.* When Peter considered the waves and the impossibility of what was happening, his trust broke down, and he began to sink like a stone.

When my trust breaks down, I break down. I am like my brother Peter, walking out into completely unknown and impossible circumstances. When my faith melts beneath my feet, I sink like a stone and cry out, "Lord, save me!"

Just when I'm sinking and drowning, the Lord says, "*Come up here and rest with Me.*" The Lord pulls me out of the mire, out of the wild and unbelieving place and into the safety of the boat, time and time again. If I never took my eyes off of the Lord, I could walk peacefully into life's impossible predicaments; into storms of slander and gross misrepresentation; into the onslaught of enticements from the enemy's targeted strategies; into the pressures of media, marketing, and overwhelming human demands. I could walk into not knowing where my next meal was coming from, without fear and despair. I could walk into the angry nations.

> *Why do the nations rage, and the people plot a vain thing? The kings of the earth set themselves, and the rulers take counsel together, against the Lord and against His Anointed* (Psalm 2:1-2).

I could walk into the time of terrible lawlessness that is upon us, the judgments coming upon our nation and the persecution of the faithful remnant, without dread. I could walk into a nation where my Jewish people are hated, beaten, and murdered, and yet the police are too afraid, powerless, or anti-Semitic to do anything to protect and defend these law abiding citizens. I could love the people in that nation so much that I would happily walk into a culture where the media does not consider the death of a Jew something worth reporting. I could walk voluntarily and with love into the raging nations, knowing what the Lord has shown me will happen there. If He has beckoned me, I will overcome all things, even fear, even death. The Lord Yeshua is the end of my journey. He is my destiny. He beckoned me.

> *Most assuredly, I say to you, unless a grain of wheat falls into the ground and dies, it remains alone; but if it dies, it produces much grain* (John 12:24).

The blood of the martyrs still speaks from the ground, and as they sowed their own blood into the soil of Israel and the nations, it will surely reap the greatest harvest ever to be brought into God's storehouses. These are the great cloud of witnesses, cheering us on across our finish line. *They are waiting for us, for they will not receive what they were promised until we have run our race, until we have reaped what they sowed.* The number of the martyrs must be completed before the Lord comes as Judge, and avenges all of the innocent blood shed on the earth.

> *And all these, having obtained a good testimony through faith, did not receive the promise, God having provided something better for us, **that they should not be made perfect apart from us*** (Hebrews 11:39-40).

> *I saw under the altar the souls of those who had been slain for the word of God and for the testimony which they held. And they cried with a loud voice, saying, "How long, O Lord, holy and true, until You judge and avenge our blood on those who dwell on the earth?" And a white robe was given to each of them; and it was said to them that they should rest a little while longer, **until both the number of their fellow servants and their brethren, who would be killed as they were, was completed*** (Revelation 6:9-11).

There are some lessons we can only learn when the Lord comes to us in a challenging way, an unexpected and frightening way, walking on water in the middle of the night. We have no natural ability to do what He does; it must be supernaturally given to us.

The Lord beckons us to come and find rest in His arms. He also beckons us across the surging sea and into the nations, where He must reap a great harvest of souls, even if this harvest will cost the martyrdom of His own ones. The Lord Yeshua knows we cannot do this apart from Him, and so His very beckoning forces us to keep our gaze on Him.

This is the song that I wrote after I saw the Lord. Whenever our forefathers had an encounter with the Living God, they built an altar to Him and offered sacrifices there. This song is the altar and the memorial I have built for the Lord's kindness to come to me. The CD I produced is my sacrifice to the Lord.

BECKON ME

Peter saw You on the water
 If it's You, Lord, call to me
 Bid me come to where You are, Lord
 Let me walk upon the sea
 I fix my eyes upon Yeshua
 Stepping into storms unknown
 I look away, my faith dissolving
 Now I'm sinking like a stone

So beckon me to come into the raging nations
 O beckon me across the surging sea
 Beckon me to come, You are the end of the
 journey
 O beckon me
 You are my destiny

I thought my eyes would never see Him
 And I have waited patiently
 Staring out into the darkness
 My tears and fears I do release
 Now my eyes have seen Yeshua
 Who bid me lay upon His breast
 With just a motion of His fingers
 That I might come and find His rest

He beckoned me to come into His peace and
 stillness
 He beckoned me to trust in His unfailing love

He beckoned me to be a child that He could
carry
You beckoned me
You are my destiny

At the speed of thought trust is broken down
My heart and strength are melted underneath
my feet
What can hold me up
What makes this solid ground
What is in Your eyes, imparting faith to me?

I know that my Redeemer lives
And I will see Him with my eyes
And though He slay me will I trust Him
This fallen seed again will rise
So bid me come across the waters
Let my eyes now meet your gaze
Let my heart be sealed in You Lord
Give me strength to run my race

Into the pain I walk, can I look straight ahead?
Why do the nations rage so hatefully?
My eyes are fixed on You, where is the thing I
dread?
And what can separate me from Your love for
me?

ENDNOTE

1. "The Art of Waiting on God," a DVD series taught by Sadhu Sundar
Selvaraj, can be found at www.jesusministries.org.

Chapter 3

The Test of Suffering

I am not worthy to tackle this most terrible of questions, nor am I qualified to answer it. In the sum of all my years, my life has been unusually sheltered from death and disease, from violent crimes and warfare, from starvation, rape, and captivity. My children were not ripped from my arms and taken away, never to be seen again. Millions of mothers just like me have experienced exactly this. The heart cannot bear the pain of even thinking about it, let alone living through it.

Even so, I have lived with chronic and, in some cases, serious afflictions in my own life and those of my family members. Some afflictions must be kept private, and only the family knows this relentless pain. These are small compared to the life-threatening conditions afflicting so many others, but I cannot deny that I have known suffering. I will know more.

I must also testify that I have experienced countless healings from the Lord, both for myself and for others I have prayed for. Some of these healings were immediate, and some were gradual, but the Lord has answered more prayers than I could ever count.

Although I have been blessed greatly, none of us can live on this earth without encountering great suffering, whether in our own lives or in the lives of those around us. My master's degree is in counseling, and so I have heard countless stories, some of which shattered me and caused many troubling thoughts in my mind concerning God's purposes in all things.

As a Jewish person, I have read and thought at great length about the unthinkable cruelty that Adolph Hitler's regime unleashed on my people in Europe. I have read terrible books, seen the photographs, heard the testimonies of survivors, and have visited two major Holocaust museums a number of times, one in Washington, D.C., and one in Jerusalem.

The Lord has spoken to me significantly over the years about suffering, in the course of various personal struggles, counseling situations, and in preparing Bible studies and writing books. With my deepest respect to all who suffer, I will now examine this subject from a biblical perspective, as well as from the existential perspective. This must not be cold or theological, nor could I ever approach pain that way. This discussion must have a heart of compassion, or it would be better not to write it.

Job: The Blameless Man

The fundamental question has always been: How can a good, loving, and all-powerful God allow (or cause) terrible suffering to come to innocent people? Both believers and unbelievers feel a great need to answer this question in a satisfying way, although some unbelievers might simply conclude that there is no God, and all of this suffering is a random occurrence.

The next logical thought says,

+ Either God is not completely good and loving;

+ Or God is not all-powerful, but is limited in how much He can help us;

+ Or there is no one who is actually innocent, and thus, we all deserve what happens to us.

The Bible makes it clear that no human is utterly pure and without sin (see Rom. 3:10-12, 23; 1 John 1:8). But the Bible also contains hundreds of references to *"the righteous, the upright, the blameless, the pure, the guileless, and the innocent* (see Ps. 1:5; 18:26; Isa. 59:7; 1 Cor. 1:8).

From this we can conclude that although there has never been a perfectly sinless person on the earth except for Yeshua the Messiah, nevertheless, in God's eyes it is possible to be blameless, upright, and without guile.

> *There was a man in the land of Uz, whose name was Job; and* **that man was blameless and upright,** *and one who feared God and shunned evil* (Job 1:1).

> *Behold, an Israelite indeed, in whom is no deceit!* (John 1:47b)

As we are introduced to Job's godly lifestyle, we see that he is truly a righteous man. After a brief introduction, the reader is permitted to observe a stunning conversation taking place in the third heaven. This behind-the-scenes dialogue is probably the most revelatory passage found anywhere in the Bible or in any other human literature, concerning the suffering of the righteous.

> *Then the Lord said to Satan, "Have you considered My servant Job, that there is none like him on the earth, a blameless and upright man, one who fears God and shuns evil?"* (Job 1:8)

I used to be somewhat upset with the Lord when I would read this. I always thought, "Thanks a lot, God. Job was doing great, and You had to go and point him out to satan! Please don't point me out to satan."

But when I read it in Hebrew, I realized that this verse may have a different meaning. Satan had already been roaming to and fro on the earth, just looking for the chance to attack someone whom God particularly loved. Instead of translating it, *"Have you considered My servant Job?"* I would translate it this way: *"I notice that you have been paying attention to My servant Job."*

Job's First Test

The enemy was already gnashing his teeth at how godly Job was, wishing he could just get at him. The Lord was such a proud parent, and knowing that satan had been watching him, He displayed His delight over Job to His enemy.

Then comes the challenge, the slander, the accusation:

> *Does Job fear God for nothing? Have You not made a hedge around him, around his household, and around all that he has on every side?...But now, stretch out Your hand and touch all that he has, and he will surely curse You to Your face!* (Job 1:9-10a,11)

Satan wants the Lord to think that we only love Him when He blesses us. This makes the Lord feel "used" for His great benefits package, and not loved just for who He is. And to silence His enemy's evil tongue, the Lord grants satan permission to ruin Job financially and to kill all of his children. This sudden devastation was Job's first test of his relationship with God. His response would put most of us to shame.

> *Then Job arose, tore his robe, and shaved head; and he fell to the ground and worshiped. And he said, "Naked I came from my mother's womb, and naked shall I return there. The Lord gave and the Lord has taken away. Blessed be the name of the Lord." In all this Job did not sin nor charge God with wrong* (Job 1:20-22).

The Second Test

Satan is utterly disgusted with Job's faithfulness to continue to love and serve God, despite the huge and unprovoked disasters He had brought upon Job. (Since Job knew nothing of the behind-the-scenes negotiations, I speak as if God had brought this disaster upon Job, because that is how Job would have seen it.)

At the next heavenly meeting, the Lord is so proud of His son, Job. He points out to satan what satan has already observed: that Job has maintained his faith, trust, and integrity toward God. Satan's snarling reply gives me the chills:

> *Skin for skin! Yes, all that a man has he will give for his life. But stretch out Your hand now, and touch his bone and his flesh, and he will surely curse You to Your face!* (Job 2:4-5)

The enemy lives to sow mistrust between man and God. He first accuses us before the Lord, trying to convince the Lord that we don't actually love Him. Then later, when the enemy cruelly afflicts the Lord's children, he accuses Him before us, making sure we know how mean and spiteful the Lord is to strike us with such sorrows. He is so jealous of our love relationship with the Lord that he will try to sow discord and mistrust in both directions.

And to silence His enemy's evil tongue once again, the Lord grants satan permission to afflict Job's bones and flesh with the most painful of all diseases, without actually killing him. This terrible plague was Job's second test of his relationship with God. His response would put most of us to shame. When his wife feels that the Lord has completely forsaken her unfortunate husband, she says, "Do you still hold fast to your integrity? Curse God and die!"

Job rebukes the foolishness of his wife's response and speaks to her with wisdom.

> *"You speak as one of the foolish women speaks. Shall we indeed accept good from God, and shall we not accept adversity?"* In all *this Job did not sin with his lips* (Job 2:10).

After some period of intense suffering, Job opens his mouth, but still does not curse God. However, he does curse the day of his birth. His misery is so great that he wishes he had never been born; surely this would have been better than this gnawing agony that never stops, day or night.

His three friends have come from afar to comfort him. When they see his hideously disfigured form, they wail and mourn, put dust on their heads, and sit on the ground with him silently for seven days. Although we speak ill of Job's comforters, we have rarely, if ever, seen such mourning and loyalty from any friends or family in our culture.

JOB'S THIRD TEST

Job's physical agony is increased by his inability to find the Lord he has loved and served all his life in this terrible trial. His friends have a great deal of insight about God, righteousness, and the justification of suffering. Some of what they say is true, but much of it attempts to find fault with Job, since there is no other logical explanation for this "punishment."

The first friend to comment is Eliphaz. Interestingly, he reports having had an eerie visitation from some kind of spirit, who gave him a word of "wisdom" for Job (see Job 4:12-21). As we read this first speech, we might conclude that this was an evil spirit who visited him, not the Holy Spirit. Essentially, he accuses Job of being a resentful fool. Even so, there are true statements mingled in with less sympathetic declarations.

Without doing an elaborate study of the cycles of speeches, alternating between Job's three friends and Job's desperate rebuttals, we will only look at a few key elements of Job's case.

As he continues to answer his friends' theological explanations for punishment and logical accusations, Job is saying,

"You don't understand. If only I could find Him. If only I could schedule a date in court with the great Judge. I know I could plead my case with Him.

I know I could show Him the life I've lived. My conscience is clear. This can't be happening to me; this isn't the God I know. This punishment is unjust.

"Couldn't you just stop accusing me, and share my pain? Couldn't you just stand with me in the terrible bewilderment and abandonment I am feeling right now? Do you have to keep telling me this is my fault? Couldn't you pray with me, instead of telling me all the right reasons that this is happening to me, none of which are true?

"I just have to find Him and reason with Him. But that's the problem! I can't find Him to talk to Him. He has disappeared, and left me dying in my rotting flesh, with only my three best friends here to tell me what I must have done wrong.

"I am so alone in my suffering, and even God has deserted me. I know I didn't sin, I can prove it. But who will hear my self-defense?"

One of the hardest aspects of Job's third test was that *the voice of the accuser came through friends*. And one of his friends received his theological wisdom from the visitation of an evil spirit. He was being used by the enemy, but thought he was "helping" Job see the error of his ways!

Oh, how the Church has fallen from her first love, her first compassion and intercessions. How often the enemy has used Christians to accuse their brothers and sisters, even gloating when those they dislike get sick and die. The greatest woundings often come from the *"house of our friends,"* from the ones who should be comforting us (see Zech. 13:6).

Recently, a woman I know sent me a long Christian article criticizing a prophetic man whom I happen to respect. She was trying to show me how dangerous this man's teaching was. The article was taking his statements out of context and deliberately making them seem heretical, when, in fact, his beliefs were biblically legitimate.

Then the writer of the article hit a new depth of cruelty by reporting that this prophetic man had a life-threatening illness and was currently in the hospital. This information was not shared out of compassion, nor did it encourage the reader to pray for him. It was mentioned to show the reader that the Lord was angry with this man and had smitten him with a terrible disease. I heard the accuser's voice in the mouth of Christians, just like Job's friends. *How far we have fallen from First Corinthians 13 love!*

It is heartbreaking to hear Job's desperate need to understand *why* this is happening. Since he knows nothing of satan's involvement, Job laments that God is sovereignly dealing harshly with the good and the wicked alike. He laments, "If God isn't doing this, who is?"

> "He destroys both the blameless and the wicked." When a scourge brings sudden death, he mocks the despair of the innocent. When the land falls into the hands of the wicked, he blindfolds the judges. **If it is not he, then who is it?** (Job 9:22-24 NIV)

SILENCING THE ENEMY WITH FAITH

Despite thinking that the Lord is unjust, Job cannot accept his friends *"smearing him with lies"* (see Job 13:4 NIV). He still believes he will be vindicated somehow, at some point. Not only that, but this man believes in the resurrection of the dead! This takes great faith, brothers and sisters. Consider these passages below:

> **Though He slay me, yet will I trust Him;** even so, I will defend my own ways before Him. He also shall be my salvation, for a hypocrite could not come before Him....Oh, that You would hide me in the grave, that You would conceal me until Your wrath is past, that You would appoint me a set time, and remember me! **If a man dies, shall he live again?** All the days of my hard service **I will wait, till my change comes** (Job 13:15-16; 14:13-14).

Job believes that he will die of this illness, which is not an unreasonable belief, given his infected condition, fever and weight loss; death seems preferable to the agony he endures night and day, for what appears to be a nine-month period.

But the passage above is remarkable. Even King David's expressions about the grave carried a grim finality. People who went to the grave would never see the light of day again (with the exception of David's prophecy about Messiah's resurrection in Psalm 22). He didn't seem to speak about the resurrection as Job did.

Consider this sentence: *"That You would hide me in the grave **until** Your wrath is past, that **You would appoint a set time and remember me**"* (Job 14:13). The word *until* tells us that he knew that death was temporary. Oh, I cannot wait to meet this man! Is he not one of the great cloud of witnesses, cheering us on through our suffering, diseases, poverty, mental afflictions, and martyrdoms? Is he not cheering us on through our doubts, when Heaven seems like a distant dream, in the midst of this cruelty and darkness?

Now, this sentence is even more incredible: *"I will wait, till my change comes"* (Job 14:14). The word for "change" in Hebrew is *chalifa*, which means *"exchange"!*[1] Job was waiting for God to exchange his old body for his new one. This really blows my mind.

Even among the prophets of Israel, have we ever seen such a revelatory, insightful prophecy about the return of the Lord Yeshua, as the following words from this tormented non-Israelite man who lived almost 2,000 years before the birth of Yeshua?

> *For I know that my Redeemer lives, and He shall stand at last*
> *on the earth; and after my skin is destroyed, this I know, that*
> *in my flesh I shall see God, whom I shall see for myself, and my*
> *eyes shall behold, and not another. How my heart yearns within*
> *me!* (Job 19:25-27)

Despite his feelings of abandonment from the Lord, Job knew that he had an advocate in Heaven, a friend, an intercessor. Job knew that even if he died, His God would raise him from the dead. Job's testimony to his friends silenced the enemy's terrible two-edged sword that he had wielded to separate Job from his Lord.

Satan tempted Job to despise the Lord for this cruel injustice. Satan incited the Lord to allow him to harm Job, by accusing Job before God's throne. Job *silenced the enemy by his faith,* against all odds, that God was good and God was loving. And Job was indeed, blameless.

> *For the accuser of our brethren, who accused them before our God day and night, has been cast down. And they overcame him by the blood of the Lamb and by the word of their testimony, and they did not love their lives to the death* (Revelation 12:10b-11).

RECONCILIATION

All tests end at some point. Job's final discourse is an incredible description of how a righteous and generous man lives his life. Chapter 31 describes Job's standards and behavior: the fear of the Lord, sexual purity, honesty, providing legal help for the persecuted, helping the poor and the homeless, and not having loved his wealth in his heart. To be honest with you, I've known of few Christians, including myself, who come close to measuring up to this standard of righteousness. No wonder satan hated him so much!

However, when Job completes this review, the author says, *"the words of Job were ended"* (Job 31:40). There always comes a point when our arguments are finished, and there is nothing but to hang on, without being swallowed up in despair and unbelief, waiting for vindication from on high. That's what the Scriptures mean when they say, *"To him who overcomes..."* Although Job may have crossed a line in attributing injustice to the Lord, he was definitely an overcomer in this terrible trial.

And so, on a day like any other, when Job was least expecting to meet his Maker face to face, the Lord Himself comes to discuss the situation with his beleaguered friend, Job. *"Then **suddenly** the Lord you are seeking will come to His temple"* (Mal. 3:1b NIV).

Interestingly, the Lord does not explain to Job the behind-the-scenes negotiations with satan that caused all this trouble—at least, that's not recorded. Given Job's continuing intimate relationship with the Lord for many years after this test, I have a feeling that the Lord did teach Job the true malicious origin of his sufferings at some point after their trust and intimacy with each other were fully restored.

We do know that when this testimony was being written, the Lord's Spirit clearly revealed this dialogue with satan to the author of the Book of Job, who, according to the NIV commentators, was an Israelite with a brilliant command of Hebrew.

But the Lord chooses to confront Job as the Creator. He spends a great deal of time demonstrating His preeminence in the universe, as the powerful Creator of the planets and constellations, and of all the awesome creatures who are fearsomely made. He discusses many of the mysteries of creation with Job, and shows him that things are not always as they appear. Job doesn't have all the wisdom needed to accurately assess what happened to him. The Lord requires Job to acknowledge God's superior power and knowledge, which Job humbly does.

At that point, the Lord reveals His anger at Job's friends, who listened to the voice of the accuser, and made Job's suffering that much worse. The Lord would have harmed them if Job had not interceded for them (see Job 42:8).

Then the Lord massively restored to Job more than what he had lost in all the terrible losses that befell him. And since he had regularly offered burnt offerings on behalf of his grown children who were killed in the calamities, one can only hope that Job was reunited with his original children in paradise when he died, *"old and full of years."* Amen.

KNOW THE SOURCE OF SUFFERING

It is more than helpful to know the source of our suffering. In Job's case, we are clearly told that his suffering was initiated by satan. However, before we explore how to combat the enemy's plans, we must understand that not all of our suffering is caused by satan. If we attribute everything bad to satan, we will not be praying or responding in wisdom, and our prayers will not be effectual. We will seek wisdom further, when we look into other aspects and causes of suffering in the next sections.

The most helpful and revelatory aspect of Job's testimony is that God did not dream up this series of nightmarish trials for His friend, Job. It was the enemy's hatred and jealousy that thrust an accusation in God's face, and the Lord was required to answer satan's challenge. The Lord could not ignore this challenge, for it cut to the very authenticity of Job's devotion to God. Was it only because the Lord was so generous to him? The Lord had to prove His servant's faithfulness and, thus, *silence the enemy's accusations.*

Beloved child of God, there are simply times in our lives when the enemy will go before the Lord and demand to plunder us, to show Him our false motives and how quickly we will turn against Him when our possessions, health, safety, or families are removed from us.

Satan demanded to harm Job, to sift Peter, and to tempt, seduce, assault, afflict, or murder innumerable other servants of the Lord since the beginning until this day. The enemy's entire job description is to steal, to kill, and to destroy. These scenarios have been played out behind-the-scenes, in the heavenly court room (see Luke 22:31-32).

The enemy accuses us before God, day and night (see Rev. 12:10). He will brazenly go before the Lord and demand to tempt, harm, kill, or plunder one of the Lord's own ones. There are three potential responses the Lord can give His enemy:

1. Sometimes, the Lord will not grant the enemy any permission to do what he has demanded.

2. Other times, the Lord will grant him permission to do what he has demanded.

3. And sometimes, the Lord will grant partial permission, but set exact limitations on how far satan can go.

This is just the biblical truth, and if we understand it, we will respond very differently concerning our sufferings and afflictions.

We do not have the scope of wisdom to always understand why the Lord chooses any one of these three possibilities in a particular case. His wisdom decides rightly, of this we can be sure.

However, we do not have a God who acts independently of His people.

> *Surely the Lord God does nothing, unless He reveals His secret to His servants the prophets (Amos 3:7).*

We were made for fellowship with the Lord and for partnership with Him. We were designed to pray His will into the earth, as it is done in Heaven, and to petition His throne for every victory in the invisible spiritual realms. We were taught to stand in prayer, knowing the schemes of the enemy, and using the sword of the Spirit, which is the Word of God, to tear down every strategy the enemy can bring to bear against the saints of the Most High. We were granted to take authority over God's enemy and his minions, to rebuke them, bind them, and subdue their arrogant and cruel onslaughts upon the people of God.

> *For the weapons of our warfare are not carnal but mighty in God for pulling down strongholds, casting down arguments and every high thing that exalts itself against the knowledge of God, bringing every thought into captivity to the obedience of Christ (2 Corinthians 10:4-5).*

That is why I love Job so much and owe him such a debt of thanks. Because of his sufferings, we have this incredibly helpful insight as to the source of these terrible afflictions that befall the Lord's children. We know that the Lord doesn't think about ways He can harm us and make our lives miserable. What kind of loving parent would have that type of motivation toward His child? The Lord is a loving parent, and He is not the author of disease, or of sin, sickness, torture, or death.

Our first parents, Adam and Eve, ate from the tree of the knowledge of good and evil, breaking the direct command of God. This gave satan dominion over the earth, which was originally given to man. That is why the Lord Jesus called satan *"the prince of this world"* (see John 14:30; 16:11 NIV).

But the last Adam, the Lord Yeshua the Messiah, bought back humanity from satan's dominion by His blood. Therefore, satan has no ownership over the redeemed, no place in them, no rulership over their lives or destinies.

> *I will no longer talk much with you, for the ruler of this world is coming, and he has nothing in Me* (John 14:30).

Satan had no foothold in the Lord Yeshua; he had neither dominion over any aspect of His thoughts or behaviors, nor dominion over His physical life. However, the Father had predetermined that His Son had to be sacrificed for the sins of mankind, and, therefore, someone had to kill Him. Satan did not understand the redemptive plan of God, or he never would have crucified the Lord of glory (see 1 Cor. 2:7-8).

Since satan hated Yeshua and didn't understand what His death would do to his evil kingdom, he inspired Judas Iscariot and other wicked men, both Jews and Gentiles, to crucify this Righteous One. The Father used satan to bring about an excellent plan of redemption, but His Son paid an unfathomable price for this awesome and necessary plan of the Father.

DEMONS OF SICKNESS

I had a powerful dream that I know was significant to my understanding of the authority the Lord has given to us over evil spirits that cause disease (see Matt. 9:32-33; Mark 16:17-18).

I was a teacher at a school. They were having a large gathering, a special party for many of the students and teachers.

In one of the larger multipurpose classrooms where I was working, there was a 14-year-old boy who was lying in a bunk bed. He was very sick with a high and contagious fever. He was suffering terribly, and the staff just ignored him and went on with the activities of the party. They were eating pizza and were very busy with activities.

I went to check on the boy, and seeing his condition, I was outraged that his mother had sent him to school like this. I began to call the other teachers to come over and help me take care of the boy. He had been lying in his own cold urine for hours, shivering and too weak to get up and go to the bathroom. When I asked why he had been brought to school like this, one of the teachers said that his mother wanted to get him out of the house because his fever was so contagious; she was afraid that she and the other children at home would catch it and die. So she selfishly left him with us and the other students, who could also catch the disease.

Everyone ignored him, and when I asked them to help me, they said they were afraid of getting sick. Even though I was a little afraid, I was more motivated to help him than worried about getting sick. Finally, with great effort, I convinced a group of teachers to help me clean him up, and his sheets and clothes. Everything was soaked, and he needed some food or liquid. After a lot of work, we got him freshened up, dry and clean, and put him in a fresh bed in a top bunk.

Then everyone immediately began leaving the room to go back to the party, feeling that he was fine now. I knew they wanted to get away from him and continue their activities. I knew instinctively that he was way too sick to be left alone. As I reluctantly started to walk out the door with the others, the poor boy began to throw up all over his fresh sheets. He tried to get up to go to the bathroom, but he was too weak. I called for the others to come back and help me, but they wouldn't; they did not want to deal with it.

Then I saw many demons coming and going from the boy and his sickbed. They were walking out of the room, between 50 and 100 of them, busy with evil and foul assignments concerning this boy; they were just arrogantly coming and going, all with some kind of destructive assignment and purpose.

I spoke up, to cast them out. No one would help me, and all the teachers ignored me. I tried to raise my voice and speak forcefully enough to command them, but because I was asleep in real life, it was hard to talk loudly enough. I opened my mouth and commanded all of these foul, evil demons of disease, infection, and death to leave this boy at once, in Yeshua's Name. My voice came out weaker than I had hoped, and I felt inadequate to cast them out. There were so many of them, but I spoke it with confidence, knowing they *had* to go.

At first, they seemed to ignore my words, continuing to file out and to carry on with their work; I wondered if I had not succeeded. But then I saw that the tallest one, who seemed to be in charge of the others, stopped and stared at me. He looked like an arrogant hippie from the Woodstock era. He started to answer me, stating that they could all ignore me, but my faith was very strong as I continued to stare back at him.

I knew in my heart that despite their outward initial response, *they had to obey me.* After we had stared at each other for a while, he gave up, realizing that he had no choice. He shrugged in defeat and disgust toward me, and immediately, he and the others left the boy, never to return.

The boy was instantly well again, and I began the chore of cleaning up the boy and his bed again from his recent mess. No one helped me.

Then I remembered that several years before, I had cast a demon out of his little brother, who had been crippled and ill, and he had been healed.

I remembered that I was known to the demons who afflicted this family, as one who rescued and set them free from these besetting spirits. I knew the demons didn't like that this was the second time I had driven them out of someone in this family.

Then I woke up and immediately saw the Lord telling His disciples, "*Do not rejoice that the demons are subject to you, but rather, rejoice that your names are written in the Book of Life*" (see Luke 10:20).

I marveled that they had obeyed me, and that their leader had acknowledged me and the authority with which I had spoken to him.

As I lay in bed, reflecting on this dream, I knew that during the time that the lead demon and I were staring at each other, he was acting like he didn't have to obey me and leave the boy. It had been vital during this staring contest that I knew beyond any doubt that they had no choice but to obey and leave. If my faith had weakened, and I had not stood my ground in my certainty that they had to go, they would not have left. *Part of the victory was connected to my absolute certainty that no matter how long they resisted, they had no choice but to leave.* I knew this was a critical lesson for all of us who might be in the ministry of casting out demons, both now and in the days to come.

Perhaps the other teachers, who didn't want to deal with the boy or his demons, represented the Church, which is "too busy" and ill-equipped to confront the demonic powers we will soon face. It is easier to continue life as we have known it than to move into this messy arena of setting people free. However, the time is coming when we will have no choice but to take up our battle stations.

REDEMPTIVE SUFFERING

It is important to clarify that not all diseases, accidents, or deaths are caused by evil spirits. It is true that death, disease, and poverty came into the world through sin, which originated from the tempter enticing our first parents. But the Lord warned us, *"On the day you eat of it, you will surely die"* (see Gen. 2:17).

Since all have sinned, we are all responsible for eating from that tree; therefore, sin and death are our responsibility: *"For the wages of sin is death, but the gift of God is eternal life in Christ Jesus our Lord"* (Rom. 6:23).

The Lord's sinless life, death, and resurrection blasted open the dread permanence of the grave. Death couldn't hold Him down, because He overcame the world, the flesh, and the devil. All who believe in Jesus Christ will have eternal life, and will be resurrected as He was. Even so, most of us must still taste physical death, which has not yet been destroyed.

> *Then comes the end, when He delivers the kingdom to God the Father, when He puts an end to all rule and all authority and power. For He must reign till He has put all enemies under His feet.* **The last enemy that will be destroyed is death** (1 Corinthians 15:24-26).

Since Paul wrote this after the resurrection of Yeshua, we know that he is speaking of the final victory over physical death, which is still in the future, and which will not come until the Lord returns.

From the example of the Lord Yeshua's redemptive martyrdom, we know that the Father can ordain the suffering or death of one of His children, in order to accomplish a redemptive purpose on the earth, which will bring glory to His name.

I am not saying that any other human death can approximate the infinite value of the Lord Yeshua's blood, which atones for us on the Mercy Seat in Heaven. Even so, the Lord prophesied to Peter the predetermined death by which he would die and glorify God. The blood of the martyrs is indeed a seed in the ground, which will spring up to salvation in the Lord's timing.

As with Peter, the Father foreknows the day on which each of His own ones will pass from this earth, as much as He has known our birth dates before time began.

> *Your eyes saw my substance, being yet unformed. And in Your book they all were written, the days fashioned for me, when as yet there were none of them* (Psalm 139:16).

The Lord can use bad things like disease, car accidents, jealous brothers, and violent martyrdom to bring many to salvation and to glorify Himself. As Joseph said to his remorseful brothers, who had brought great evil upon him,

> *But as for you, you meant evil against me; but God meant it for good, in order to bring it about as it is this day, **to save many people alive*** (Genesis 50:20).

The cruel suffering they thrust upon their innocent brother was used by God to save many lives! The Father had a redemptive purpose in this terrible event, and brought salvation to many as a result. The Lord needed to get Joseph into Egypt to save many lives. His father Jacob would never have sent him there.

But if Joseph had not been sent there to prevent the starvation, which would occur many years in the future, Jacob and his sons would have starved, because Egypt would have had no grain to sell them. The whole region would have starved if Joseph hadn't been there.

If Joseph hadn't been a slave, he wouldn't have been in prison to meet the cupbearer to Pharaoh, who would end up bringing him into Pharaoh's courts. I could continue with this fascinating logic, but I've made the point sufficiently.

Beloved, we must understand this truth: God can use seemingly evil events for great works of salvation. They murdered the Lord Jesus, and look what happened! The enemy's strategies were defeated, and *billions* of souls, (when the final harvest is counted) will now occupy the places prepared for them before the foundation of the world.

> *Most assuredly, I say to you, unless a grain of wheat falls into the ground and dies, it remains alone; but if it dies, it produces much grain* (John 12:24).

LAWLESSNESS CAUSES SUFFERING

The innocent suffer when they live in a lawless society. If a nation adopts legal policies, or supports software and entertainment products that promote or tolerate violence, abortion, pornography, sexual aggression, and the breaking of God's covenants, it is often the innocent who suffer. Two examples of this are child molestation, which has affected a staggering proportion of children and teens in our nation; and human trafficking, which not only enslaves thousands of boys and girls in foreign countries, but which also takes place behind locked doors in our own nation. The perpetrators are largely fueled by lust and greed: what they see in books, magazines, television, and the internet causes them to act on their poisonous lusts. Their cruel selfishness has left multitudes of casualties, who bear indescribable pain and damage (see Chapter 7 on sexual brokenness). And in the case of human trafficking, the motivation is profit, where the lives of poor foreigners, teenagers, and even young children are sold to the highest bidder, who is driven by lust.

Much suffering is due to a nation turning its back on the laws of God, which were given to us for our own good and protection. In at least some cases, we have to admit that our own personal "lawless" choices have caused or contributed to our suffering. I will give a few examples for individuals and families. Please do not think this section is meant to produce guilt; I have not made upright choices for much of my life, and I have suffered to some extent for these choices, though not as much as I should have.

I also know that upright and responsible believers get terrible diseases, or are victimized, or are in accidents. I also know that we live in a toxic environment; this is not our personal fault. The air and the water are not clean and pure, as Lord created them. The food we eat has been tampered with genetically—something the Lord never intended, since He created all the seeds of life with their perfect DNA. This also is not our fault, and can give us nightmarish and hard-to-trace health problems.

In providing this list of questions, I am not judging anyone who is struggling with disciplining their habits. Even so, we have to take a look at our contribution to our own suffering. The following questions are highlighting a biblical standard of obedience, in a few areas that affect the health of our minds and bodies.

- Do we smoke cigarettes, drink alcohol, or use drugs?

- Do we engage in sexual behavior outside of marriage?

- Do we eat foods that are obviously unhealthy?

- Do we break the laws of the land, such as the speed limits?

- Do we curse or use foul or abusive language?

- Do we have an uncontrollable temper?

- Do we watch or read filthy things, fill our minds with violent images, or fuel demonic lusts and covetousness in our souls?

- Are we full of resentment or bitterness toward others? This is a recipe for illness.

- Do we take communion lightly, without examining our hearts and meditating on Yeshua's suffering? Paul says this will make us sick, and some of us will die.

- Do we take a day of Sabbath rest with the Lord, as our bodies were designed to do?

You may have noticed that I did not include, "Do you exercise?" This is because I do not exercise, and if I write this in the list, the Lord might call me a hypocrite! If you exercise, that is awesome!

"THE RIGHTEOUS ARE TAKEN AWAY"

There is an appointed time for each of us to depart this earth, and the transition can often involve pain and suffering. Each child of God has a time to be born and a time to die (see Eccles. 3:1-2). None of us want to suffer or die, but we all want to go to be with the Lord. It is hard to bear, but we must not love our lives unto death, and we will be rewarded as overcomers.

Elijah was taken up in a chariot of fire; however, Elisha, who had a double portion of Elijah's anointing, suffered and died of disease (see 2 Kings 13:14).

Hezekiah was a righteous king, but while still young, the prophet Isaiah told him to prepare to die of his disease. After Hezekiah wept bitterly, the Lord relented, and added fifteen years to his life. But he still died relatively young, and well before having to see the destruction of Jerusalem by the Babylonians, which was the Lord's mercy (see 2 Kings 20:1-6).

Josiah was a devout and righteous king of Judah. He was the most zealous for God's law of all the kings of Judah. When the neglected Book of the Law was found and read to him, he tore his clothes, knowing that great wrath was going to fall upon Judah and Jerusalem. Josiah was afraid for what would happen to Judah and Jerusalem under his reign, and he sent his priest and several others to consult with a trustworthy prophetess of the Lord. She prophesied against the city and its inhabitants, because they had forsaken the Lord. After she completed this prophetic word of God's decision to judge Judah for her idolatry, she then gave them the word of the Lord for King Josiah.

Because your heart was responsive and you humbled yourself before the Lord when you heard what I have spoken against *this place and its people, that they would become accursed and laid waste, and because you tore your robes and wept in My presence, I have heard you, declares the Lord. **Therefore I will gather you to your fathers, and you will be buried in peace.** Your eyes will not see all the disaster I am going to bring on this place* (2 Kings 22:19-20 NIV).

After receiving this word, Josiah put all of his zeal into removing idolatry from Judah, and walking in the laws of the Lord. Nevertheless, the Lord did not turn away from His fierce anger against Judah, because of King Manasseh's evil practices.

In fulfillment of the word spoken by the prophetess, King Josiah was killed at age 39, in a battle with Pharaoh Neco in Megiddo (the Valley of Armageddon). This passage makes a very stunning theological point about Josiah's early death. *Because Josiah was righteous, because he tore his robes and wept, because he was zealous for God's law, the Lord took his life early!* The Lord caused him to die because He loved him, and wanted to spare the righteous king's eyes from seeing the horrible disasters He was going to bring on Judah and Jerusalem at the hands of the Babylonians. He gave his servant rest, although he died young and in the violence of battle. Consider this passage from Isaiah:

*The righteous perish, and no one ponders it in his heart; devout men are taken away, and no one understands that **the righteous are taken away to be spared from evil.** Those who walk uprightly enter into peace; they find rest as they lie in death* (Isaiah 57:1-2 NIV).

The Lord could not bring the terrible siege of Babylon against Jerusalem while this zealous and righteous young king was serving Him with all his heart. There was no other king who made such stringent efforts to root out every source of pagan worship and child sacrifice in Judah as King Josiah. At the age of 26, after reigning for 18 years, the young king sent a trusted priest and several others to the house of the Lord, where they found the Law.

Until that moment, Josiah was unaware of the standards that the Lord required of Israel, as well as the curses that would come upon them if His laws were disobeyed. Israel had provoked God to fierce anger in her brazen idolatry.

But from the moment his awareness was kindled, Josiah was utterly driven to clean up the filth and perverse harlotry from Jerusalem and the surrounding region. How could God send His judgments with such a tender-hearted and worshipful king on the throne? Therefore, the Lord determined to cause Josiah's death early, so that there could yet come four more wicked kings after him. The fourth king was Zedekiah, whose eyes saw the destruction of Jerusalem and the death of his sons, before those same eyes were gouged out by the Babylonians.

It is important to the Lord that all of his judgments are acknowledged by His people as just and true. He does not want to be misunderstood in His motives or His actions, and the Lord needed Judah's wickedness to reach its climax before the destruction, so that no one could ever accuse Him of injustice, or unjustified slaughter.

In Genesis, the Lord prophesied to Abraham that his descendents would be enslaved in Egypt for 400 years before the Lord would bring the people out of bondage and into their Promised Land. People might wonder, "Why did the Israelites have to wait 400 years before they could be granted their Promised Land?"

The answer is found in this passage:

> *Know for certain that your descendants will be strangers in a country not their own, and they will be enslaved and mistreated four hundred years. In the fourth generation your descendants will come back here, for **the sin of the Amorites has not yet reached its full measure** (Genesis 15:13,16 NIV).*

In a similar vein, one could say that Jerusalem was destroyed in the fourth "generation" of evil kings after Josiah, although the number of years was considerably fewer. Wickedness had to be shown as fully wicked for the Lord's judgments to be just.

JOSIAH, A TYPE OF MESSIAH

Our Lord Yeshua was actually one of the royal kings of Israel, in the direct lineage of the kings of Judah. Did you ever think about this? He was a youthful, zealous king in the line of Judah, not completely different from His ancestor Josiah. Josiah had come to the throne as a little boy, but grew in wisdom and stature until it was time for him to assert his authority.

But if the Lord Yeshua was a legal king of Judah, why was Herod's dynasty on the throne when the Messiah was born in Israel? Why wasn't Yeshua actually on the throne instead of the corrupt Herod, who was not even descended from Jacob, let alone from the tribe of Judah?

After Nebuchadnezzar invaded and besieged Jerusalem, there was a great exile and captivity from the land of Judah. We see that the prophets Ezekiel and Daniel were among those taken captive into Babylon. After 70 years, a portion of the Israelites returned to the land from what was then the Persian Empire. However, the kingdom of Israel, according to the royal line of Judah, was never reestablished after their return. The king of Persia was ruling over the entire region, and although he graciously allowed Ezra and Nehemiah to tend to the rebuilding of the walls and the worship institutions, he did not permit the setting up of the former system of David's dynasty.

Following the rule of Persia, the Greek Empire conquered the Middle East; following that, came the Roman Empire. When Rome conquered a region, there was no king permitted but Caesar. Rome would appoint clients as puppet kings in each region it ruled, according to political expediency and financial payoffs. And so, Rome appointed an Idumian, Herod the Great (37-4 B.C.), to be its limited ruler in that province of its empire.

The Father chose for His Son to be born into a Gentile empire that would not respect the Davidic line of kings, so that Yeshua would not reign as an earthly king over His people. If He had been the rightful king of Israel, He could not have been handed over as a sacrifice, and we would all be dead in our sins.

As this humble and gentle king staggered up the hill with the wood of His own sacrifice on His back, He was not thinking of Himself. He knew of the terrible judgments of God which would fall on Jerusalem in 40 years, essentially one generation later. As a prophet, Yeshua could see the future scenes of starvation, bloodshed, and the crucifixion of young children, even as He was being led to His own crucifixion. And He mourned for the generation whose eyes would see the destruction of the city He loved and died for.

> *A large number of people followed Him, including women who mourned and wailed for Him. Jesus turned and said to them, "Daughters of Jerusalem, do not weep for Me; weep for yourselves and for your children. For the time will come when you will say, 'Blessed are the barren women, the wombs that never bore and the breasts that never nursed!'"* (Luke 23:27-29 NIV)

God could not send destruction upon Jerusalem while the righteous young king Josiah was serving Him wholeheartedly. Similarly, the Father could not judge His city while His Son, the Bridegroom, was walking the streets of Jerusalem, teaching in the temple courts, healing the sick, and binding up the broken-hearted. He could not permit the Roman army to destroy Jerusalem and the temple, to starve and crucify hundreds of thousands, and to exile the Jewish people to the four corners of the earth, while the Light of the World was zealously bringing God's Word and righteousness back to Israel.

Both Yeshua and Josiah lived in a generation that preceded each of the two primary military invasions and destructions of Jerusalem and God's temple. Both of them died in their thirties, violently. Both loved the God of Israel, and were zealous to see the Jewish people worship the God of Abraham, Isaac, and Jacob, and to put away idolatry, complacency, and self-righteousness.

We are living in the best of times and the worst of times. If our generation is approaching a time of great judgments and devastations, we might see precious believers removed from the earth at a younger age than we might think reasonable. Some of their deaths might seem terribly unjust or cruel. Please remember that things are not always as they seem. The Lord may be sparing their eyes the judgments that will fall on their beloved nation.

The Lord Suffers With Us

It was very painful for the Lord to watch the enemy ruin and afflict His righteous servant Job, while He was "required" to watch and listen to all of Job's responses, without lifting a finger to rescue him. After the first test, the Lord pointed out to satan that He had permitted him to perpetrate a gross injustice upon Job, and yet Job had maintained His integrity.

> *And he still maintains his integrity, though you incited Me against him to ruin him without any reason* (Job 2:3b NIV).

This is one of the most perplexing mysteries about human suffering: If God is all-powerful, how can He watch us without healing us? Why wouldn't He intervene sooner than later? Why does He permit the enemy to plunder His people without intervening in so many instances? How can we believe He cares if He doesn't heal and rescue us?

While I am certainly not able to answer this mystery completely, I believe Scripture gives us a few clues. They concern the *righteous judgments of God*. This subject is so important to the Lord that I believe He directed me to include an entire chapter on it, where I will fully present His case. For this chapter's purposes, we will look at the subject only briefly.

It is important to the Lord that all His judgments be seen and acknowledged as just, true, and righteous. The angels and even the altar of God declare the righteousness of His judgments during the worst moments of the wrath of God being poured out on the earth (see Rev. 16:4-7).

In the parable of the wheat and the tares, the Lord tells us that He will not rip up the "tares," the sons of the evil one, before the harvest has reached maturity. He clearly teaches the disciples that both the good and evil crop must be permitted to come to its full state of ripeness before the harvesters separate the good from the wicked and burn the tares at the end of the age (see Matt. 13:30).

Just before the writing of this book, the Lord gave me a disturbing dream. In it, I was the mother of a dear son, a boy about 10 years old. He seemed to be my only child, and I loved him tremendously. Every day, my son went off to a school environment that treated him cruelly and shamefully. The other children continually tormented him in a variety of ways. The parents of these children did not discipline their unkind children; in fact, they also treated my son harshly. I watched each day as he endured some form of physical and mental abuse.

At one point in the dream, they were about to do something really bad to him, which could have killed him. At that moment, I "stepped in" momentarily, and spoke to the perpetrators, both adults and children. In a forceful voice, I said, "Treat him right, or you'll hear from me about it!"

When I said this, I knew that I had the legal authority to bring great penalties against them if they harmed my son, and yet I knew that the moment of punishment would come at a later time. I also knew that they did not have to heed my threat. I hoped that they would, and I knew that they recognized my authority to punish them later, but they did not have to obey me. They could have been defiant and killed him, and I would not have punished them until a later time. I almost held my breath to see what they would do. They feared my threat and backed off from the severe abuse. I felt relieved.

My son was afraid and unhappy at school as he faced this relentless cruelty. He loved me and knew that I loved him. He never complained about going to school each day, nor did he ask me why I didn't protect him. Somehow, I had the power to intervene, and yet the school was not my domain to "micro-manage." Justice would have to wait.

When I woke up, I felt sad and disturbed. I wondered why I let my sweet and obedient son go into this rotten school every day to be mistreated, without stopping them every time they were about to do something to him. How could I love him and watch everything he went through, wanting with all my heart for him to be safe and well, and yet not intervene most of the time?

It occurred to me that the Lord gave me this dream so that I would have a small sense of what He feels as he watches the evil ones abuse His beloved children. He hurts, He watches, He desires for the abusive rebels to see the error of their ways and respect His children. But except in certain cases, He often does not intervene. He will bring to bear all of His legal power and authority at a later time if they don't repent.

Why Believers Need to Repent for Their Nation

I wrote in my first book about the intercessory and repentance conferences I attend under the leadership of Nita Johnson.[2] The Scriptures warn both nations and individuals that shed innocent blood. As righteous Abel's blood cries from the ground, so all innocent blood cries out to God from the ground (see Gen. 4:10).

I have met several people who were permitted to hear in the Spirit the horrifying cries of the innocent blood that has been shed from the beginning. If not for the Lord's mercies in limiting the experience, these unbearable wails could make someone lose his mind. In Revelation, we see the martyrs in Heaven crying out for God to avenge their blood, which was shed by the wicked (see Rev. 6:9-11).

The purpose of these repentance gatherings has been for the believers to allow their hearts to be broken over the cruel injustices committed by our nation, even as our Lord Jesus' heart is broken. Without repentance, the Lord will not heal or forgive a nation which is heavy with blood guilt.

> *If My people who are called by My name will humble them-*
> *selves, and pray and seek My face, and turn from their wicked*
> *ways, then I will hear from heaven, and will forgive their sin*
> *and heal their land* (2 Chronicles 7:14).

For those who might think that only unbelievers need to repent, take note of this verse. The word *repent* in Hebrew is *yashuvu*, which means to turn.[3] The Lord is saying that *His people* need to seek His face, humble them-selves, and turn from their wicked ways. The first word is "if." This means that *if not*, He will not hear, He will not forgive, and He will not heal our land.

Over a number of years, we have wept over these issues: the broken trea-ties and slaughter of the First Nations people; the enslavement of innocent Africans, who were kidnapped and brought in chains and slave ships to this soil; the treatment of "freed" African Americans during the 100 years fol-lowing the Emancipation Proclamation; the cruelty inflicted on Chinese immigrants; the legal abortions of roughly 50 million unborn babies; human trafficking, targeting children and teens as sex slaves, even in America; and other abominations too terrible to mention. Much more about these issues and the repentance work that was done can be found on the World for Jesus Web site.

The repentance that takes place in these painful gatherings is vitally important for the delaying of God's judgments against our nation. He can-not ignore the blood of the innocent that has been shed in a nation's history, even if He waits many years. There will either be repentance or judgment; this is a fully biblical truth. Even so, the coming judgments, while having been delayed by God's mercy, are not cancelled against this nation.

The emotional and spiritual pain we entered into at these gatherings took a toll on our souls and well-being. The Lord gave us what we could bear from His heart, and protected us from going into a pit of depression, anger, and uselessness. The Lord's glory was present, but so was loud wailing, as we find in the Book of Lamentations. The Lord always strengthened us, knowing when we could handle more tears and when we needed to rest. He deeply appreciated what we offered and will move mightily to overturn this great evil and bring true revival to America.

Sometimes, the pain of what we heard was hellish, and I wanted to escape from the knowledge of such evil and cruelty committed in our beloved America. I felt caught between the ideal of "righteous, patriotic American Christianity" and the realities of satanic greed and depravity, operating with great profits under the nose of law enforcement, and with high-level corruption protecting these activities.

The Lord has shown unspeakable restraint in not pouring out wrath upon our violent, idolatrous, and blood-soaked nation. Nevertheless, the Lord loves America, and will bring us revival fire before the fires of judgment. Praise His great mercies!

The Lord is very close to the forgotten people, the victims, the slaves of human trafficking, the oppressed, the aborted, the poor, the prostitutes, the disenfranchised members of this world's populations. He expects His people to share His burdens and His concerns for these forgotten ones. If we don't care for them, we are not His friends.

THE HARDEST CONVERSATION

I am now including a section that originally appeared in my first book.[4] It is a journal entry about suffering, which includes a conversation I had with the Spirit of the Lord; it took place over several days surrounding September 11th, 2006. It was, by far, the hardest conversation I have ever had with the Lord. It was triggered by a dream, in which I suffered. The pain this revelation caused me is almost indescribable, but I needed to understand this matter.

The Lord has begun to speak to me about a terribly hard reality we will all have to face. Lawlessness will come upon our way of life, and His children will suffer intensely as a result of this oppression, injustice, and violence. It should not seem strange to us. Large numbers of His beloved children are suffering at the hands of lawless and brutal men, as well as merciless and cruel governments, at this very moment in other parts of the globe. Likewise, His people have suffered this way throughout the pages of the Bible, and these sufferings are documented in much historical literature since the New Testament was written.

> Dear friends, do not be surprised at the painful trial you are suffering, as though something strange were happening to you. But rejoice that you participate in the sufferings of Christ, so that you may be overjoyed when His glory is revealed (1 Peter 4:12-13 NIV).

Recently, the Lord gave me a most disturbing and realistic dream in which the unthinkable happened: I was victimized by a lawless man, and despite my repeated cries to the Lord to rescue me, He did not. When I awoke, the first question the Lord asked me was,

"Are you angry with Me?"

I replied that I was not angry, but was stunned and could not understand why He did not rescue me when I called upon His name for help, over and over. The Lord told me to record the dream in my journal, and then He would speak to me about it. I wrote down every painful detail and read it aloud to Jesus.

The Lord then led me to the eleventh chapter of Hebrews, and began to speak to me about Cain and Abel, as well as the multitude of beloved saints described in this densely packed passage. Abel is commended for having faith, and Hebrews asserts that God was pleased with his offerings. We also see that Abel's testimony still speaks and lives, despite his removal from the earth at the hands of a lawless brother.

The Lord then asked me if I thought He loved Abel less than Cain because He did not rescue Abel from this lawless one, with whom God was most displeased, while Cain lived for a long time after this event. I replied that the opposite was true; that I believed God loved Abel more than Cain, but nevertheless allowed him to be bludgeoned to death without rescue.

I then studied the "heroes of faith" who escaped the edge of the sword, did not burn in the flames, were not devoured by fierce beasts, had miraculous victories over enemies and armies too strong for them, and even experienced resurrection from the dead! The writer commends all of these for their great faith.

He then draws our attention to another group of believers, who also had great faith. These were tortured, scourged, chained, imprisoned, starved, driven out of their homes into the caves and open pits of the earth, went without clothing, food, or shelter, were sawed in half, stoned, and stabbed to death with knives and swords. The writer then commends these as well for their faith, but asserts that neither the victorious ones nor the persecuted ones received what they had been promised by God. *"Only together with us would they be made perfect"* (Heb. 11:39-40 NIV). This great cloud of witnesses is waiting for *our generation* to finish our race; only then, will they receive what they have been promised!

As the Lord and I honestly confronted my stumbling block concerning the distinct "lack of rescue" I had experienced, as well as the murder, rape, and torture of countless believers throughout time and geography, He began to teach me about the coming suffering and the falling away of His people.

This conversation caused me much pain and many tears, but the Lord was insistent that I become prepared to trust in His goodness no matter what might happen to me, or anyone else. I now record portions of that life-altering conversation. Referring to my dream and the lack of rescue, I asked the Lord what I had done wrong; He answered,

"*You were a victim. You did not do anything to cause it or deserve it. Sometimes righteous people are victims.*"

"Are You saying that sometimes even calling on Your Name will not rescue us from the situation?"

"*Yes, sometimes I will not answer in the form of rescuing you. It will not be what you wanted Me to do. I do this for My own purposes in your life. Sometimes I will rescue My children, and they should always call on My Name, as you did repeatedly. That was good and right, but I allowed this to take place so you will understand how it feels to be a victim, and not blame yourself for something over which you had no control.*

"*My children will be victims of lawlessness in these last days. Brutal and selfish men will do worse to My children than what this man did to you. This is already happening to Christians in other countries, as you have read in the e-mails.*

"*Do not be surprised and do not be angry at Me when it happens. My people will be victimized. Sometimes I will sovereignly and miraculously drive off their attackers. Sometimes I will not. I am still a good God, even when men are evil.*

"*You will need to comfort My children who are victims, and you need to know it was not their fault. You will love them more because of this and will not question My goodness.* [The Lord then named a brutal scenario that is occurring to some of His children now.] *This can and does happen, and I am still a good God, and I love My children. Is this hard to believe?*"

"Yes, I wish You would stop these acts of violence and protect Your own ones."

"*Sometimes I do protect My own ones. Sometimes I allow My servants to suffer. I do not love them any less because I allow them to suffer at the hands of evil men. The protected ones are not loved any more than the victims. Do I love My martyrs less than the ones I keep alive until the Catching Up? Surely you do not believe that!*"

I attempted not to start crying and answered, "It feels that way to my emotions, I must admit. I believe what You are telling me, but in my heart it feels like You love less the ones whom you allow to be beaten, raped, tortured, and killed. Forgive me, Lord, but it *feels* that way."

At this point, I could not stop the tears, and wept bitterly. I was unable to grasp that He could love the victim just as much, and yet not stop the cruelty. I added, "My heart can't take it."

The Lord replied, "*If you do not fully grasp My love and goodness, even when I allow you and those you love to suffer and be victims, your faith will not survive the cruelty of the lawlessness and invasion that is coming. I **am** good when men are evil. I **am** good when men behave well. I do not change, but men hurt My children. It has been so from the beginning, since I allowed Cain to bludgeon Abel to death with an iron plow. I loved Abel more, and he was the victim.*

"*My people do not know what was done to My prophets or My saints, and what is being done right now to some of My most beloved sons and daughters on the earth.*

"*Are you better than My other children in other cruel places and in other cruel centuries? Is My American church so much better than all of these other people who suffered, and suffer daily for My Name and testimony?*

"*Why am I a good God when it happens to someone else, but a mean God when it happens to you or your loved one? My Church in America needs to get real! This will happen to all of My Bride wherever and whenever she dwells on the face of the earth. She will be hated and will share in the fellowship of My suffering.* [Here He reminded me of Matthew 24.]

"*I love you, Jill, and I will keep you. No matter what happens to you, I love you and will keep you. Keep fighting and resisting and rejecting and rebuking the evil one. Keep calling on My Name, and above all, keep trusting in My goodness when lawlessness increases and much harm comes to My most beloved ones.*"

This conversation continued the following day, on September 11, 2006. I was crying, as I thought of the victims of "9/11" and our previous talk about all victims.

The Lord Jesus asked me, *"Does your heart still hurt from yesterday?"*

In response, I cried, because I felt so sad that some of His children are allowed to be harmed so terribly, but He loves them just as much as the ones He protects supernaturally.

The Lord said, *"My heart hurts, too. I cry when My children suffer; don't you think I cry? Is My heart harder than yours?"*

"No, Lord, You have a tender heart; of course You cry." However, I was thinking, "You are the only one in the world big enough to stop it, and yet even though it hurts Your heart, You allow it."

He knew my thoughts, of course, and we both sat in silence as the pain raged within me for a while. It is unlikely that I will understand why He allows these things until I see Him face to face, outside of this earth's limited perspective.

I am ending the excerpt here. Despite my lack of understanding, the Lord did heal and comfort my heart before this conversation and struggle were completed.

> *For I am convinced that neither death nor life, neither angels nor demons, neither the present nor the future, nor any powers, neither height nor depth, nor anything else in all creation, will be able to separate us from the love of God that is in Christ Jesus* [Messiah Yeshua] *our Lord* (Romans 8:38-39 NIV).

"GIVING MY SERVANT REST"

In closing this chapter, we will look at a very basic, obvious reason for some of the suffering and death of God's people. The Lord will simply choose to take His servants home to Heaven, in order to grant them rest. And so, we must never assume that the Lord is punishing someone who dies early. It may be exactly the opposite. We must not assume it is satan who is killing the person, because the Lord may be giving His servant rest. That is why wisdom is needed in knowing how to pray and respond to each situation.

Within the last few years, one of the greatest and godliest evangelists on the earth died. Shortly before his death, some believers who were close to this man, gathered to weep and pray to the Lord for his life to be spared. One particular prophet was among those praying for his life. This prophet was taken to Heaven during the prayer time, and found himself standing before the throne of God, interceding for his friend. He also saw the spirit of the dying (yet still living) man, standing near him before the throne. The Lord said to the prophet, "*Your request cannot be granted.*"

The prophet asked the Lord why not. The Lord answered, "*I want to give My servant rest.*"

The prophet was then returned to the prayer meeting on earth; he did not tell the people what he had heard from the Lord. The man of God passed away by the next morning. He had worked hard for the Lord, and it was simply his time to go to His Father's house and rest until the resurrection of the dead.

The Lord uses physical death as the way of separating our bodies from our spirits, and bringing our spirit-person to Heaven to be with Him. For our spirit to leave our mortal body, most of us have to experience death. There are some Scriptural exceptions to this, and I will now summarize two of these exceptions:

1. Paul tells us that in the last generation, not all believers will physically die, but some will be kept alive until the catching up of the prepared Bride. At this moment in history, the righteous dead in Messiah will be raised first, and then the living will be caught up to meet the Lord in the air (see 1 Thess. 4:13-17).

2. There are special cases in both the Old and New
    Testaments where individuals have been/will be translated
    alive without tasting death. Some have been kept alive and
    will remain alive until the coming of the Lord Jesus Christ
    (see Gen. 5:24; 2 Kings 2:11; Luke 9:27; John 21:22).[5]

THE GOD OF ALL COMFORT

*He is despised and rejected by men, a man of sorrows and
acquainted with grief....Surely He has borne our griefs and carried our sorrows....He was oppressed and He was afflicted, yet
He opened not His mouth....Yet it pleased the Lord to bruise
Him; He has put Him to grief* (Isaiah 53:3a,4a,7a,10a).

There is no sorrow, pain, or anguish we can experience on earth that is
worse than what our Lord Jesus bore upon Himself for our sakes. He is not
a cold, distant God, watching us dispassionately as we struggle to survive,
like a half-crushed insect on the ground. He is personally involved in our
suffering.

People often cannot feel His presence when they are in a period of intense
grief or pain; I know that feeling myself. We wonder, "Where are You when I
need You the most? Why didn't you stop that person from harming me? You
don't know how terrible this pain is, Lord. I can't bear this anymore!"

Despite what we feel or perceive, the Lord is surely close to those who
are in trouble and who call upon His name:

*This poor man called, and the Lord heard him; He saved him
out of all his troubles....The Lord is close to the brokenhearted
and saves those who are crushed in spirit. A righteous man may
have many troubles, but the Lord delivers him from them all*
(Psalm 34:6, 18-19 NIV).

If we could see how intently the Lord feels all that we feel, if we knew His compassion upon all that we endure, we would never feel abandoned again. He Himself knows what it feels like to hunger, to thirst, to walk for miles with blisters, to be scorched in the heat of the day, and to shiver in the cold night air. The Lord knows what it feels like to be sleep-deprived, and to not know where His next meal will come from; He knows what it feels like to be harassed, humiliated, grilled, insulted, misunderstood, and accused of having a demon. He knows the exhaustion and demands of mobs of people, who could not give Him a moment of rest or privacy.

The Lord knows what it is like to have the skin ripped off His back by sharp metal hooks, piece after bloody piece. He knows what it is to carry an unbearable load of rough, heavy wood on His shredded shoulders, walking up to His crucifixion, though He had done no wrong.

The Lord knows what disease, cancer, infection, fever, dislocated joints, muscle spasms, and slow suffocation feel like; all of these were laid upon Him on the cross, the infirmities of the world and the cruelty of His atrocious hanging.

The Father in Heaven knows the pain of losing a child, an only Son. He watched Him cry out in agony, helplessness, and humiliation, and could not lift a finger to rescue His beloved Son. We will never know the pain the Father suffered that day.

And the Son knows abandonment as we will never know it. The Son knows what it is to die as a vile sinner, bearing every filth, blasphemy, perversion, iniquity, theft, murder, and child abuse ever committed. The Son knows hell as we will never know it. Where He has gone, there we will never go. The Son knows the blackness of feeling His Father's radiant face turn away in rejection of the unclean thing His Son has become.

We will never feel what the Father experienced as His only Son was taken away from the land of the living. We will never taste a grief or a pain that our Lord has not tasted before us, for us, with us, in our place, and for our good. Each time we take communion, we should remember Him. It will lessen our suffering each time we remember His.

> *For we do not have a High Priest who cannot sympathize with our weaknesses, but was in all points tempted as we are, yet without sin....Therefore He is able to save to the uttermost those who come to God through Him, since He always lives to make intercession for them* (Hebrews 4:15; 7:25).

Sadhu Sundar Selvaraj was once taken to Heaven, and he saw the Lord Jesus on His knees before the altar in Heaven. The Lord was holding onto the horns of the altar, and He was weeping rivers of tears. He was pleading and interceding for us in our desperate situation, before the Father. He continued to intercede until the Voice from above the Mercy Seat said, "*It is granted.*" This is the kind of Savior we have, who ever lives to intercede for us.

The wounds and gashes in our hearts are the places through which the Lord's light and comfort shine the brightest. The very areas where we were wounded become the source of comfort to countless others. When I am going through a very painful or overwhelming season, it is a great comfort to talk to someone who has been through the same thing. This fellowship of suffering is precious, because only someone who knows what we are feeling can truly comfort us.

For parents who have lost a child, it is not helpful for us to say, "I know what you are feeling," if we ourselves have not lived through that type of pain. Sadly, we really do not know what they are feeling, although we mourn with them and sympathize deeply. They can often receive deeper comfort from someone else who has lost a child, and has received God's comfort.

The Lord permits these afflictions in our lives and uses them to bring comfort to others. I've seen this in my own life so many times. After going through an affliction or grief, whether emotional or physical, I later realize that the Lord carried me, even when I couldn't feel His help. Then, I will encounter someone who is going through a similar trial, and it will be obvious that the Lord has given me exactly what they need to be comforted. If I had not gone through the trial, I would not be equipped to help to pull them out of the same pit.

> *Blessed be the God and Father of our Lord Jesus Christ, the Father of mercies and God of all comfort, who comforts us in all our tribulation, that we may be able to comfort those who are in any trouble, with the comfort with which we ourselves are comforted by God* (2 Corinthians 1:3-4).

ENDNOTES

1. See http://www.studylight.org/lex/heb/view.cgi?number=02487.

2. See www.worldforjesus.org.

3. See http://www.studylight.org/lex/heb/view.cgi?number=07725.

4. Jill Shannon, *Coffee Talks With Messiah: When Intimacy Meets Revelation* (Theodore, AL: Gazelle Press, 2007).

5. For an astonishing true account of a man who has been kept alive until the coming of the Lord, read "The Maharishi of Mt. Kailash" by Sadhu Sundar Selvaraj; www.jesusministries.org.

Chapter 4

A Change in Destiny

For those who believe that the Lord is still speaking to us today, there is an issue that the Lord would like me to explore, to help us understand the nature of prophetic words.

Many Spirit-filled believers and leaders operate in the realm of the prophetic. It is common in churches and conferences for people to wait in line to receive a personal word from someone who is ministering prophetic words. It is also common for us to "hear" inner words or impressions in our private prayer times with the Lord. Sometimes, we see inner visions; at times, though not as often, we might see "open" visions right before our eyes.

These words may be general, biblical words of correction or encouragement, which would not cause us any confusion. However, at times we get a specific, directional word about our destiny or our future. These words can either be gloriously productive—or confusing and disruptive in our lives. My purpose in this chapter is primarily to deal with *true* prophetic words that do not seem to "come true," or that are changed at a later time in our lives. However, I must first address the issue of false prophetic words.

A LYING SPIRIT

The wicked King Ahab was surrounded by hundreds of Israeli prophets whose guidance he liked and trusted. In First Kings 22, we read that he asked these prophets if the Lord would bless a military campaign against Ramoth Gilead. They all assured him that the Lord would grant him a great victory.

However, the Judean king Jehoshaphat was visiting Ahab at this time, and he suggested that Ahab inquire of one of the Lord's true prophets before proceeding into battle. They brought in Micaiah, whom Ahab despised, because *"he never prophesies anything good about me"* (1 Kings 22:8 NIV). When Micaiah prophesied a disastrous defeat, the other prophets mocked him cruelly, and insisted that Ahab would be successful. Before being dragged off to prison, the righteous prophet said this:

> *Therefore hear the word of the Lord: I saw the Lord sitting on His throne with all the host of heaven standing around Him on His right and on His left. And the Lord said, "Who will entice Ahab into attacking Ramoth Gilead and going to his death there?" One suggested this, and another that. Finally, a spirit came forward, stood before the Lord and said, "I will entice him." "By what means?" the Lord asked. **"I will go out and be a lying spirit in the mouths of all his prophets,"** he said. "You will succeed in enticing him," said the Lord. "Go and do it." So now the Lord has put a lying spirit in the mouths of all these prophets of yours. The Lord has decreed disaster for you* (1 Kings 22:19-23 NIV).

Most people wonder if this "volunteer" lying spirit was an angel or a demon. I'm not sure; it could have been a righteous angel, merely lying for God's good purposes to destroy Ahab. But it could have been a demon as well, since God may have permitted this evil spirit to serve His good purposes. Paul writes that God Himself will send a *"strong delusion"* into the earth in the latter days, and thus, I can't be sure which type of spirit it was (see 2 Thess. 2:11).

Another troubling biblical account is found in First Kings 13:1-25. A prophet from Judah was sent with a rebuke to the idolatrous king Jeroboam. The Lord had warned this prophet not to eat bread or water after delivering the word, nor to return by the same route on which he came.

On his way home, an elderly prophet found him and enticed him to come to his house to eat and drink. At first, the Judean prophet refused, due to the fear of the Lord. But the elder prophet told him,

> *I too am a prophet, as you are. And an angel said to me by the word of the Lord: "Bring him back with you to your house so that he may eat bread and drink water." (**But he was lying to him**.) So the man of God returned with him and ate and drank in his house* (1 Kings 13:18-19 NIV).

While they were eating and drinking, the true word of the Lord came to the lying prophet, and he decreed that the disobedient prophet from Judah would be killed by a lion on his way home because he had disobeyed the word of the Lord. Indeed, the young prophet was killed by a lion for his disobedience. I always felt sorry for the deceived prophet, who was killed.

In this case, a false prophet gave a false word to a true prophet. The elderly man may have been a true prophet in the general sense of hearing God's word accurately, but he had a severe character flaw. In this case, he created a false prophecy, knowing it to be a lie. He misused his gift to entice an innocent man, and thus, I would categorize him as a false prophet. However, this false prophet also delivered the true word of the Lord after he had deceived the young prophet. The lying prophet was used by the tempter to ensnare the godly prophet. However, the one who lied had a genuine prophetic gift, since he could also hear a word from the Lord, as could Balaam (see Chapter 11).

After the death of the young prophet, the elderly, lying prophet was seized with remorse for his role in this man's death and mourned for him deeply. He had a conscience, despite having lied. Why he lied is not entirely clear; it seems he did not expect the prophet to get killed because of this lie. Not everything is black or white in the realm of the prophetic.

Even Judas Iscariot was seized with remorse after he saw the horrible results of his betrayal of the Lord Yeshua. Satan had filled him to do this thing, and yet when he came to his senses, he was desperately sorry. Even so, his remorse was too late. This "son of destruction" was unable to repent unto salvation and committed suicide (see John 17:12).

As a side note pertaining to Judas, we find a profound warning for all of us in this terrible story. Cain was given a chance to repent before sin got the better of him. Sapphira, not knowing that her husband had been struck dead a few hours earlier, was given a chance to repent before repeating the fatal lie to Peter. Pharaoh was given many chances to repent before the Lord hardened his heart. *It is important not to miss the opportunity to repent while it is still available.* This warning is true for Christians as well as non-Christians (as with Ananias and Sapphira, who were Christians). A moment comes when it is too late, and we do not know when that moment will come.

I have read testimonies of believers who were at the deathbed of someone who had resisted previous offers to repent, and was now unable to repent before death. These were people who had been offered the Lord's salvation many times and had continually refused, saying, "Maybe later."

As they lay dying, Christians would sit at their bedside, pleading with them to accept the Lord while there was still time. But in more than one account, the dying person said, "I waited too long. *My heart is like stone. I cannot repent.* Leave me alone. I already see the hellish fiends waiting to take me."

Then, as they neared death, they would scream in terror as their spirits were dragged away by overanxious demons bearing chains. *The ability to repent is a gift from the Holy Spirit, not something we can choose anytime we want.* This is a mystery, but from these frightening deathbed testimonies, I realized that if the Lord hardens someone's heart, that person becomes a doomed "son of destruction." God forbid! Do it *today*, for we may not have tomorrow.

> **Today** *if you will hear His voice, do not harden your hearts as in the rebellion...so I swore in My wrath, "They shall not enter My rest"* (Hebrews 3:7b-8a, 11).

Now, returning to the story of the lying prophet, this is the point we can take from it: prophets can lie to us, whether knowingly or unknowingly. We must be extremely cautious, prayerful, and discerning as to which prophetic words we believe and act upon.

Within the Spirit-filled community of believers, many prophetic words have been spoken that were not actually the word of the Lord. In many cases, the believer who gave the word was not deliberately opening himself up to a lying spirit. He or she "heard" a word, and did not discern it correctly. This word could then harm the believer who receives it and acts upon it. In some cases, prophets are speaking out of their own deceived imaginations, which is terribly harmful to naïve and trusting young believers (see Jer. 14:14).

If someone prophesies a specific, "directional" word over our lives, destinies, or futures, we must go to our prayer closets and pray until we know that this word is truly from the Lord. There is a very small company of prophets on the earth whose words never fail and are sure and trustworthy (see 1 Sam. 3:19). However, most who prophesy still make mistakes from time to time, and we must be in prayer over each word given to us.

Unfulfilled True Prophecies

Some Christians are very quick to condemn anyone whose prophecy does not seem to come true. They refer to the Book of Deuteronomy, where it tells us that false prophets must be stoned if they lead us after other gods or if their words do not come to pass. In their zeal to condemn false prophets, these people are not taking into account the whole counsel of Scripture.

There are numerous biblical prophecies that did not come to pass in the generation that the prophet spoke them. We know that some of Isaiah's predictions about the coming Messiah's future kingdom did not come to pass in his day. These words would only be vindicated in a future generation. Likewise, Daniel and the other prophets prophesied some words that will not be fulfilled until the last generation. This by no means makes them false prophets.

In addition, there were words spoken that did not come to pass in the timeframe that the prophet predicted; however, these were true biblical prophets who were not wrong in their prophecy. Let us look at a few such cases, because these will help us in our own situations:

Jonah walked the streets of Nineveh and prophesied, *"Forty days and Nineveh shall be overthrown"* (see Jonah 3:4). He did not say, "if you do this," or "unless you do that."

In response to his dire warning, the entire city repented in sackcloth and ashes, and as a result, the city was not destroyed for over 100 years. Thus, Jonah's prediction of 40 days did not come to pass. And yet no one in the Church would call Jonah a false prophet. We also see a changed prophecy given by Isaiah, concerning king Hezekiah.

> *In those days Hezekiah became ill and was at the point of death. The prophet Isaiah son of Amoz went to him and said, "This is what the Lord says: Put your house in order, because you are going to die; you will not recover." Hezekiah turned his face to the wall and prayed to the Lord...and wept bitterly. Before Isaiah had left the middle court, the word of the Lord came to him: "Go back and tell Hezekiah...I have heard your prayer and seen your tears; I will heal you....I will add fifteen years to your life" (2 Kings 20:1-2; 3b-5a, 6a NIV).*

The Lord changed Hezekiah's destiny in response to his prayers and tears. And yet Isaiah's original prophecy was the word of the Lord.

The Lord told Abraham to sacrifice his son Isaac on Mount Moriah. At the last second, the Lord told him not to slay his son. In this case, Abraham was being tested, although he did not know it at the time. For a test to be genuine, the person being tested cannot know it is a test. He or she must believe it is a fixed reality in the Lord's mind. Abraham heard the Lord correctly, but the Lord changed the outcome at the last moment, for His own redemptive purposes.

The Lord told Moses that He would destroy the children of Israel for their disobedience. It was an unequivocal, *"Let Me alone, that I may destroy them and blot out their name from under heaven; and I will make of you a nation mightier and greater than they"* (Deut. 9:14).

Moses fasted for 40 days and nights, pleading before the Lord that He might not do this thing. The Lord heard Moses' costly intercession and relented from His plan to destroy them.

We can glean from these examples that the word of the Lord for an individual or a nation can be changed, delayed, or cancelled, due to people's prayers or responses. Unlike a fatalistic Greek drama, where everything must come to pass, no matter what, our God is a living, responsive, and reasonable God, who listens to His people. He acts in conjunction with their prayers and tears and can change His decree.

Therefore, we must be very careful not to call people false prophets unless we know for sure that they are leading the Lord's people astray into idolatry, deception, or sin.

My Coffee Talks Destiny

Those who read my first book will likely remember two dramatic testimonies I shared. One was when my heart stopped with a violent jolt in the fall of 2003; there was no pain, but I felt it stop suddenly and with great force. I then saw a year written before my eyes. This was not a heart attack because there was no pain, and I was fine moments afterward. From that moment until now, I have always believed that the Lord was showing me the year of my physical death. I could not think of any other prophetic meaning for this strange event.

The second testimony was that of my future martyrdom in a country in Europe. This took place during three days of seclusion in April 2006. The Lord showed me this destiny in an inner vision and in a "glory visitation," which is an encounter where the tangible weight of God's glory falls and remains over me for a significant period of time. In addition, I received three external confirmations from people who did not know me, that this word was truly from the Lord. Putting two and two together, I have always connected these two testimonies, though they were separated by three years: the stopping of my heart and the martyrdom vision. Thus, since 2006, I have believed without wavering for over three years that this would take place as the Lord revealed it to me, and in the year I was shown in 2003.

I have been accountable to my pastors about this destiny, and have struggled mightily with it. I did not doubt that it was true, and I had fully agreed to it before the Lord. However, I did not particularly want to die this death in a few short years, nor did I want to face the feeling of abandonment that the Lord had warned me about. Although I knew the Lord would not truly abandon me, He told me that I would feel that way. I would need to hang on by faith and to overcome fear.

> And they overcame him by the blood of the Lamb and by the word of their testimony, and they did not love their lives to the death (Revelation 12:11).

I also felt afraid of leaving my family to minister abroad and die. I would be alone, and who would bury me? I wondered who would take over my ministry, concerning the distribution of my books and CDs. I felt terrible for my husband, who would be alone, since our children have grown up and moved out. There were many tearful sessions, as I fought the need to imagine this final scene over and over. I conquered this to a large degree over time and did not allow my mind to go there. However, there were times during long, sleepless nights that I would worry about the event and would feel depressed about the prediction of abandonment.

After awhile, I began to consistently thank the Lord for the honor of martyrdom and in my prayers, I contended hard for my destiny. I was concerned that if I felt afraid for too long, I would disqualify myself from this high calling. I reasoned that the Lord would then assign me a different kind of ending, which would be less glorifying to His name, and that would result in a lesser reward when I reached Heaven. I was more afraid of losing my reward in Heaven than I was of the dreaded scenario.

I also wanted to please the Lord in the deepest motives of my heart, and I prayed regularly and sincerely that He would send me to this nation. I prayed that my life and my death in this nation would glorify Him and save many lives. The Lord gave me a love and a burden for this nation, and I spent over a year studying the language and taking private lessons to improve my preaching of the Gospel in this language.

This year, as I write this book in 2009, I made my peace with my destiny. While I cannot say honestly that all fear disappeared, I reached a point where I was trusting the Lord to carry me through that time and to take my spirit at the perfect moment. I accepted it with a measure of joy and resolve that I had not achieved until this year. In fact, I prayed regularly that He would not remove this honor from me due to my unworthiness and fear.

THE LORD PREPARED ME FOR CHANGE

When I began writing this book, this chapter was not in the plan. This is because when I began, I had no idea that the Lord was going to bring a massive change into my life, purposes, and destiny. He knew, of course, but I knew nothing of it.

Looking back on it, I now see the ways the Lord was preparing me for what He was about to surprise me with. I will share with you three things that happened just before I left for a particular prophetic conference, where everything changed in a moment.

1. One week before this conference, I was having a coffee talk. As you know, one of the hardest things about the martyrdom revelation was the warning that I would feel abandoned, like a lost child on a crowded city street, who could not find her father. I would feel that way, just as the Lord had felt abandoned by His Father on the cross.

In once sense, the Lord Yeshua really was abandoned, because all of our sins were laid upon Him. But in an eternal sense, He was not truly abandoned, because the Father had predetermined to raise Him from the dead into glorious exaltation, the moment His hideous ordeal was over. So He had told me, *"I wasn't really abandoned, but it felt that way. You will feel that way, too."*

I cannot express to you how much that hurt me and scared me. I felt I could go through anything if I could just feel the Lord's presence wrapped around me, giving me grace to overcome the fear and the pain. But the thought of not feeling Lord at all—it just overwhelmed me with despair. There was one time I had lain on the floor, weeping hysterically and pleading with the Lord, "Please, please don't make me do this without Your presence. I can't do it; You know I can't!" And I went on and on, pleading with the Lord not to let me feel abandoned.

I sensed in my heart that He was not going to respond to that kind of faithless pleading, and in fact, He did not respond, although He calmed me down with His peace. *I know that the Lord is much more moved by our faith than our fear.* When I was finished with my hysteria, I got up and went back to my chair, knowing that the Lord had heard me but had probably not appreciated my lack of faith.

That was two years ago. But now, one week before this particular conference, I was back in my chair with more faith in the Lord's goodness than I had in my previous meltdown. I knew that the Lord is a gracious and compassionate God, who hears and responds to the faith-filled prayers of His children. And so I decided to approach Him one more time about the terrible abandonment issue, which still disturbed me enormously. However, this time I approached Him as a friend with a proposition, rather than as a pleading, terrified, and lost child.

This time, I calmly and rationally told Him, "Lord, I'd like You to consider changing one aspect of my destiny. I am honored to be a martyr for You, and I definitely don't want You to remove this honor from me because of my fear and sadness. But I am deeply disturbed by this prediction of abandonment. If Your Father would consider my request, could You please change just that part? I'm not asking You to add 15 more years to my life, as You did with Hezekiah. That wouldn't even be good for me." (In this I was saying that with all the evils coming upon the earth, I was so fragile that it would be better for me to leave sooner than later.)

I continued, without crying, "If You are not pleased to grant this request, I will accept that. I know that I will hang on and be an overcomer, but if it pleases the Father, I am asking You to change this one part of my destiny."

The Lord did not answer me at that time, but I absolutely knew He had heard me because He always hears us. I thought in my heart, *Who knows if the Lord will be gracious and change this part of the prediction? Maybe I won't even know if He has granted my request until the time of my death, but maybe I will feel His presence then, because of this prayer.*

I was content that I had brought this matter before Him in faith, not in fear. I knew this is the kind of prayer that moves Him to respond. I had no idea how hugely my Lord would respond only ten days later!

2. After my friends and I arrived at the conference on a Wednesday night, we were talking in the hotel. I shared with them that night that I had finally made peace with my martyrdom. I told them that I still had some fear, but I was finally at a point where I completely trusted the Lord to carry me through it, and that I knew I would overcome. I embraced my destiny as the

absolute best plan for my life, or the Lord would not have ordained it for me.

3. The next day was Thursday, and we were in sessions all day. But at 4:00 in the afternoon, we were released for a dinner break, and we returned to the hotel, exhausted. Shortly after coming in, I received an unscheduled phone call from a close prophetic friend who did not know I was at a conference. This call came at the one moment in the day when I had turned on my phone and was free to talk.

He told me that he had seen a brief vision that depicted the place in Heaven that the Lord had prepared for me. My friend didn't know this, but months earlier, I had made a private request of the Lord, concerning my place in Heaven. My friend told me something that precisely answered my private request, which the Lord alone had heard. This vision showed my assigned place setting at a banqueting table, a place that was prepared for me long before I was born. When I entered and saw my name inscribed at my place, I would know that it had been waiting for me all this time. I would be joyful because this place fit me perfectly and was what I had asked of the Lord. The Lord felt it would help me to know this now because it would help me to run my race, and He prompted my dear friend to call me at that time.

Little did I know what would happen 24 hours after hearing about this vision. But this information would later help me to process a huge shift that was about to take place in my understanding of my future.

My "Changed" Destiny

Three days before writing this chapter, I attended the conference just discussed. When I go to these conferences, I almost never get in lines for prayer or to receive a prophetic word. This is not because I am opposed to this practice in any way. I appreciate the tireless ministers and prophetic teachers who stand for hours, praying for the Lord's children. My reasons for not going up are private, and yet I will tell you anyway.

The Lord has brought me to a place where, for the most part, I need to receive my healings, instructions, and blessings from Him alone. I rarely desire for a man or woman to lay hands on me and impart something to me, unless the Lord leads me to go up for prayer. I have received many healings and blessings; it is time for me to be a blessing to His flock. Of course, when I am ill, depressed, or suffering pain, I would welcome prayer.

However, there are a few prophetic leaders whose integrity, humility, and spiritual authority are like unto the fathers of our faith in the Bible. If one of these ministers would receive a word from the Lord for me, I would gratefully and humbly receive it. One of the speakers at this conference was such a man, who lives a consecrated life of continual prayer and fasting. Like Samuel, none of his words fall to the ground. Although I have heard him speak before, I have never asked him for a word from the Lord. I glean enough treasures from his messages to the entire audience attending the conference. His words bring the fear of the Lord to anyone who listens with a teachable heart.

At this conference, after preaching the message, he prayed a closing prayer over the audience. This lengthy word was more than a prayer; it was a strong exhortation from the Lord. As is frequently the case, he saw the Lord Jesus standing before him, speaking this word to His people. It was about forsaking our concerns about our material things. We were exhorted sternly to pursue the Lord's Kingdom purposes and not our own comforts and selfish desires.

During this word, the prophet saw a large treasure box being placed at the foot of the stage. It was full of scrolls that contained the destinies of all of the participants in the room. He saw our angels holding our scrolls, and they desired to reveal to us God's purposes and destinies for our lives. However, the Lord said that His people were not asking or seeking to know these sealed destinies, and thus, they still remained unknown to us.

At that moment, to my utter astonishment, I heard the prophet speak my full name into the microphone. He began to deliver a personal word to me publicly, revealing my life's purpose and destiny, as the Lord was speaking to him my destiny at that very moment. Everyone in the sanctuary heard my destiny revealed at the same moment that I was hearing it.

When I realized he was speaking over my life, I knelt down to receive it. The destiny he spoke was not martyrdom in Europe at all. In fact, it was almost the opposite. It was a consecrated life of fasting and prayer in another nation, similar to the prophetess Anna, who fasted and prayed in the temple until the first coming of the Lord (see Luke 2:36-38). It would not be unto death, but unto life. The sacred destiny he was declaring over me was contingent on my obedience to go to this nation and "give my life in fasting and prayer for the coming redemption of the Lord Jesus Christ." He saw a beautiful bridal canopy stretched over me, "as a Jewish bride" would stand under the *chuppah* on her wedding day. This material was light and transparent, being made of gold dust.

As I listened to this lengthy personal prophecy, I was stunned, awed, and a little confused. I knew this man's walk and history, and I knew that the words and visions he receives are from the Lord, who stands before him. And yet I wondered as he spoke: *The Lord had confirmed my "earlier" destiny to me with several outside confirmations. Could this really be happening?*

When my personal word finally ended, the man of God continued speaking warnings and loving exhortations to the entire flock in the room. Neither before nor after my word did he give any other personal words to individuals. He spoke about martyrdom and consecration, and most of us ended up on our knees, doing sacred business with the Lord, as he prayed for us. I hardly heard what he said after my word. I was processing this information at high-speed thought, and my head was reeling with the implications. I felt I had to talk to this prophet after the meeting. I was so worried he would be ushered away the moment the meeting ended. I silently pleaded with the Lord to let me talk to him.

The moment he left the platform, while others were still in prayer, I approached him and begged for a moment in private. He graciously agreed, and I was permitted to follow him and his aides to a private room for a few minutes.

During that rare private conversation, I quickly shared with him my prior revelation about my martyrdom in Europe, which I had received three years and three months before. I told him this had been confirmed to me by three different people who were neither connected to me nor to each other. I asked him if I had "heard wrong." He replied that I had not heard wrong, but that the Lord had changed my destiny.

He reminded me that Abraham had to be completely willing to sacrifice Isaac, but after he passed the test, the Lord changed His instructions. Likewise, I had proven that I was solidly committed to give my life for the Lord's purposes in this other nation, and now I was receiving my new destiny. He also shared that at a particular moment in his own life, the Lord had changed his destiny, and it took him a long time to adjust to the new plan.

I tell you the truth, precious reader: if this word had come from someone else, I could have thought that a lying spirit was tempting me to avoid the high cost of martyrdom, offering me this helpful prophetic escape from death.

If the Lord had revealed this change of plans to me privately, I might have thought it was the enemy in my mind and would have rebuked it. I was absolutely certain about my prior revelation and had taken tangible steps to prepare for ministry in this nation. But the Lord, in His mysterious dealings, knew that there was a man I would believe.

I didn't ask anyone for a prophetic word, nor did I desire any change in my seemingly ordained martyrdom. I had agreed to it of my own free will. The Lord chose to astonish me with this revelation in front of hundreds of people I did not know and to have it captured on DVD.

As an additional confirmation, I realized several weeks later something so remarkable, that there is no one but the Lord who could have orchestrated it. This astonishing word was spoken **20 years to the day** since my family and I left Israel permanently. Although I shared about our returning to America in *Coffee Talks With Messiah*, the month and day of our departure was never detailed. In fact, if one allows for the time zones, this word was spoken on the same day, and even at the same hour that we boarded the plane for the United States in 1989.

My Lord Yeshua, being satisfied that I had prayed and prepared diligently for three years and three months (39 months) to minister and then be killed in this other nation, chose to rescue me as He rescued David from Saul's spear. As He rescued Isaac from the knife. As He added 15 years to Hezekiah's life. This word came in the fortieth month from the prior revelation.

Though I did not ask the Lord for this, He changed my destiny for His own sovereign purposes, which I might not understand until the end of the age unfurls. In the Lord's mind, this is not truly a change. Rather, it is the result of my heart's gradual transformation, which allowed Him to open up what He had prepared for me before the worlds were formed. In other words, if I had not reached a point of full and unequivocal submission to martyrdom, I would not have qualified to walk out this "new" destiny. It will be so challenging, that it will require the mature fruit of one who has completely died to her will and her rights. *A test cannot reveal itself to be merely a test; only through walking out its absolute certainty, can our heart be proven.*

In the last few days, I have been thinking about other cases where someone's death has been averted through prayer. Two testimonies stand out in my mind. In one case, there was a Christian mother with a husband and a three-year old son. She developed a long and debilitating heart condition, which caused her to waste into skin and bones, and was at the point of death. She was in the hospital, awaiting one last operation, which had almost no chance of success, but her husband wanted to try anything to save her. They called for a godly man to pray for her healing. As he prayed, he sensed that the Lord was telling him it was her time to die. However, as he looked at her little son playing in the hospital hallway, oblivious to the terrible loss he was about to suffer, he began to fervently pray with great compassion for this woman and her son, who would be motherless in a few hours.

He then saw the Lord Jesus sitting on the bed with them, and He was intently watching her weep her heart out for a long time. After some time, the Lord told this man that He had seen her tears and would grant her life back to her. She was completely healed after this operation and is still beautiful and healthy all these years later.

The other testimony was of an elderly man who was dying, and his two grown daughters begged this same man to come to his bedside and pray for healing. As he prayed, he heard the Lord tell him that this man would not be healed. That day was the man's decreed day to die, and it was settled. The prophet plainly told the daughters what the Lord had decreed, thinking that this settled the matter. However, they did not accept his answer and explained with great sorrow and desperation why their father *couldn't* die. They needed him too much, and they shared all of the terrible consequences that would befall their family if he died. They asked the prophet to go back to the Lord yet again, and so he did.

This time, after he had prayed with great pity and compassion for this family, he saw a calendar on the wall. He watched the pages flipping ahead to a new date in the future. The Lord told him that He had heard their cries, and would extend his life until the day revealed by the flipping calendar.

For the work of His Kingdom, if I will be obedient to go where He has called me, the Lord Yeshua has graciously granted me life. And yet, many of my brothers and sisters will indeed be martyred, even as I was bracing myself to undergo martyrdom in a few short years. The Lord loves all of His children, both His martyrs and those He keeps alive. Each one of us has a precious and glorious destiny. The Psalmist wrote, "*Precious in the sight of the Lord is the death of His saints*" (Ps. 116:15).

But also precious are the *living* sacrifices His children are asked to offer: fastings, hardships and persecutions, tears and intercessions for His people. This is also a difficult and sacrificial path.

There is a scroll of destiny in heaven with your name on it. Have you earnestly sought the Lord to reveal to you what is written in Heaven of your life's purpose? It will remain sealed unless you seek and ask for your heavenly blueprint to be revealed to you. The Lord desires to reveal it to you more than you desire to know it! Go for it, dear reader, go for it! It is yours, reserved in Heaven for you! Amen.

THE SEASONS OF THE TREES

The Lord gave me a prophetic dream, whose meaning I have not fully understood. However, I believe it connects to personal seasons and destinies, possibly changing destinies in particular. It may relate to changes in the seasons for the Church in general. It had a hi-definition, biblical feeling, like a Daniel-type dream as I experienced it.

In this dream, my husband and I lived in an older house, like those built in the 1950s. We seemed to spend a lot of time alone, sitting in the modest living room, and we didn't seem to have the children.

I saw my rocking chair in the corner of the living room. I know that this rocking chair represents my intimate relationship with the Lord, because this is where I meet with Him, and this is where He appeared to me on March 23, 2007.

My husband and I were sitting on the couch, looking at the chair. Suddenly, the chair disappeared, and in its place, I saw a large pot with dirt in it, one which used to have a potted plant. I knew that the plant had died a long time ago, and we had never bothered to replace it. This may represent destinies, ministries, and callings in our lives and marriages that we missed, due to selfishness or disobedience.

I was sadly looking at the empty pot when suddenly, a large, magnificent tree appeared in the pot. It was lush and full of branches, covered with hundreds of small white flowers with pink centers, something like apple blossoms, only with a deep pink center. They may have been more like almond blossoms. (The almond tree is the earliest tree to bud and flower in Israel.)

Then the tree and its pot began to rotate slowly and deliberately, in one full circle, allowing us to admire it from all angles. I felt it was "showing off" its beauty for us. After making one full circuit, it stood still again.

I was astonished and delighted that the Lord had given us this tree and excitedly pointed out this miracle to my husband. At first I thought it was a fake plant, which can often look so real. But as I touched and smelled the blossoms, I knew it was a real tree the Lord had given us. I was overjoyed and seriously thought this would be our beautiful miracle plant forever.

But after a few moments, the tree began to be transformed before our eyes. Quickly, it morphed into a lush evergreen tree, like a pine tree, covered in full green branches. It was as beautiful as the flowering tree, but was a completely different species of tree. I knew this was a "winter tree" and that the seasons were changing. As I continued to look at the evergreen tree, I was expecting the Lord to put some beautiful clumps of white snow on the branches, to complete the winter scene.

However, to my shock and great disappointment, the needles began to drop from the tree. Thousands of pine needles rained down rapidly onto the ground, and within moments, the branches were left bare. This made me sad; I felt the tree must have died, but I wasn't convinced it was really dead. I still felt some hope left in the tree.

As soon as the branches were bare, the Lord Yeshua appeared, standing among the lower branches of the tree. At first, He seemed so small that I thought He couldn't be real, but as I looked, I realized He was truly the Lord. He began walking among the bare branches of the tree, earnestly searching for fruit on the bare branches.

Then for a moment, the scene changed: I saw the full-sized Lord in a forest of evergreens, and He was padding skillfully through the thick woods like an Indian scout, moving purposefully through the forest. The Lord was pushing aside many branches as He walked, searching for fruit on tree after tree.

Then the scene returned to our living room, and the Lord was back to walking and searching for fruit among the bare branches of our potted tree. I looked down at Him, overwhelmed with love and happiness to see Him, and cried out, "Beloved!"

Yeshua looked up at me, and began to walk out of the tree, toward where we were seated on the couch. As He came out, He grew larger and larger. The Lord looked at me, reached out His hand, and briefly squeezed my hand with affection; His hand was normal size, warm and soft. But He moved past me quickly, like a man on a mission, and headed toward my husband. He then began to do a transforming work in my husband.

When I woke up, this is the verse that immediately came into my mind:

> For the time will come when you will say, "Blessed are the barren women, the wombs that never bore and the breasts that never nursed!"... **For if men do these things when the tree is green, what will happen when it is dry?** (Luke 23:29,31 NIV)

There are different seasons in our lives and in the history of the Church. In many cases, including my own, much of our lives have produced no lasting life or fruit for the Lord, nothing to show Him but an empty pot full of dirt. This pot represents the place where our destinies should have flourished like flowering and fruitful trees, but we did not seek them, nurture them, or pay the price to walk in them.

This pot also represents the lack of life and true fruit in the Western church over the past generation. At the conference, the prophet saw many scrolls of destiny, one for each believer in the room, but they will never know their destinies unless they seek and ask for them to be revealed. If they don't, their futures will not flourish with the Lord's ordained purposes for them.

In His kindness and mercy, despite our negligence and carelessness, the Lord has sovereignly granted us one last life-bearing cycle, during which we must produce fruit and reap a harvest of souls for His Kingdom. This last chance is extended to all individuals, churches, and ministries. He has first given us a leafy tree, full of fragrant blossoms, which represents a season of abundant, undeserved blessings, wealth, youthful beauty, growth, and fragrant offerings to the Lord. He is showing off His beauty and generosity to us, and we are twirling before Him like a well-adorned Bride, showing off our magnificent blossoms. I believe this lush and flowering season is almost or completely behind us at this point. Many of us enjoyed the flowers without maturing for the time of fruit.

After this season, comes the season of maturity. The evergreen tree is a symbol of the mature Bride. She displays a less flamboyant beauty, for she is a sturdy, unwavering, mature, soldierly, and stately tree. She does not twirl in girlish vanity, nor does she flower or show off, but she is fruitful, bearing the fruit of hard, "armored" pine cones; these carry her seed for the next generation of harvested souls.

We would like the Lord to crown her with the "icing" of white snow to adorn and decorate her branches. This would be like a ripening into a princely old age, full of years. However, He is accelerating everything, and this maturity will not be a long season. The Lord is allowing the darkness of these final years of the church age to strip away all her needles, all her comforts and support structures. He must shake everything that can be shaken, and the Church will be purged, pruned, tested, and examined for fruit.

I hate to say this, but I believe the bare branches might represent losing our money and homes and enduring great hardships for the Kingdom of God. I hope it does not mean this, at least not in all cases. For believers who have been comfortable, this will be so difficult that many will be tempted to join the enemy's system and ultimately, take the mark of the beast to receive physical sustenance. This would bring temporary relief, but our eternal souls would be damned. God forbid!

See that you do not refuse Him who speaks. For if they did not escape who refused Him who spoke on earth, much more shall we not escape if we turn away from Him who speaks from *heaven, whose voice then shook the earth; but now He has promised, saying, "Yet once more I shake not only the earth, but also heaven." Now this, "Yet once more," indicates the **removal of those things that are being shaken, as of things that are made, that the things which cannot be shaken may remain.** My son, do not despise the chastening of the Lord, nor be discouraged when you are rebuked by Him; **for whom the Lord loves He chastens, and scourges every son whom He receives** (Hebrews 12:25-27;5b-6).*

Beloved ones, the Lord is searching for fruit among our branches. Even when the twig is dry and bare, and all of the normal supports of this world system have been stripped away from us, the Lord Jesus expects us to bear fruit. How He searches among the branches for the lasting fruits of His Holy Spirit. He searches as a father for his missing child.

Both the destinies of martyrdom and the sacrificial life of fasting, prayer, and reduced circumstances are costly and painful lifestyles. Both of these special destinies feel like death to our flesh; they hurt our human strength, pride, and any sense of controlling our own lives. They are both very humbling paths, full of tears. If we agree to either of these destinies, which only the Lord can determine, we will feel like a mature pine tree which has been stripped of its beautiful covering of protective needles.

Even so, the Lord expects us to bear fruit, even the armored pine cones bearing the good seed of the Son of Man (see Matt. 13:37-39). These pine cones represent putting on the full armor of Messiah in the last-days' battle against evil (see Eph. 6:13-18). We might feel like a dry, dead stick for a season, but we are very much alive in Messiah Yeshua and will continue to bear much fruit if we abide in Him!

Ask the Lord now to examine the fruit of your life; ask Him to prune or strip away everything that hinders you from bearing fruit that will hold up under Heaven's fiery scrutiny and the world's cruelty on that day. Ask Him to pull out the "tares" in the field of your heart so that the good seed may flourish and not be choked out by soulish strongholds, woundedness, and offenses. May our Vinedresser find lasting fruit on our bare branches in that day. Amen.

I wrote this song as a parable for the lives of individuals, as well as for Israel and the Church.

WHERE IS MY SON?

When I saw you in the desert, you were early fruit
    to me.
    In the spring your branches blossomed, in the
    winter, evergreen
    As a newborn, no nation loved you, then I
    washed and gathered you
    When you grew to love's awakening, with My
    wing I covered you

Where is My son that he might run to Me?
    Where is My son that he might come?
    Open your heart that you would cling to Me
    I AM your rock, the only One

Oh my son, there is a river, I would plant you by
    My streams
    The branch is bare, your roots are withered,
    how can you bear fruit to Me?
    Though father and mother forsake you, I will
    gather you
    Still I love you, still you grieve Me, still I wait
    for you
    For you desire to be My chosen, and hold My
    word in high esteem

But My tears are ever falling, why is My son
far from Me?

Though you treat Me like a stranger, relentless I
pursue
Still I call you, still you pierce Me, still I weep
for you

Let us spend the night together, and in the
morning we will seek
For the vines of summer's blooming
For the late fruit on the tree
Where is the flower and fragrance?
Where is the fruit of your desire?
How I search among the branches as a Father
for His child

Chapter 5

The Anonymous Healer

In 850 B.C., Aram was one of the predominant military powers in the Middle East; it had even gained victory over the Assyrians, thus increasing its prestige in the region. Aram inhabited the territory of modern-day Syria. Its army was commanded by Naaman, a valiant soldier who was highly esteemed by his king, Ben-Hadad, and by the people of Aram. But Naaman had incurable leprosy.

His wife had an Israeli servant girl, who had been captured by an Aramean raiding band. This girl told her mistress, "If only my master could visit the prophet who is in Samaria! For he would heal him of his leprosy."

Naaman reported this to his king, who sent him to Joram, the king of Israel. King Ben-Hadad assumed that this Israeli prophet would obey Israel's king, and that if he paid Joram a large sum of money, he would order the prophet to heal his leprous military official. And so, Naaman arrived in Israel with a letter of introduction, 750 pounds of silver, and 150 pounds of gold.[1]

When the king of Israel read the letter that demanded that in return for payment, he would heal the foreign commander, he tore his clothes and cried, *"Am I God, to kill and make alive, that this man sends a man to me to heal him of his leprosy?"*(2 Kings 5:7). He suspected that the powerful rival king was setting him up in an impossible situation, as an excuse to make war against Israel.

When the prophet Elisha heard that the king had torn his robes, he sent word to him, assuring him that the leprous man should be sent to him, *"so that he will know that there is a prophet in Israel."* Elisha wanted this pagan commander to understand that the God of Israel was real and could heal through His chosen prophets.

> *Then Naaman went with his horses and chariot, and he stood at the door of Elisha's house. And Elisha sent a messenger to him, saying, "Go and wash in the Jordan seven times, and your flesh shall be restored to you, and you shall be clean"* (2 Kings 5:9-10).

Elisha was a humble man of God. Naaman, who had come all the way from Syria to be healed of an incurable and infectious skin disease, was an important man. In fact, his armies had demonstrated military dominance over Israel, although the two nations were in a period of relative peace. If Elisha had wanted to display his greatness, he could have healed Naaman in such a way that would have shown his superiority over this worldly military leader.

He could have stood there and loudly and publicly proclaimed the God of Israel over Naaman, and could have said "Thus saith the Lord, thou art healed of thy leprosy, O great general!"

Instead, Elisha did not even come out of his bedroom. He said to his servant, *'Tell him to go wash in the Jordan seven times, and the God of Israel will heal him.'* His heart said, "I don't even need to be involved in this healing; I don't even need to make my name known in Aram. He will know there is a prophet in Israel and that the love of his Israeli slave girl brought him to Israel to be healed by the one true God." Elisha's only motivation was to give glory to God.

GOD RESISTS THE PROUD

*But Naaman became furious, and went away and said, "Indeed,
I said to myself, 'He will surely come out to me, and stand and
call on the name of the Lord his God, and wave his hand over
the place, and heal the leprosy.' Are not the Abanah and the
Pharpar, the rivers of Damascus, better than all the waters of
Israel? Could I not wash in them and be clean?" So he turned,
and went away in a rage (2 Kings 5:11-12).*

The proud Naaman went away very angry. It was an insult to his position not to be granted an audience with the prophet, and then to be asked by a servant to dip in the humble Jordan river seven times. There were larger rivers in Damascus; if all it took was a river, he could have stayed home and dipped in a more impressive body of water. He felt he deserved more attention than this. But what he needed was healing from the invisible God, not a big fanfare. He was ready to storm off to Aram, but was counseled by his servants, who loved their master and wanted him to be healed.

*And his servants came near and spoke to him, and said, "My
father, if the prophet had told you to do something great, would
you not have done it? How much more then, when he says to
you, 'Wash, and be clean'?" (2 Kings 5:13)*

Naaman needed to humble himself to receive from the God of Israel. Elisha had set an example of humility for him, by not taking glory to himself for this healing. But in his anger, Naaman wouldn't have recognized or appreciated the prophet's humility. He was too busy feeling proud and offended. However, he heard the wisdom in his servants' encouragements.

*So he went down and dipped seven times in the Jordan, according to the saying of the man of God; and his flesh was restored
like the flesh of a little child, and he was clean (2 Kings 5:14).*

In this amazing story, we also see the humility of God Himself. Having observed Naaman's pride as he stormed away from Elisha's servant, the Lord could have withdrawn his offer of healing. Naaman could have gotten to the river, only to hear the Lord say, "Too late. You should have obeyed the first time." But the Lord was gracious, and when Naaman's heart became humble like a child, he received the perfect, new skin of a little child.

THE ANONYMOUS HEALER

Let us now fix our eyes on the healing ministry of One greater than Elisha. The Lord Yeshua was a humble prophet in Israel. He was much more than a prophet, and yet He usually called Himself "the Son of Man." In Hebrew, the word for "man" is *adam*, and so this title actually means, "Son of Adam." This preferred title of Jesus gives us a picture of this man's humility.

An even greater manifestation of the Lord's humility is seen in His desire to remain anonymous as He performed healing miracles. It is so obvious that this man did not want acclamation, but only wanted Israel to give glory to the Father. One example of this humility is found in Matthew 8.

> *When He came down from the mountainside, large crowds followed Him. A man with leprosy came and knelt before Him, and said, "Lord, if You are willing, You can make me clean." Jesus reached out His hand and touched the man. "I am willing," He said. "Be clean!" Immediately he was cured of his leprosy. Then Jesus said to him, "See that you don't tell anyone. But go, show yourself to the priest and offer the gift Moses commanded, as a testimony to them* (Matthew 8:1-4 NIV).

The Lord honored the Law of Moses and required that the man offer the sacrifice that the Torah prescribed (*Torah* is the Hebrew word by which Jewish people refer to the first five books of the Bible). But He did not want publicity over this healing; His motivation was compassion, not recognition.

Before we continue looking at Yeshua's humility, let me share something that the Lord showed me, that has changed the way I look at the ministry of healings and miracles.

Once I was praying during the night for a woman I had heard about who had an advanced crippling disease. I knew that I would be meeting her soon, and I was wondering if the Lord would want me to pray for her healing. She was a strong Christian with genuine faith in God's ability to heal her and had received much prayer from believers. However, some of the people who had prayed for her had been abusive in their behavior. The abuse took place in Christian meetings with people she did not know. She had not asked them for prayer, and yet they hauled her out of her chair and commanded that she walk; when the poor dear could not walk because she was not healed, they berated her for lack of faith.

Even though I wish I could heal every afflicted person I see, I know that I have no power to heal anyone. If the Lord is not showing me that it is His intent to heal them at this time, I would rather minister to them in the way He shows me. Perhaps He might only wish me to sing a worship song to someone, or to sit and talk together, or just to make them laugh. (I love to make people laugh!) What is my Father asking of me in each case?

> *Then Jesus answered and said to them, "Most assuredly, I say to you, the Son can do nothing of Himself, but what He sees the Father do; for whatever He does, the Son also does in like manner* (John 5:19).

If my Lord Yeshua did not heal of His own initiative, I should not do so either. And so, I did not want to be one more Christian putting pressure on this dear sister. She already had faith for healing and had an amazingly cheerful and uncomplaining disposition, though she suffered greatly.

As I lay in bed, I was pondering these thoughts and wondering what the Lord's purpose was for this visit. Then I felt the Lord's Spirit say to me, "*If you did pray for this woman in her house, privately, and she was completely healed of advanced multiple sclerosis, and her spinal cord and myelin sheath were completely restored, would you be willing to tell her that you never wanted anyone to know that you even prayed for her, as I did? Will you do what I did on earth? Would you instruct her that no one is to know that you prayed for her? She can go and testify of her healing, she can jump for joy in the temple courts, she can tell everyone that the God of Israel healed her, but are you willing to be completely anonymous now and forever?"*

And from this amazing word, the Lord began to show me His healings throughout the Scriptures. For the first time, the force of His humility confronted me. I noticed that the healing methods used by Yeshua were mundane, unspectacular, and even embarrassingly unhygienic. And I was surprised at how many times the Lord instructed those He healed not to tell anyone. The Lord took me to so many incidents where He demonstrated an unusual degree of humility. This teaching is a result of that revelation.

As the Lord questioned my motives that night in bed, He did not promise me that I would receive the gift of healing at that time, nor did He promise me that this sister would be healed. But Yeshua wanted to understand my heart's motives right up front. *The Lord tests our heart before He trusts us with His power.* If we cannot be trusted to remain humble with the small miracles, how will He trust us with great power, wherein we might be tempted to make a name for ourselves?

The Pool of Siloam

In John 9, we see the story of the man born blind, whom the Lord Yeshua passed on the road. Although His disciples assumed that he was blind due to his own sin or that of his parents, the Lord explained to them that his blindness was for the purpose of revealing God's glorious works to Israel. This was a setup to glorify the Father through the works of the Son.

> *When He had said these things, He spat on the ground and made clay with the saliva; and He anointed the eyes of the*

blind man with the clay. And He said to him, "Go, wash in
the pool of Siloam."…So he went and washed, and came back
seeing (John 9:6-7).

Like the ancient prophet before Him, we see Yeshua sending the man to
a small, humble body of water, where he would simply wash and receive his
healing far away from the crowd, and thus, far away from those who would
praise Yeshua for the healing.

The Lord could have healed this man any number of ways; He could
have publicly and loudly proclaimed, "In the name of Adonai, let this blind
man who was blind from birth, see! You are healed, brother! O, Glory to
God!"

But the Lord didn't do that. Instead, He crouched down and spat on the
dirt, rubbed the mud together with his fingers, and placed it on the man's
eyes. Then He told him what Elijah had told Naaman: "*Go, and wash yourself
in the pool of Siloam.*" The man was led away to the pool with his eyes plas-
tered with moist mud. He washed in the pool, came up seeing perfectly, and
went home. He didn't come back to Yeshua, shouting his praise; he just went
back to his house. I believe the Lord Yeshua wanted it this way.

Sadly, this healing caused persecution for the man and his parents at
the hands of the leaders of my Jewish people. While there is much more we
could say about the Pharisees' grievous responses, it is not the purpose of
this section to delve into that. Because of his truthful testimony, the man
was evicted from the synagogue. This may sound like a small punishment to
the modern reader, but in first-century Roman-occupied Israel, being evicted
from the synagogue was very harmful.

First, it cut the person off from his Jewish community and all of his
prayer life, spiritual nourishment, and fellowship. He obviously could not
frequent the local Roman temple with its statues of Jupiter, temple prostitutes, and the regular slaughter of pigs.

Second, since his fellow Jews were the only people he could do business with, it cut him off from his livelihood. We need to understand the cost to an Israeli Jew of following Yeshua, which is as true today as it was in Yeshua's day.

Third, Israelis lived in a hostile environment, surrounded by Roman soldiers who did not need much excuse to arrest, scourge, or crucify Jews. Therefore, the love and support of friends and family were part of survival, both physical and emotional. Being cut off from the only group of people they could associate with was dangerous and depressing.

The Lord made a point to search for this rejected Jewish man, after hearing about the persecution that had befallen him. In verse 35, we read,

> Jesus heard that they had thrown him out, and when He found him, He said, "Do you believe in the Son of Man?" "Who is He, sir?" the man asked. "Tell me so that I may believe in Him." Jesus said, "You have now seen Him; in fact, He is the one speaking with you." Then the man said, "Lord, I believe," and he worshiped Him (John 9:35-38 NIV).

Yeshua healed this man by a lowly method and then sent him away so that the moment of actual healing would remain anonymous. Later, the Lord searched for him privately, to make sure that the man would be able to withstand the hardship of being excommunicated from the Jewish community, while under Roman rule. The Lord was revealing Himself, not to gain credit, but to give the man a revelation of who had healed him; He wanted to ensure that the man would not deny Him under intense pressure and, thus, lose his heavenly reward. And so, the compassionate and humble Lord Jesus revealed His identity privately to His newly healed Jewish brother, but not publicly.

We notice in verse 35 that the Lord chose to call Himself by the humblest of all titles: "the Son of Man." He could have said far better things, and they would have been completely truthful, but He identified completely with the race of Adam. It is interesting that the King James Version translates this verse "Son of God," even though the Greek text clearly says "Son of Man." Perhaps the translators felt that "Son of Man" was too humble, and they changed the English title to honor the Lord more. However, we honor the Lord more by using the title He chose to call Himself, for that was the title His Father chose.

Son of David, Have Mercy!

We see another example of the Lord's anonymity in Matthew 9:27-31. While traveling on the road, two blind men followed him and cried out, "*Son of David, have mercy on us!*" These men were using a Messianic title and were shouting it at the top of their lungs on a public road. Only the Messiah could be called "Son of David," and all of Israel knew it. Because the Lord did not want praise and fanfare, He did not acknowledge their request until He could remain anonymous. While Yeshua could have healed them right there, He chose to wait until He had entered the privacy of a house.

> *And when He had come into the house, the blind men came to Him. And Jesus said to them, "Do you believe that I am able to do this?" They said to Him, "Yes, Lord." Then He touched their eyes, saying, "According to your faith let it be to you." And their eyes were opened. And Jesus sternly warned them, saying, "**See that no one knows it**"* (Matthew 9:28-30).

A Partial Healing

In another unusual case of healing the blind, we see yet another private miracle, which was deliberately performed outside of the village and coupled with a command to tell no one.

> *Then He came to Bethsaida, and they brought a blind man to Him, and begged Him to touch him. So He took the blind man*

by the hand and led him out of the town. And when He had spit on his eyes and put His hands on him, He asked him if he saw anything. And he looked up and said, "I see men like trees, walking." Then He put His hands on his eyes again and made him look up. And he was restored and saw everyone clearly. Then He sent him away to his house, saying, **"Neither go into the town, nor tell anyone in the town"** (Mark 8:22-26).

The Lord Jesus spat on the man's eyes. Was there life in His saliva, in His DNA and bodily fluids? I would say, "Yes, I'm sure there was life in every part of His sinless body." But spitting is an undignified thing to do; in our culture, it might seem like an unhygienic contact.

I have two questions for you: How would you feel if a godly person with a gift of healing spat on you? And, how would you feel if you were praying for the sick, and the Holy Spirit told you to spit on someone? To be honest with you, it seems unthinkable to me. To obey the Lord on that one would take tremendous courage for me, and I hope I could do it. And yet, if Yeshua had not obeyed the Father and performed the healing in the exact way that the Father desired, that man would not have been healed.

Yeshua was the humblest man on the face of the earth. Despite knowing that the Father had sent Him straight from Heaven's glory, he was humble in a way that we cannot fully grasp. If we could walk in that humility, our lives would be turned upside down, and so would our public and private ministry.

After placing His hands on the man, the Lord did not proclaim any great healing. Rather, He said, *"Do you see anything?"*

The man said, *"I see men walking around like trees."*

Incredibly, this is the only recorded biblical account that describes a partial healing by the Lord. After the Lord placed His hands on the man a second time, he received his complete healing, and could see clearly.

Why do you think the Bible included this testimony of even our great Lord Yeshua obtaining only a partial healing after His first attempt? I believe this account is there to encourage us, and also to keep us humble.

When we pray for people, we desire to see great and instantaneous healings. Naturally, we want to see miracles follow our prayers of faith. It is good to desire these types of healings, which encourage and thrill us. But those who are active in healing ministries report that many supernatural healings do not take place in a dramatic and instantaneous manner. Sometimes, we see an instant miracle, and this gives great glory to God. But more often, the healing might come the next day, or the next week, or gradually over some passage of time. It is still supernatural healing, particularly if the affliction was not one that would have naturally disappeared over this time frame.

If this partial healing could happen to our Lord Yeshua, how much does that encourage us to persist when we do not get the perfect or complete results we desired? We might see nothing right away, or we might see some small improvement at first; but later, we might hear about the complete restoration of that person. Are we willing to accept that? I think it is very humbling.

The Lord says in Zechariah 4:10, *"For who has despised the day of small things?"*

If the Lord can trust us to rejoice and appreciate the day of small things, He will trust us with great authority. I believe that the Father Himself limited His Son's first attempt at healing this blind man, in order to encourage His flock that the servant is not greater than his master. If the master persisted until the healing was complete, without growing discouraged or being offended at His Father, then we must do likewise.

Finally, Jesus sent him home, saying, *"Don't tell anyone."* If you prayed privately with a blind person in a little alley and saw him receive his sight immediately, would you be willing for no one to know that you prayed for him? Even if you testify publicly that this blind man was healed, are you willing to leave yourself out of it and to be anonymous? This is the exact question the Lord asked me that night in bed, as I prayed about the sister with crippling affliction.

I know that it wasn't the Lord's time to be revealed to the world. Many people think this is the reason why the Lord continually told people not to report what He had done. I do agree that this was a part of the picture. However, the Lord showed me that His overriding reason was that *He only wanted the people to give glory to God, for He came to earth to reveal and glorify His Father in the eyes of Israel.* Below are three examples, where we see that the Lord Yeshua's only motivation was to give glory to God.

> *Now behold, one came to him and said to Him, "Good Teacher, what good thing shall I do that I may have eternal life?" So He said to him, "Why do you call Me good?* **No one is good but One, that is, God**" (Matthew 19:16-17a).

> *Then Jesus said to him, "Receive your sight; your faith has made you well." And immediately he received his sight, and followed Him,* **glorifying God. And all the people, when they saw it, gave praise to God** (Luke 18:42-43).

> *Now when the multitudes saw it* [the healing of the paralytic man] **they marveled and glorified God,** *who had given such power to men* (Matthew 9:8).

When the crowds saw the paralyzed man carrying his mat, they were filled with awe, and they praised God because He had given such authority to men. This is precisely the response the Lord Yeshua desired. He was the Son of Man; He had emptied Himself of equality with God, and He performed miracles as a devout man who was relying on His heavenly Father for the power to do miracles (see Phil. 2:6). His humanity would encourage us that we too would be sent out to perform miracles, relying on the Spirit of God to do the supernatural. Surely, God has given such authority to the sons of men.

The Lord Jesus didn't have false humility, for He knew who He was and where He came from. The Lord told the truth about Himself, but His heart was not to glorify Himself, but to glorify the One who sent Him. That should be our heart, too. Sadly, much in our flesh wants to call attention to ourselves. That is human nature, and it is the opposite of the Lord's heart. *God is asking us to be the opposite of ourselves.* In a moment, we'll explore how we can train our hearts to be humble, as our Lord's heart is.

WILL WE DISQUALIFY OURSELVES?

As we look toward the great healing revival that is coming soon, we need to know that it will be a nameless, faceless revival, where no great healer makes a name for himself. This massive wave of healings and deliverances will involve countless unknown servants of the Lord. They are those who have no desire to be known or sought after, and *whose deepest heart motive is only to glorify God and disappear quietly into the next task. "I must decrease that He might increase"* (see John 3:30).

We will see unlikely people, those whom our culture does not esteem, healing the sick quite naturally and unselfconsciously. Little children will be involved in this revival, and it is happening already in some places; I have seen the evidence myself. There is an awesome DVD called *Finger of God* that documents some of the miraculous work of God being done around the world.[2] It is an excellent resource for those who are skeptical about the healings and resurrections being reported to us from other nations.

For the Lord to trust us with His great power, we have to have a meek heart, the heart of the anonymous healer. Perhaps some have received these gifts, even if they have not cultivated a meek heart; that is the Lord's decision. But I do believe that this is going to become a requirement across the board; I also believe that in my case, for my own good, the Lord will require this heart before I receive the full measure of this coming power.

If my heart would become proud because of the abundance of power and revelations, it would separate me from the Lord. It would ruin my intimate relationship with Him and jeopardize my eternal destiny, and *He's not willing to risk that, even for the healing of His children.* If I can't be trusted, the Lord will find lowly people who He can entrust with the powers of the age to come. Will we sign a contract of anonymity with *Adonai,* in the privacy of our prayer closets?

Sadly, there are some who are operating in great power gifts but are using this power to gain fame, ministries, or finances for themselves. Perhaps they were humble in the past, but have now built their own kingdom. Does their God-given gifting mean that the Lord approves of their motives, their hearts, or their deeds? Does it mean that they will occupy a great throne in Heaven?

Indeed, it does not mean that. The Lord does not withdraw His gifts, because Romans 11:29 tells us that the gifts and the callings of God are irrevocable. The flock so desperately needs people with enough faith to heal the sick that the Lord will use these servants to help His children, even if they are making a name for themselves. Remember that the Lord warned us that many who ministered for the Lord in miraculous signs would be rejected by Him on judgment day, because they were lawless and He never knew them (see Matt. 7:21-23).

It is right to publicly glorify God for all healings and deliverances, both emotional and physical. These testimonies must not be kept secret. *However, the point of our testimony should not be how anointed our ministry is; rather, the focus should be on the Lord receiving glory.* Some sow and others reap. Perhaps we might pray for someone and see an immediate healing, which is like reaping wonderful fruit. But who planted, who watered and fertilized before we got there? Let us remember in humility that others sowed the seed, prayed and fasted, and watered the earth with their tears, but did not see the results that we were granted to see at that moment. Our prayer was part of a Kingdom process, and we must remain humble.

> *Even now the reaper draws his wages, even now he harvests the crop for eternal life, so that the sower and the reaper may be glad together. Thus the saying, "One sows and another reaps" is true. I sent you to reap what you have not worked for. Others have done the hard work, and you have reaped the benefits of their labor* (John 4:36-38 NIV).

I have heard preachers with a healing or revival ministry come to a church, who somehow never find the time to open the Word of God. They spend their allotted preaching time talking about themselves, how blessed their family is, and how much the Lord is doing through their ministry. It is good to share what the Lord is doing in our lives, but who is the focus of the preaching? We need to hear the Word of God preached in the power of the Spirit, to build up our faith.

The greatest ministering servants on this earth are the most humble. When I am privileged to hear them preach, I feel the reverent fear of the Lord, and my thoughts are about how I can please the Lord more. They glorify the Lord Yeshua and do not call attention to themselves. The testimonies they share show the audience that any believer can walk this closely with the Lord, if he or she will be obedient, transparent, and humble. One of these godly preachers is Sadhu Sundar Selvaraj.[3] He always glorifies the Lord alone. I heartily recommend to you his teaching CDs and DVDs. They have changed my life.

I believe that anyone who desires to exalt his or her own ministry through the supernatural gifts will be disqualified from participating in the great harvest. We must seriously adjust our hearts in order not to fall into this perilous snare of pride.

Go Low!

From the law to the prophets, from the gospels and epistles to the Book of Revelation, we are warned that we must humble ourselves; clothe ourselves in humility; become like a little child; walk in lowness and meekness of heart; consider others better than ourselves; and know that, having done all, we are merely unprofitable servants and were only doing what was expected of us. These urgent admonitions are continually presented throughout our Bibles. I will provide only a few examples here, but if I were to include all of them, this chapter on humility would consume the whole book.

> *Blessed are the poor in spirit, for theirs is the kingdom of heaven....Blessed are the meek, for they shall inherit the earth* (Matthew 5:3,5).

> *Yes, all of you be submissive to one another, and be clothed with humility, for "God resists the proud, but gives grace to the humble"* (1 Peter 5:5b).

> *I dwell in the high and holy place, with him who has a contrite and humble spirit, to revive the spirit of the humble, and to revive the heart of the contrite ones* (Isaiah 57:15b).

> *Now the man Moses was very humble, more than all men who were on the face of the earth* (Numbers 12:3).

We must remember that we are but dust, and the Lord could remove from us the breath of life at any moment of His choosing. We are owed nothing and guaranteed nothing, other than eternal life, if we continue to trust in the atoning work of the Lord Yeshua and to walk with Him.

The Lord explained this amazing parable about humility to Sadhu Sundar Selvaraj: when sunlight streams into a room, and we see thousands of dust particles hovering in the air, it is not actually the dust we are seeing. It is the light of the sun reflected off of each particle of dust. Without the light, one cannot see the dust in the air. The Lord told Sadhu that we must all remember that we are just like that dust. We are nothing and cannot be seen, apart from the light of God, reflecting on us and from us.

We have been warned by many prophets that Pride will be one of the most sneaky and destructive onslaughts that the enemy will bring to bear against God's most fervent and powerful servants; those who have been entrusted with great anointing, power, and authority will not notice Pride coming up from behind them. Pride comes like a thief in the night.

I have experienced this myself. I can be walking with God and producing much work for His Kingdom in a humble state of mind. Suddenly, I will hang up the phone from a conversation, and to my dismay, I will hear one of my sentences played back in my mind by the Holy Spirit, who is the world's best tape recorder: I will realize that this statement is sheer pride. I didn't plan to say or think anything proud. It just popped out of my mouth. When this happens, I feel very upset with myself, and I immediately go before the Lord and repent.

Rick Joyner has written in *The Final Quest* that we must constantly put on the mantle of humility, which, although it looks drab and unappealing, will be our sign of great honor in Heaven.[4]

I will now share a small lesson on how to do this in a practical way. When I first began attending the repentance conferences under the direction of Nita Johnson, she would have the intercessors spend time "going low," before we could move into the phase of weeping, interceding, and repenting for the sins of our nation (this ministry is also discussed in the chapter on suffering).

Nita would instruct us to physically get as low as we could in the room, whether kneeling at our chairs, or lying prostrate on the floor. We usually met in hotel conference rooms, and the carpets were truly filthy. But at that moment, you don't care about your freshly washed hair or the clothes you put on that morning. You remember that in Bible times, they tore their clothes, put on scratchy, dirty sackcloth, and placed a handful of dirt from the earth on their heads to display their sorrow and humility. As I lay on my face on the well-worn carpet (or when in Jerusalem, on the dirty and dusty cold stone floor), I would wonder, *How do I go low? What thoughts should I think?*

After awhile, Nita would say, "When you've gone as low as you can, go lower still." I would make a deliberate effort to think accurate, humble thoughts about who I was before God. I would picture myself as dust, sinking into the floor. I would try to think very lowly and humble thoughts about the life I've lived, the years I've wasted not being loving, the selfishness of my soulish comforts, and my petty and arrogant offenses at others. I must admit that I often had no idea if my efforts were pleasing to the Lord, or if I was successfully going low.

After attending many of these conferences, it became easier to quickly adjust my mental assessment of my sorry self. I found that I was able to honestly enter a tearful, grateful, truly humble estimation of the unworthiness and unholiness of my innermost thoughts and motives, and of the years I have spent in selfish pursuits. It gets easier, beloved brothers and sisters!

Recently, the Lord had me spend several months meeting with Him for two hours in the middle of every night, specifically for the purpose of doing "go low" exercises. He wanted to work with my heart and train me in true humility. I would spend these two hours thinking the kinds of thoughts I described above. I would picture my heart sinking lower before the Lord. I would choose to think deliberately lowly thoughts about who I really am, and what my thought life has looked like before His face.

There was one night when I got "stuck." I had gone low in my heart for at least half an hour, but I felt He wanted me to go lower. And I simply could not budge. I couldn't make my heart do anymore than I had already achieved. I sat there, mentally stuck, as if I had hit a plateau, and there was no where to go from there. I said, "Lord, I can't go any lower." His Spirit responded, "*It's surprising how much the human heart lifts itself up.*"

Because of the Lord's loving character, I didn't feel hurt or offended by this comment. I knew that He only speaks the plain truth for our own benefit. He didn't even say it in a derogatory way; it was just so matter-of-fact. I felt He was saying that even He is surprised by the hidden recesses of pride in every human heart. It must be pretty bad if it could surprise *God*.

The Lord then kindly added, "*You might as well go back to bed. There isn't any more work we can do right now.*"

He did not sound angry or disappointed in me at all. He was just being a good teacher, who knows when their student has had enough for one day.

I went back to bed, feeling a little bit like I had failed my teacher, and the moment my head hit the pillow, a most amazing thing happened. Instantly, my heart was plunged into a new depth of realization of who I really was! I began weeping and praying at this new understanding of the depth of my unworthiness and inherent uncleanness. His Spirit did for me what I could not do for myself! After a period of weeping and completing the "going low" exercise, I went back to sleep eventually, knowing my heart was more pleasing to the Lord.

HUMBLED BY A KISS!

The Lord will sometimes surprise us with His absolute and sovereign initiative in our lives. I think He enjoys keeping us "off-balance" with His surprise visits, which are very humbling for me. It gives me a sense that the Lord is in total control of my life. The following testimony is one of those humbling surprises, which reveals the Lord's unique and unsettling sense of humor. This event is actually shocking in its implications, even though it almost seems to be a "divine joke." I think the Lord would like me to share it, because it has enlarged my understanding of the Lord's great power, as well as His unpredictable ways.

When I have my coffee talks with the Lord, I close my door for privacy. We have always had cats, and one of my cats would make it impossible for me to concentrate on the Lord if she was in the room. She would either walk on me, or playfully bat the prayer shawl off my face, or play with its hanging fringes, or generally do something to demand that she be the center of attention. Her name was Snowflake, and sadly, as of this writing, she has gone on to cat heaven. This is why I am writing in the past tense.

I have always fed the cats before meeting with the Lord, so I knew that Snowflake was not in need of food. Each day as I would talk to the Lord, I would always see her white paws under the door and hear her voice whining to get in. This was distracting, and I would pray, "Lord, tell her to go away until we're finished."

The Lord would respond, and I would see her paws withdraw immediately, as she sadly walked away from my door. All creation must obey His Word! As time went by, the Lord trained me to use my authority to silently "command" her to leave us. I would whisper in an inaudible voice, "Snowflake, go away until the Lord and I are finished."

Within a few seconds, she would obey the spoken word that she had not heard with her ears, but was nevertheless obligated to obey. I watched this happen many times and marveled at the authority of a spoken command, and at the obedience displayed by a normally disobedient cat. This was good training for me to understand the authority that the Lord has put in our mouths.

One day, as this same pattern was happening, I said something a little different. I said, "Lord, tell her to go away." Then, not wanting the Lord to think I was unkind, I added, "You know I fed her, and I'll kiss her when we're finished."

The cat left, and I spent close to two hours with the Lord. Later, after doing some chores downstairs and not seeing Snowflake, I went up to my room to work on some e-mails. I deliberately left my door open, so that the cats would know I was available now. I looked around the hallway and saw no trace of the cats. I began answering e-mails on my laptop, sitting on my bed. That was the last thing I remember. I never saw the cat come in or jump up on the bed. I only knew I was working on my computer.

In the next moment of conscious awareness, I found myself huddled over Snowflake on the bed, embracing and kissing her zealously, over and over. I didn't know how or when I had gotten this way. The computer was set aside. And I was "unconsciously" kissing this cat, without knowing she had arrived, and without making any conscious decision to leave my computer, hug her, or kiss her. As I came to my senses, I felt her in my arms and heard her purring loudly as I was repeatedly kissing her. I was stunned as I remembered my promise to the Lord: "I'll kiss her when we're finished."

To be honest, I couldn't believe the Lord would do such a thing to a person. To realize that I had been so out of control was kind of demeaning, and yet it was also funny. I felt very small and helpless when I realized that the Lord could do such a thing, and yet I was aware that He loved me and was playing a joke on me.

Why in the world would the Lord do this? When He put Peter in a trance, it was to reveal the salvation of the gentiles (see Acts 10:10-48). When He put Paul in a trance, it was to warn him to leave Jerusalem (see Acts 22:17-18).

But for me, it was to make me kiss a cat who I would have kissed eventually of my own free will. Was the Lord revealing the salvation of the feline kingdom? Or was it simply to show me that He heard me when I said, "I'll kiss her when we're done"?

I believe the Lord wanted to show me that even the little promises we make are important to keep. Since I did not seek her out to fulfill my vow to the Lord, He caused it to come to pass without my participation. And more importantly for my faith, it was ironclad proof that the Lord is really with me all these times that I imagine Him to be, and He hears every word I say. I believe this was the Lord's humorous, yet "heavy-handed" way of showing me that He is real and very present for our conversations.

In addition, I learned that the Lord can cause me to go somewhere and do something while in a trancelike state, while having no knowledge of doing it. This was one of the most surprising lessons about God's supernatural power I have learned, even though it concerned such an inconsequential matter as kissing a little white cat.

THE HUMILITY OF OUR MASTER

The Lord Yeshua lived out humility in everything that He said and did. He spent three-and-a-half years healing the sick, raising the dead, and casting innumerable demons out of bound humanity, and all without ever calling attention to Himself. He tried to avoid the fanfare and the crowds, but they followed Him. He commanded people not to tell who had healed them, but they spread the word anyway. He sought private places to teach His disciples, but behold, the multitude was never far behind.

The Lord used His own saliva and common dirt to heal the eyes of a man born blind. He was willing to walk for miles into the house of a Roman soldier who had exhibited love for the Jewish people in order to heal his slave.

There was only one moment in His earthly ministry, where the Messiah had to be presented to Israel as her king, as His father Solomon had entered Jerusalem before Him. The Son of David was required to ride into Jerusalem, rather than walk, for His final ministry before suffering an unjust and excruciating death.

Although the Lord Yeshua had walked into Jerusalem many times, this would be His last pilgrimage to the temple mount, where He would become the human Passover lamb who would take away the sins of the world. The Father needed His Son to fulfill Zechariah's familiar prophecy, just as the Lord had already fulfilled many of the other messianic prophecies by that point.

Rejoice greatly, O daughter of Zion! Shout, O daughter of Jerusalem! Behold, your King is coming to you; He is just and having salvation, lowly and riding on a donkey, a colt, the foal of a donkey (Zechariah 9:9).

If there was ever a moment for Yeshua to receive the honor and grandeur He was due, riding triumphantly into the holy city as the King of Israel, this would have been that moment.

"Go into the village opposite you, and immediately you will find a donkey tied, and a colt with her. Loose them and bring them to Me." So the disciples went and did as Jesus commanded them. They brought the donkey and colt, laid their clothes on them, and set Him on them (Matthew 21:2, 6-7).

And they threw their own clothes on the colt, and they set Jesus on him (Luke 19:35b).

The Lord asked His disciples to bring both the mother donkey and her colt to Him. I believe that the Lord, knowing the intense bonding between a mother and her young, did not want the mother to be fearful as men came and took her baby away. He could only be seated on one animal, but He asked for both animals.

They brought both of them to Him, and Jesus chose the lower one to ride on, so that Zechariah's word about the humble king would be fulfilled that day. He could have ridden on the taller animal, but He rode in on the colt, the lowest creature.

May we go and do likewise. Amen.

ENDNOTES

1. Zondervan: NIV text notes on 2 Kings 5:5.

2. *Finger of God*, produced by Darren Wilson (Wanderlust Productions, 2007), is available on Messianic Vision's Web site at www.sidroth.org.

3. See www.jesusministries.org.

4. Rick Joyner, *The Final Quest* (New Kensington, PA: Whitaker House, 1996).

Chapter 6

Outside the Gates

One day Peter and John were going up to the temple at the time of prayer—at three in the afternoon. Now a man crippled from birth was being carried to the temple gate called Beautiful, where he was put every day to beg from those going into the temple courts. When he saw Peter and John about to enter, he asked them for money. "Peter looked straight at him, as did John. Then Peter said "Look at us!" So the man gave them his attention, expecting to get something from them. Then Peter said, "Silver or gold I do not have, but what I have I give you. In the name of Jesus Christ of Nazareth, walk" (Acts 3:1-6 NIV).

PETER lifted him up to his feet, and his feet and ankles became strong. This man, who had been crippled since birth, began leaping and jumping. This one, who was carried daily to the temple gate to beg, now leapt into the temple courts, clinging to his new friends, Peter and John.

He was always on the outside of the gate of the religious people. Day after day, the worshipers streamed in and out of the temple courts, but did anyone look him in the eye before that moment? No! Hundreds of religious people passed him everyday. He neither made eye contact with them, nor did they make eye contact with him. He was outside the gates, and they were inside the gates, giving their service to God.

But on this one chosen day, someone said "Look at us!" Someone stopped and looked into his eyes and required him to make personal eye contact. The cripple did not want to look back at them; he just needed money, not relationship. Eye contact was of no use to him. But it is very important that Peter insisted that he look at them. Peter said, "Look at me, because I'm going to give you something that you never dreamed or expected on this day. Something much better than a few dollars!"

IN THE TEMPLE COURTS

After the publication of my first book, I was asked to attend a huge yearly convention for Christian booksellers, publishers, and authors. In 2007, it was held in Atlanta, in the largest building in Georgia. Since my husband was not able to make this trip, I was permitted to bring Katya, my ministry partner.

As we prayed in the hotel room on the night before the convention, Katya and I were nervous about what would be expected of us. I knew I would be signing books and meeting many people, and I felt way out of my element. I had never been to a professional gathering this large and was not comfortable in crowds; it was also not my style to be an aggressive promoter of any product, including my new book. I had never wanted to be in business, but the Lord had instructed me to begin a small business after I had completed my first book.

The next morning, I woke up at 4:00 A.M. and began to wait on the Lord to prepare me for the day's massive responsibilities. For the next hour, the Lord showed me how I would be representing Him throughout this convention if I would abide in the heavenly realm with Him.

I saw Jesus walking in the marketplace of His day. I was able to perceive His mind-set as He walked, taught, prayed, and ministered to large crowds as well as individuals.

His head was in the heavens, but his feet were on the earth. In all of the Lord's sojourns to Jerusalem during the three-and-a-half years that He ministered publicly, He was in the temple courts. The Lord showed me that the environment I would be walking into was very much like the temple courts. There were scribes, who were writers; there were Pharisees, who were religious leaders and teachers; there were Sadducees, who were the priestly "aristocrats" of society, with power and political sway. The Hebrew word for Sadducees means "the righteous ones." However, in the first century, this group had become a worldly and politically driven force within Judaism; they neither believed in angels, nor in the resurrection of the dead, nor in the afterlife.

And there were Essenes, devout mystics, who shunned the politics of religion and lived in selfless communities in the Judean desert. They desired personal intimacy and holiness with the Lord, and lived an austere lifestyle. Except for the austerity, I could definitely relate to the Essenes.

Unfortunately, there were also those who engaged in commerce in the temple courts. The Lord walked among them, as He mingled and taught in the midst of all this business and religious activity. I could see Him walking among the merchants in this convention, teaching, commenting, picking up books and looking over them, and always speaking the Father's heart to the merchants, priests, and seekers.

The Lord showed me that He was always about His Father's business for every moment that His feet were in the place of the world's business. This was the secret the Lord gave me, to show me how to behave that very day at the book fair. The Lord showed me in a very deep way that He chose to place me in business at this late stage of my life, although it was the last thing I desired.

The Lord put me in the marketplace to minister to all kinds of normal people, and also to Christians who buy and sell, although these were activities I had never wanted to do. The Lord said to me, "*I put you in the place of business, but you will be about My Father's business.*"

This insight endued me with a huge infilling of the Holy Spirit, which would enable me to go into this big, scary place of commerce. The Lord filled me with a servant's motivations, full of compassion for His flock. He lifted me above caring whether I buy or sell anything and above caring about my name, my book, or my promotion. Although I loved my publisher's family, I was not there to please man; doing the Father's business was all I cared about.

Katya had also been praying during those early morning hours, and we took time to pray together after the Lord had spoken to each of us separately. With tears, we covenanted with the Lord to always represent His heart in the place of business. We knew we would be praying for many people we would encounter. And this strong desire to do our Father's business lifted us from the previous night's fear into courage, resolve, and trust that we were walking into a holy assignment. My desire to run away from all this, as well as my ambitions and my ego, disappeared.

For the first time, I stopped fighting this path the Lord had placed me on. I stopped complaining and saying, "I hate this!"

Rather, I started to say, "I will walk this walk, the crucified life in the marketplace, for every day that You give me to do so." Our two days at the convention were thus supernaturally ordained, and we were strengthened and led to our divine appointments at each moment of the day.

Naomi

Peter and John had encountered a man outside the gates of the marketplace, and had shown concern for him; they looked him in the eye and ministered the Lord's life-changing healing to the crippled man. This bears some resemblance to what happened to us on that first morning in the Convention Center. As we walked toward the huge exhibition hall, we saw hundreds of attendees with their badges being ushered into the biggest room I have ever seen in my life.

And standing just outside the "gate" was a uniformed security guard, a delicate African American woman. She made no eye contact with the mobs that streamed by, nor did anyone make eye contact with her. Everyone walked past her, for she was not their destination. I was immediately drawn to her because she seemed to be ignored, and I wondered how she felt about all the Christian business men and women flowing into the great hall.

We approached her and I looked into her eyes and greeted her as a child of God who deserves to be greeted with love. This should not be such an exceptional act, except that no one else was doing so. She had a very stern face, and there was nothing light or happy about her expression. For some reason, the first thing I said to her was, "I'll bet everyone just walks past you, don't they?"

She answered, "Yes, they do."

I continued, "You really don't deserve that."

She agreed, "No, I don't."

I immediately liked her spirit. She knew that she was a person who was no less worthy of a greeting than anyone else who walked by. I sensed she was happy to be engaged in conversation.

I asked her what her name was, and her answer really surprised me when she said that her name was Naomi. We Jewish people have a little expression we use when we meet someone who claims to be Jewish, but it doesn't seem possible from their race or appearance.[1] We say, "Funny, you don't look Jewish!"

As I looked at this woman, it was hard to imagine that her parents had named her Naomi, and I was thinking, "Funny, you don't look like a Naomi!"

I realized later that she had adopted this Israeli name, but I didn't know that at the moment.

When she said "Naomi," I felt an unusual connection to her as if she was a fellow Jew, even though I was fairly sure that she was not of Jewish origin. I accepted the identity she presented to me; to do otherwise would have been disrespectful. All I said was, "May Adonai bless you," and I hugged her. "Adonai" is one of the most frequently used Hebrew names for the Lord in the Bible.

We had a total of four encounters with this lady. In this first one, we didn't know if she was a Christian, and I did not feel led to ask her. That first conversation was simply acknowledging her name and value. That small kindness meant a lot to her.

Then we entered the marketplace and spent hours on our feet. We did a book signing and prayed for many people. The Holy Spirit guided our encounters, and we always put others' needs before our own. God filled us with that "non-commercial" feeling, because it was just pure ministry.

The second time we saw Naomi was around lunch time. When people needed to go out to the restrooms, they would pass this guard. This time, we stopped and greeted her again, and Naomi made a request. She asked, "Can you find me a Star of David?"

In this huge marketplace of hundreds of booths, we had seen three booths that were of a Messianic Jewish flavor. However, Naomi added, "I don't want the kind of Jewish star with a cross in the middle of it, but just a plain Star of David."

I was tempted to ask her why she didn't want a cross, but I sensed the Lord just wanted us to bless her and search for a plain Star of David.

Many Messianic Jews and non-Jewish believers wear a Jewish star with a cross in the middle of it. I appreciate that symbol, even though I realize it could potentially offend a Jewish person who doesn't believe in Yeshua. Naomi told us that she had asked someone else, but he had brought her a star with a cross in it, and she did not want that. (I assume this other kind person was able to return the item.) And so, Katya and I set off to find this gift.

THE STAR OF DAVID

Before I continue Naomi's story, I feel the Lord would like me to address a controversial issue that has arisen among believers. It concerns the nature and origins of the six-pointed blue Star of David. This star is a symbol of Judaism and appears on Israel's national flag, as well as its airline and countless other cultural and religious articles. I have received some questions and e-mails about this issue, and I believe the Lord is asking me to briefly address it here, so His flock will not be confused or misled.

There are teachings and Web sites that claim "evidence" that this symbol is of ancient and satanic origin, and some add that it is the "mark of the beast." They claim that this six-pointed star was part of Canaanite idolatry, which Israel was enticed by during the years of her apostasy, despite the fact that the Bible does not tell us this.

Some "Christian" Web sites display a Jewish star with Yeshua's Hebrew name written from right to left in Hebrew letters in the middle of the star, and the caption underneath reads: "The Mark of the Beast." When I saw this, a shudder went through me. This was so outrageous that I wondered how anyone could accept such a blasphemous accusation against the Lord's name and His people. I felt the enemy had overplayed his hand with such an obviously false accusation. As if the holy Son of Man would allow His name, which means "salvation" in Hebrew, to be inserted into the final economic mark of allegiance to the antichrist. And yet, there are Web sites and publications promoting this slander.

Some groups go further, presenting an elaborate theory that uses reinterpretations of Bible verses and of history. This theory states that the Jews have satan's DNA in them; they claim that there was a sexual relationship between Eve and the serpent, resulting in Cain and his "demon seed" that produced, of course, the Jews. This is utterly unbiblical and doesn't even make sense. Therefore, I will not explain the innumerable ways that this theory is wrong, heretical, and a damnable lie. I will just give one proof, and then I will let you pray about it and read your own Bible. Genesis clearly and unequivocally states that Adam knew his wife, and she bore him Cain, their first child.

> *Now Adam knew Eve his wife, and she conceived and bore Cain, and said, "I have acquired a man from the Lord." Then she bore again, this time his brother Abel* (Genesis 4:1-2).

There are others calling themselves Christians, who claim that we Jews of Eastern European origin are not Jews at all, not even descendents of Abraham, but are imposters from a completely different Gentile lineage. (During the Holocaust, our enemies certainly felt we were Jewish enough to attempt our complete liquidation.)

From what I can discern, some of these presentations are coming from professing Christians, who have been horribly misinformed. Some are coming from anti-Semitic groups that use Christian vocabulary to enhance their slanderous case against the Jews. I have looked at "Christian" Web sites that make me sickened and horrified by what they write about the Jewish people.

Like their spiritual father, Adolf Hitler, these haters have made the Jewish people the scapegoat for all of America's sins and financial woes. We were blamed for the Bubonic Plague during the dark ages and are now blamed for every governmental and financial agenda that is harmful to America's future. We are accused of controlling all of the world's wealth and running the world's media. I will not enumerate the logical reasons why this scapegoating of the Jewish people is demonic, false, and unjust. Just know that it is, and ask your precious Israeli Messiah how He feels about His Jewish people.

The Lord Yeshua will not look on Christian anti-Semitism lightly, and I would urge you not to be deceived by these hellish lies against His brothers and sisters. More will be presented on the Lord's coming judgments against Christians who hate the Jewish people in the chapter on His righteous judgments. If you feel confused by the enticing words coming from these anti-Semitic groups, contact Sid Roth's ministry, which has done much homework on these topics.[2]

I have only researched the Star of David to the extent that genuine sources are available. It seems there is no ancient documentation that is authentic, as to its origins. Some groups make statements, such as, "This star was used by King Solomon in his idolatrous practices. Thus, it is called 'the Star of Solomon.'" The problem is that there is no evidence in the Bible or any other reliable ancient texts that this is true. Rather, these statements seem to originate in medieval Europe. I have read the accusations, but have never seen credible documentation.

We know that Solomon was led astray by his foreign wives and their idolatry, but nothing is said of a six-pointed star. In occult circles, it is common knowledge that the pentagram, or *five-pointed star*, is the symbol used in pagan ceremonies. I witnessed this myself in a "religious" ceremony I was required to attend in my past. This group's rituals contain outward elements of Christianity, yet are in fact, occult. I sensed immediately that it was false, and I hid under the Lord, while praying quietly in tongues through the whole affair. I saw on the floor a large, five-pointed, upside-down star, with initiates standing in the center of it.

Since a number of Christians have questioned me and even warned me about the evil of the six-pointed Jewish star, I became troubled about it. I would never want to promote any symbol that had satanic origin, even if it was connected to my own biblical heritage as a Jew. Since I own items with the blue Star of David, I sought the Lord in prayer. If He had wanted me to throw away everything I own with this symbol, I would have done it. As much as my heart is connected to Israel and my Jewish people, I would not grieve the Lord, for the sake of any other loyalty or allegiance. I hate paganism, idolatry, and all occult practices, and I bear much accountability as a teacher of God's flock. After prayer, the Lord was gracious to give me a word. I will summarize for you what He told me.

The Lord showed me that the enemy hijacked a symbol that was not intrinsically evil. The enemy knew that if people, and Christians in particular, would connect the six-pointed star with satanic activity, they would hate the Jews and treat them as agents of satan. This would justify the persecution and murder of the Jewish people.

This would promote Christian anti-Semitism in particular, because Christians would treat the Jewish people as their enemy, since they are allegedly in a conspiracy with satan. This would promote the enemy's ongoing desire to destroy the Jewish people, who are an integral part of the Lord's past, present, and future redemption of the world.

The Lord requires His Bride to love Israel and to pray for her salvation, both physical and spiritual salvation. The Lord yearns for His Jewish people to be in a loving relationship with Him, which is impossible if "Christians" who bear His name hate and persecute them. This would make them hate Jesus because His people are so hateful.

The Spirit of the Lord showed me plainly that when He looks at the blue Star of David, He sees it as a symbol of the Jewish people being regathered to the land of their fathers, the land He gave irrevocably to Abraham, Isaac, and Jacob. He sees it as a picture of solidarity with the people and the land of Israel; He has never rejected this nation, nor has He revoked His promises to them.

> Thus says the Lord, who gives the sun for a light by day, the ordinances of the moon and the stars as a light by night, who disturbs the sea, and its waves roar (the Lord of hosts is His name): "If those ordinances depart from before Me, says the Lord, then the seed of Israel shall also cease from being a nation before Me forever." Thus says the Lord: "If heaven above can be measured, and the foundations of the earth searched out beneath, I will also cast off all the seed of Israel for all that they have done, says the Lord" (Jeremiah 31:35-37).

The Lord's covenants with Israel and His future redemptive purposes, as well as the relationship between Israel and the Church, are covered in the final chapter of *Coffee Talks With Messiah* (Gazelle Press, 2007). I have also presented them in various degrees in *A Prophetic Calendar: The Feasts of Israel* (Destiny Image Publishers, 2009).

In the final chapter of this book, we will take another look at how the Lord feels about Christians who hate His Jewish people. When you have studied these matters thoroughly, you will know the Lord's undying heart of love for His Jewish people. He desires for the Bride of Messiah to show them unconditional love and to cover them with an umbrella of intercessory protection from the devices of destruction being planned against them.

EVERY TRIBE AND NATION

We now return to the search for Naomi's desired star. For more than two hours, we walked through this enormous building. Finally, we found a booth that sold beautiful Israeli products, and there was a star, perfect for Naomi. The woman at the booth was a believer, and her Messianic Jewish business partner was not at the booth at that moment.

After buying the necklace, it took me a long time to find Naomi. None of the other guards recognized that name, and I began to wonder it that was her real name. After 15 minutes, I found her and burst out, "Naomi, I found the star!"

Her face lit up as she treasured her new star. I just hugged her and said, "May Adonai bless you."

When I returned to the jewelry booth, I found Katya talking with the other owner, an American-Israeli woman whom I had known when I lived in Israel! I had not seen her since 1985, and she not only remembered me fondly, but she told us that they still sing my Hebrew worship songs in their congregations. That surprise was a precious reconnected friendship, which never would have occurred if we hadn't been searching for a star.

The next morning we walked up to the "gate," and saw dear Naomi sitting in her security chair, wearing her Star of David on a golden chain. She was very happy to see us; we had become friends quickly. We didn't think she was a Christian, because she had not wanted the cross. After we exchanged greetings, I asked her what her last name was. She seemed almost angry at this question and answered, "I'm in the middle of a legal name change."

When I heard this, I wondered if she belonged to a religious group, where all members have adopted the same last name, which identifies them as part of the lost tribes of Israel. I felt a fresh word springing up in my heart, which the Lord was giving me for her.

I hugged her and asked, "You want to become a daughter of Israel? Don't you know the nations hate us? Don't you know you are signing up for persecution?"

She replied, "That's OK, I want to become a part of Israel."

I didn't ask her about her group. Instead, I looked her in the eye and said, "Naomi, do you know Jesus?"

This was our third encounter, and she looked at me with a very strange look on her face. She answered, "I know about Him, but I don't know Him. He was just a carpenter; the Bible says so."

At that moment, the Spirit of God gave me the exact Scriptures that Naomi needed right then.

One of the words He put in my mouth came from Isaiah 49. First I told her with great intensity, "Oh, He was more than a carpenter, Naomi; He received worship." After telling her more about the Lord, these are the passages that I combined into one message:

> It is too small a thing for you to be My servant **to restore the tribes of Jacob** and bring back those of Israel I have kept. I will also make you a light for the Gentiles, that you may bring My salvation to the ends of the earth (Isaiah 49:6 NIV).

> *Then I saw another angel flying in midair, and he had the eternal gospel to proclaim to those who live on the earth — to every nation, tribe, language and people...and with Your blood You purchased men from God **from every tribe and language and people and nation*** (Revelation 14:6; 5:9 NIV).

> *Now Israel loved Joseph more than all his children, because he was the son of his old age. Also he made him a **tunic of many colors*** (Genesis 37:3).

When I said that the Lord has opened his arms to every tribe and every nation, she stopped me and said, "*Every tribe?*" That word caught her attention, which might have been because of what her group was teaching her.

I said, "Yes, Naomi, every tribe. Why do you think Joseph wore a coat of many colors?"

Then I spread out one arm over Katya on my left and over Naomi on my right and said, "Joseph had a coat of many colors, because the Father has opened his arms to every tribe and every nation. This Yeshua I'm talking about is this same Jesus who hung on the cross. Naomi, do you keep the Ten Commandments?"

She said, "I sure try."

I said, "I try too, but none of us can keep them perfectly. In the Old Testament, it says that only the blood of animals can atone for sin, and the One we are talking about is that same Jesus who was more than a carpenter. Only His blood can atone for the fact that none of us can keep the Ten Commandments for even one day. Will you please consider His claims?"

She was getting it! The love that we showed her was so obvious that this precious woman heard something different that day from what she had been taught.

"I KNOW AN AUTHOR!"

In our next encounter at the gate with Naomi, she saw my newly published book sticking out of Katya's purse, and she was staring at it. She said, "I'm looking at your book."

Katya, who is my best press agent, whipped out the book and said, "This is Jill Shannon; she wrote the book!"

Naomi looked at me in astonishment and said, "You're an author?"

At this revelation, this beautiful little security guard started laughing and dancing for joy across the lobby, her face lit up like a thousand suns.

"I know an author! I know an author!" As she danced further away from us, I chased her and hit her with my magazine, calling, "Stop that dancing, Naomi; we need to talk to you!" We were laughing like we were best friends.

I would imagine that dozens of authors must have walked by her over those two days, and yet she was thrilled to know an author. She didn't know the others, because they hadn't made eye contact with the one who stands in the gates, outside of the temple courts. And so we gave away our last copy of my new book to Naomi.

I told her, "The first thing I want you to read is page 158, 'Receiving Eternal Salvation.' After you read that part, then go back and find out how a Jewish girl found Jesus, found Yeshua the Messiah."

Our last glimpse of Naomi was as we were leaving. We just watched her from behind, without her knowing it. She was standing, reading my book, and dancing in place with a big smile on her face as she read.

And we snuck up behind her and said, "Naomi, what are you doing?" And she just laughed and laughed; she was so happy, so transformed.

We never saw her again, nor have I heard from her. Because she gave us a different name than her legal name, I was unable to track her down later.

We are still praying for our new friend, who stood outside the gates of the Christian marketplace. If my precious little sister finds this book, I hope she will write to me.

Just as Peter and John looked intently into the crippled man's eyes and made personal contact in the gate outside the temple, we had to connect with Naomi's eyes. Our Lord Yeshua walked in the place of business every day, while being about His Father's business. We finally learned how to live out this revelation in this place of business, where we were about our Father's business. Our heads were in the heavens, but our feet were on the earth.

The Wretched of the Earth

I had a dream that helped me to understand what attitudes the Lord requires of me toward the least-esteemed populations in the earth.

I was in an inner city, which was, not surprisingly, dirty and crowded. I sensed it was in Europe. I was alone, searching intently for a believers' meeting that I knew was taking place in that city. I knew the meeting was called "Holy Spirit."

I was asking various shop people if they knew where I could find the meeting called "Holy Spirit." One shopkeeper pointed out a man who was standing on the sidewalk, and he said that this man could take me to the meeting. I looked at the man, and immediately knew that he was an alcoholic and that he also had some nasty fetish concerning razor blades. I was repulsed by his unclean condition and was afraid to go off alone with him. I was afraid of his razor blades, even though I sensed he only used them on himself.

As I looked at him, I thought, "I don't think so. This is not the person I would like to take me to find this meeting." So I politely said to the shopkeeper, "That's OK. I'll find it by myself."

Then I set off down the alleys to look for the meeting. As I was leaving, I noticed the alcoholic man being mentored by a Christian shopkeeper. The godly man was teaching him the ways of the Lord and taking him under his wing. I felt convicted that I had rejected the man due to his disagreeable addictions, and that another Christian was caring for him and doing for him what I should have thought to do.

Then I went down an alley that had a sign over it: "Alley of the Prostitutes." I saw many girls lining the streets, drumming up the obvious business. I needed to pass by them in order to get to the meeting called "Holy Spirit." I only wanted to get past them, to get where I wanted to go. But they were very territorial, and wouldn't let me pass. They said this was "their alley."

I said, "I just need to get past here to get to my meeting," but they insisted this was their territory, and I would just have to find another way around. I was getting frustrated. I didn't care about these girls' souls; I just wanted to get past them.

Then I went down another alley. I came to a door leading into a room, and I knew I needed to go through that room to get to the meeting. I opened the door, and was horrified. In the room were at least 100 women, maybe several hundred. These women were more hideously wretched, poor, mentally ill, dazed, and unclean than anyone could dream up, even in the slums of a Charles Dickens novel. They all stared at me with vacant eyes—needy, yet zoned out—missing teeth, dirty... Some seemed schizophrenic, and some looked like alcoholics or drug-users. I looked at them in horror, backed out of the room, and shut the door. I then continued on my way to find the anointed meeting.

Then I came to a smaller door that I hoped would lead me where I wanted to go. I opened the door and saw about 100 men in the same wretched condition as the women I had just seen. They didn't just look awful on the outside, but they also seemed awful on the inside. I couldn't have imagined a more repulsive group of people, who seemed frightening in their mental state, as well as filthy and dazed. They were all staring right at me, either expecting something from me or just too dazed or crazed to know what else to do. This was the ugliest group of people I have ever seen, beyond normal human imagination. Again, I backed out in horror and shut the door. This was *not* what I wanted to see.

Then I woke up, with a terrible, sinking feeling of "Please let this not be a prophetic dream about my real future work, Lord."

POSSIBLE INTERPRETATION

I have not received a direct interpretation from the Lord, but this has been my impression since the dream. There were four encounters: the man, the prostitutes, the room of women, and the room of men. I backed away from all of them, the most wretched of the earth. I shut the door. The people I saw did not have the Holy Spirit yet, because they were lost, hopeless, poverty stricken, and diseased (inside-and-out) individuals.

I wanted to be on the mountain top with God, basking in an anointed meeting. I wanted to be with other kindred spirits, worshiping the Lord and bringing down the indescribable pleasure of His glory. I wanted to be in the place of safety, peace, glory, and worship, in a heavenly atmosphere. That desire is represented by a meeting called "Holy Spirit."

It is probably obvious to you what the Lord was trying to show me about myself. These sick and broken people are a heavy burden on the Lord's heart. He cares as much about each one of them as He does for me.

> "Go out quickly into the streets and lanes of the city, and bring in here the poor and the maimed and the lame and the blind." And the servant said, "Master, it is done as you commanded, and still there is room." Then the master said to the servant, "Go out into the highways and hedges, and compel them to come in, that my house may be filled. For I say to you that none of those men who were invited shall taste my supper" (Luke 14:21b-24).

The Lord needs laborers to go out to the highways and the hedges, to love and serve the disenfranchised people and communities. Godly people who know His heart need to bring them God's life, light, healing, health, wholeness, and rescue. I don't know what my assignments will be, but I cannot make my highest priority finding an anointed meeting without wanting to offer help to those around me.

This was the work that Mother Teresa gave her entire life to in the streets of India. When she was asked how she could bear to do such disgusting work as wiping maggots out of their eyes, she said, "I imagine I am cleaning Jesus' eyes, and then I don't mind."

I wanted to bypass the unpleasant encounters with the "untouchables." I wanted to be on the highest place of God's mountain. However, what I didn't understand is that being in the lowest place is the path to heavenly glory. So everywhere I turned, God forced me to confront the lowest element of humanity, which I need to care about, rather than escaping to an anointed meeting.

I needed to make a serious mental adjustment after the dream, and none of it has left me. It is not what I desire to do, but if I do it to the least of these, I do it to Yeshua. I do not live to please myself, and I must lay down my will and my rights to be in perfect union with the Lord.

As we have seen in Acts 3, no one ever looked at the crippled beggar lying in the gate; they walked past him, and when they were in a charitable mood before worshiping Adonai, they might pull out some coins for him. But they did not look him in the eye and connect with his spirit. After Peter and John looked him in the eye, they gave him the Lord's healing and brought him into the temple courts. He was no longer an outsider, lying in the gate.

Isn't this what Messiah's sacrifice has done for us? He has taken us, who were filthy beggars outside the gates of God, and cleansed us, healed us, and made a way for us to be brought near to the Master's court. He has done exactly this for us, but it is hard for us to see ourselves that way. When we do, our compassion for others outside the gates will grow into genuine love. Then we will stretch out our hands to the outcasts of the earth.

I wrote this song about the Lord's broken heart for such ones. He desires us to share His pain, and enter the anguish He feels over the oppressed, the sex-slaves, the aborted children, the impoverished and starving. The hopeless ones. If our hearts are not broken, how can we dance upon injustice? How will we have the authority to call down God's justice for these victims of injustice, until our hearts are broken, as the Lord's heart is broken? The song was inspired by a dream given to Julie Meyer, a precious and anointed songwriter and worship leader at the International House of Prayer in Kansas City, Missouri.[3]

THE DOOR OF YOUR HEART

When Your heart breaks, who will comfort You?
    And who can know the sorrow in Your eyes?
    Gazing on injustice in the earth
    On the hungry ones, the helpless ones

And who are they that You would call Your
    friends?
    For those the world despises, who will cry?
    Imprisoned and impoverished in the dust
    The voiceless ones, the hopeless ones

We enter the door of Your heart, into the gate of
    Your pain
    And when our souls are torn and broken we
    can dance upon injustice
    Your kingdom come, Your will be done, Your
    justice reign

For the first door is a portal to salvation
    And the second door the inner court of love
    But few would choose to enter the chamber of

repentance
Rachel weeping for her children

If Your cup of wrath would overflow
   Who could bear Your judgment on our land?
   Who will hear the blood cry from the ground?
   The mourning ones, the broken ones

For the tears of Your people are an offering
   And our weeping as the evening sacrifice
   But few would wear Your sorrow, though none
   could bear Your anger
   Or the harvest swept away with fire

How the heavens tremble when You groan
   Your weeping sends a shaking in the earth
   Who will come to fill the cup of tears?
   O Holy One, O Righteous One

Enter the door of His heart, into the gate of His
   pain
   And when our souls are torn and broken
   We will dance upon injustice
   Your kingdom come, Your will be done, Your
   justice reign

Endnotes

1. Despite our little joke, in reality, there are many descendants of
    Abraham, Isaac, and Jacob who are scattered across the earth, and
    most of them do not look like "typical" American Jews like me, who are
    of eastern European or Russian extraction. Some are black, some are
    oriental, and many Israelis look North African or Middle Eastern. So
    who can determine who really "looks Jewish"?

2. Sid Roth's Messianic Vision and *It's Supernatural!* TV are found at www. sidroth.org.

3. Julie's outstanding worship music can be found at www.ihop.org.

Chapter 7

Sexual Brokenness

M ANY Christians have acquaintances or relatives who are in the gay life-style, or who struggle with thoughts in this direction, although they are not sexually active. I know several such people and have known more over the years of my life. But the ones who are secretly struggling would not have told me unless they felt I was a safe person to tell.

Therefore, you might know someone who is struggling, but you are unaware of it because they are understandably afraid to tell anyone, particularly a Christian. Maybe it is the teenage son or daughter of a friend, who is contemplating suicide over this secret shame. Teens who struggle with this issue have a tragically high suicide rate, and many are in the churches. Some have heard hatred preached, and they don't know where to turn with these unwanted desires. This causes the Lord great pain because He wants to show love to these young people; He wants His people to show them His rescuing love.

I do believe that preachers must preach the truth about Heaven and hell, sin and judgment. Even so, it is important not to inadvertently condemn the lambs under our care, the young and struggling ones who will not realize that Yeshua's love and mercy are fully extended to them. It is even more important not to single out homosexuality as the "worst sin" in our preaching when we do not condemn ourselves for practicing equally unrighteous things. These are people we know and, in many cases, people we love. The Good Samaritan helped a stranger as if he was his own brother. *Likewise, gay people must not be the outcasts of Christian communities and churches!* For if that is the case, where will they turn for acceptance and love? They will turn to others in this lifestyle and will reject this hateful version of Christianity. They will think Jesus is just like us and will reject Him. Then who will be held accountable for the peril of their eternal souls?

This is the most important starting point for moving from fear and hatred into compassion and merciful love: *Homosexuality is only one form of sexual brokenness.* Other forms are fornication, adultery, incest, rape, child-molestation, masturbation, pornography, sadomasochism, and lust and uncleanness within marriages. Are any of us truly pure? Was there anyone pure but our Jesus?

Our holy God looks upon all the twisted versions of the beautiful human sexuality that He created. The Lord sees untold numbers of people committing all of these forms of sexual sin and is grieved to see sin abound under the eyes of Heaven. These acts lead to diseases, addictive behaviors (enslavement), unwanted and fatherless children, abortions, broken families, wounded young people, shame, secrecy, and all manners of defilement in our society.

Many of these behaviors are kept secret, and the believers who are committing them hate themselves. Christian research tells us that a great number of pastors are addicted to pornography, and many Christians are drawn to one or another form of sexual activity that is impure in God's eyes. We cannot think that homosexuality is the unforgivable sin, but that Christians who engage in other sins can be beloved members or leaders in our churches. This is hypocrisy. As we judge, so we will be judged. Paul warns us, *"You who judge others, do you not do the same sorts of things yourselves?"*

> *Therefore you are inexcusable, O man, whoever you are who judge, **for in whatever you judge another you condemn***

yourself; for you who judge practice the same things (Romans 2:1).

Some Christians feel safe telling their pastors about their struggles or secret sins; this is a good and healthy thing, for secrets are terribly destructive. In these cases, the person knows that his or her confidentiality would be respected.

But I fear that many do not feel safe telling their church leaders, particularly in the area of homosexuality. If they come in for counseling with this issue, would they be rejected, or judged as worse than the people who come with other problems?

A formerly gay friend of mine put it this way: *"It doesn't matter how you've been twisted...the solution is the same. We're all bent."* He meant that the only solution is the kindness, mercy, and blood of Yeshua. He is the only answer to all of our brokenness and impure desires.

Who Will Cast the First Stone?

*Then the scribes and Pharisees brought to Him a woman caught in adultery. And when they had set her in the midst, they said to Him, "Teacher, this woman was caught in adultery, in the very act. Now Moses, in the law, commanded us that such should be stoned. But what do You say?" This they said, testing Him, that they might have something of which to accuse Him....So when they continued asking Him, He raised Himself up and said to them, "**He who is without sin among you, let him throw a stone at her first**" (John 8:3-6a, 7).*

There is no one without sin, except for the sinless One. The Pharisees wanted to test the Lord in matters of Torah observance. If He showed excessive mercy to this adulterous woman, they could accuse Him of disobeying

Moses. And if He disobeyed Moses, then He Himself could be judged as a sinner—who could not possibly be the Messiah.

Before we continue, it should also be noted that Moses actually said to put both the male and the female adulterer to death. Since they caught her "in the very act," it is hard to picture that the man was hard to catch. So why did they only bring her, when they clearly could have seized the man who was also in the very act? Could it be because this sin hit a little too close to home if they seized the man? Might that mean that one of their own party could be next in line for stoning?

Everyone in this group of devout Jews desired to condemn this woman, except for one man, who was the only one present without sin. In fact, in His righteousness, the Lord Yeshua was the only man who had a right to stone her. But in His sinless character, He was merciful and knew that mercy would be a greater motivator for her to repent than judgment would. God will judge all people in righteousness, but for now we are called to show mercy. Yeshua the Messiah did not come to condemn, but to save sinners.

The goodness of God leads you to repentance (Romans 2:4b).

For the Son of Man has come to seek and save that which was lost (Luke 19:10).

Those who are well have no need of a physician, but those who are sick. But go and learn what this means: **"I desire mercy and not sacrifice." For I did not come to call the righteous, but sinners, to repentance** (Matthew 9:12-13).

The Lord desires mercy in the hearts of His people toward everyone. Mercy is more pleasing to God than sacrifice. As we have been shown mercy, we must show mercy to our fellow sinners. The teachings of Jesus command us to love one another, even those who have made themselves our enemies. If we do not show mercy, we will not be shown mercy on the Day of Judgment. What part of this is hard for us to understand?

> *Beloved, do not avenge yourselves, but rather give place to wrath; for it is written, "Vengeance is Mine, I will repay," says the Lord* (Romans 12:19).

> *For the wrath of man does not produce the righteousness of God* (James 1:20).

Will hatred and condemnation bring sinners to repentance? There is a Christian Web site that declares that "God hates fags"; they think they are representing the heart of Jesus to the gay community. It sickens me. After the brutal murder of Matthew Shepard, this Web site depicted a simulation of this precious young man burning in hell, announcing daily how many days he allegedly has been in hell. These merciless ones have no fear of the Lord to do such a thing. They have no idea how much the Lord Jesus loves this young man.

Matthew Shepard lingered in a coma for five days after he was viciously beaten and left for dead on that fence.[1] How can we know what comfort and communion his spirit was receiving from the Lord Jesus during those last days of his life? How can we know what inner works the Lord granted to his spirit during his last hours? The human spirit remains strong and very much alive, even when the body is so close to death. Many who have come back from death or from near-death have reported this.

Some of those who think they are righteous and claim to know who is in hell and who will be received into Heaven will be very surprised on the day they meet Yeshua. Those who show no mercy will not receive mercy on that day.

Blessed are the merciful, for they shall obtain mercy. But many who are first will be last, and the last first (Matthew 5:7; 19:30).

If the Lord did not love sinners, where would we be? If He did not look with compassion upon those who practice a vast array of sinful behaviors, thoughts, and words, where would we be right now? If He loves drug users and men who secretly look at pornography, why would He hate gay people? Are they worse than anyone else? Some might think they are, but in fact, this is one sin among many that will require repentance and the atoning blood of Yeshua to enter the Kingdom of God. *Do we want Him to judge us as harshly as we judge homosexuals?*

> *Therefore you are inexcusable, O man, whoever you are who judge, **for in whatever you judge another you condemn yourself; for you who judge practice the same things.** But we know that the judgment of God is according to truth against those who practice such things. And do you think this, O man, you who judge those practicing such things, and doing the same, that you will escape the judgment of God? **Or do you despise the riches of His goodness, forbearance, and longsuffering, not knowing that the goodness of God leads you to repentance?*** (Romans 2:1-4)

What the Lord Considers an Abomination

Someone might say, "But the Book of Leviticus tells us that to lie with a man as one lies with a woman is an abomination." Yes, this is absolutely true, and we will shortly look at some of the other behaviors the Lord considers to be abominations. Only then will we decide what our response will be to those behaviors and the people who commit them. First, let us look at the Bible's instructions for sexual behavior.

We see that the Book of Leviticus presents a large number and variety of sexual activities that are forbidden for people to do. The Lord our God is a holy God, and He has created and blessed the human body. We are made in His image, male and female.

He has given us prohibitions against many variations of incest; bestiality; rape; anal intercourse, whether with another male or a female; and marital intercourse during the woman's monthly cycle, as well as for a period after childbirth. We would do well to honor these boundaries, for they were given for our own good and health.

The Lord did not want fathers or grandfathers, stepfathers or stepmothers, uncles, aunts, children and grandchildren, brothers or sisters engaging in sexual activity with each other. These family relationships were not designed for that type of activity. To do so is to step out of God's healthy and holy boundaries. This will cause generations of misery, torment, woundedness, mental and physical illness, shame, guilt, secrets, suicides, hatred, and sexual dysfunctions throughout the lives of both the perpetrators and the victims of such things.

Likewise, the Lord created every body part for a particular function. Some parts are created to function in the digestive system. Others parts function within the reproductive, endocrine, neurological, muscular, circulatory, or respiratory systems.

And some pertain to the system of eliminating toxic wastes from our bodies. There are two openings in the body that are designed to carry toxic wastes out of the body. Nothing should ever enter these openings, but matter should only exit from these parts.

If we came with a User's Manual from the One who created us, it would spell this out clearly. Actually, He did give us a User's Manual…it's called the Bible. That is why Paul says these acts are *"contrary to nature"* (see Rom. 1:26). It is like going the wrong way down a one-way street.

The Lord designed the original and natural form of sexual intercourse that He instituted at the creation of male and female. Apart from any political arguments or agendas of social justice, this is simply the way we were created. And now we will focus on one particular form of sexual activity that the Lord has prohibited, for our own good and our health: "*You shall not lie with a male as with a woman. It is an abomination*" (Leviticus 18:22).

The Hebrew verb for "to lie with" is *tish'kav* (*shachav*).[2] This verb is always used in the Bible to refer to intercourse, even though it literally means "to lie." It is interesting that when the aged King David could not keep warm, they brought him a young girl to lie near him in bed to give him her body heat. However, since the king did not have sexual relations with Abishag, the Hebrew description does not say that he *shachav* with her, even though she did technically lie down next to him (see 1 Kings 1:4).

The first thing we should notice is that it is the act that God calls an abomination, not the person. There are a few places in Scripture where a person is called an abomination, but most of these are not connected to sexual activity.

Now, let's look at some other behaviors that God considers an abomination. The most-used Hebrew word for *abomination* is *to'evah*.[3] I found 116 references in the Old Testament, and Proverbs alone contains 20 uses of this word. Out of this large collection of abominations people commit, only a handful refer to sexual behavior.

Here are 15 other activities or people that the Lord calls *to'evah*, an abomination:

1. Carved images of gods (see Deut. 7:25)

2. Sacrificing our children (see Deut. 12:31)

3. Serving other gods (see Deut. 13:13-14)

4. Offering a defective animal to the Lord (see Deut. 17:1)

5. Witchcraft, soothsaying, interpreting omens, sorcery, mediums, spiritists, contacting the dead (see Deut. 18:9-12)

6. A woman who wears a man's clothing or a man who wears a woman's clothing (see Deut. 22:5)

7. A divorced woman going back to her first husband after marrying someone else, even if the second husband dies (see Deut. 24:4)

8. Unequal weights and measures—cheating customers in the workplace (see Deut. 25:13-16)

9. A perverse person (see Prov. 3:32)

10. A proud look

11. A lying tongue

12. Hands that shed innocent blood

13. A heart that devises wicked plans

14. A false witness

15. One who sows discord among the brethren (see Prov. 6:16-19 for 10 through 15)

I did not write out these cases in order to justify sinful sexual activity. I wrote them because I have been guilty of more than one item on this list. If the Lord would wish to destroy homosexuals, He would have to destroy me as well. After I got saved, did I ever have a proud look or a lying tongue? Yes, I did, even though I was saved. Do you know anyone who has sown discord among the brethren? Can any of us say we have not committed any of these abominations in our lives? Even if we did not sin, we're still not allowed to condemn anyone. Remember, only the sinless One did not wish to condemn the adulterous woman.

In the same way, a great number of people are either struggling with same-sex attractions or they slip into the lifestyle from time to time, but they are brothers and sisters who have prayed to the Lord for salvation and desire to live upright lives. We will look at this issue in the coming sections.

> *Do you not know that the unrighteous will not inherit the kingdom of God? Do not be deceived. Neither fornicators, nor idolaters, nor adulterers, nor homosexuals, nor sodomites, nor thieves, nor covetous, nor drunkards, nor revilers, nor extortioners will inherit the kingdom of God.* ***And such were some of you.*** *But you were washed, but you were sanctified, but you were justified in the name of the Lord Jesus and by the Spirit of our God* (1 Corinthians 6:9-11).

And such were some of us. The Lord has washed us clean, if we have accepted His rescue and salvation, *and if we do not persist in these behaviors.*

MATT'S STORY

Recently, I talked with a dear brother in the Lord, who was so kind as to share with me his life's testimony concerning this issue. He will be "Matt" in this story. I know that every person's thoughts and struggles are unique to their upbringing, chemistry, emotional needs, and the events in their lives. However, I also believe that there are a number of common factors.

In addition, from those I have known personally, there is a big difference between male and female homosexuality. The way men and women process emotional and physical needs are extremely different, and therefore, sexual brokenness has a different form and texture in the two groups. To learn more about these differences, see the section called Helps and Resources at the end of this chapter. In particular, there is much teaching available from Exodus International, which is referenced in this section.

Matt was raised in a liberal denomination in the South. He was the oldest of six children, and he told me, "I always knew there was something different about me." He went to church, loved God, and prayed to Jesus all of his life.

There was one very traumatic event in his young life. One night when Matt was seven, he was awakened by his baby brother, who was crying in the middle of the night. This crying went on, and it was keeping Matt awake, but his parents did not hear it. At one point, Matt paced back and forth outside the baby's room, whispering, "Oh, please go to sleep so I can go to sleep." He did not go get his parents.

In the morning, Matt's mother found the baby dead. He heard her screaming into the phone, "My baby's dead!"

He never told anyone what had happened during the night, and Matt carried terrible guilt from this event. Whenever anyone in the family would mention his baby brother's name, he would cover his ears and run out of the room. He doesn't know if this trauma could have contributed to his sexual orientation, but it was definitely one more indication that "there was something wrong with him."

He didn't know it, but for years after this terrible shock, his dad would wake up and go to the door of each child's room to listen for their breathing.

Matt was much closer to his mother than his father. He felt his father wanted a more rugged son, but Matt was not interested in sports. He was always a very intellectual boy, did a great deal of reading, and had long conversations with his mother. His father had some anger issues, which caused Matt to keep some emotional distance from him.

Meeting Matt now as a middle-aged adult, I perceive him as a warm, articulate, and relational person. He is a gentle, loving, and masculine man, who is in touch with his need to be loved. As we talked about his life, he mentioned frequently that although his sexual urges were very strong as a teen, he had a stronger emotional need to be loved. We will see that distinguishing between these two needs is one of God's Kingdom keys to walking in freedom and purity.

Sex or Love?

Before I continue Matt's journey, let's look more closely at these two different needs. We were made for love, and all people need to be loved. However, in both the heterosexual and homosexual populations, there are people who have allowed their sexual needs and pleasures to dominate their relationships. These people choose to live a promiscuous, uncommitted lifestyle, in order to receive the maximum sexual gratification without covenant, commitment, or heartfelt love.

This lifestyle makes them more like animals than men created in God's image. There is a great deal of promiscuity in the gay community, but is it any greater than among heterosexuals? If we could see the statistics, I would guess that both populations contain a similar level of promiscuity or non-marital fornication.

However, among both populations, there are many individuals who are looking for true love, as well as feeling sexual attractions. They are looking for one person to whom they can give their heart completely, and with whom they can remain in a committed love relationship. Obviously, this desire is a response to the way God designed us, according to the biblical account of our creation.

Many have not received sufficient nurturing from their parents, whether from the same-sex parent or the opposite. And so, as we enter puberty, we begin to look for someone who will love us and gratify us in the emotional arena, as well as the physical, to greater or lesser degrees.

Matt explained to me that as he approached his teens, he felt both the sexual and the emotional needs, but he could not distinguish them. He very much needed love, but as his body began to experience sexual chemistry, he told me, "I sexualized my emotional needs." He used sexual contact as a substitute for the actual love he was craving. It was very easy to confuse these two areas, especially as a 12- or 13-year-old.

THE TEEN YEARS

In the third and fourth grade, Matt experienced the usual flirtations with the girls, but as he moved toward puberty, the same-sex attraction was there. He told me that from his experience, the world of athletics and locker rooms is a highly charged atmosphere for teenage boys. It was here that his attractions began to develop. He believes that in the locker room, many more boys than we realize are open to same-sex experimentation.

As an interesting historical note, the ancient Greeks developed the Gymnasium, competitive male sports, and matches where they wrestled naked. Much of our modern sports and the Olympic games are derived from ancient Greece. This culture also bred a high level of homosexual behavior. Matt observed that the world of male athletics and locker rooms seemed to contribute to the development of same-sex attractions. Is it possible that this modern phenomenon is connected to the spirit of ancient Greece, a fallen principality who opposed God's covenants (see Dan. 10:20; Zech. 9:13)? Could this spirit still influence our culture?

I was surprised to learn that he began same-sex experimentation at age 12, during camping trips with an organization for boys. This continued until high school. Somehow, the boys who were interested found each other, while others remained unaware. Matt did not feel any guilt about this activity, although he realized he had to be very careful about who he told. He did not see it as a conflict with his church upbringing, because he had never heard or read anything in the Bible on this topic. He thought, "This is just how I feel."

His attraction to boys grew to a point of more than just physical desire. He was feeling a need for genuine relationship with an individual person, "Mr. Right." He wanted to be loved.

Matt explained to me that he was not trying to play a female role. Some gay relationships involve this type of role-playing, but he just felt like a guy who was attracted to guys. He had no negative value judgments about who he was at that time, but hearing other guys' remarks about "fags" made him realize it wasn't cool. He learned how to guard his secret.

Being a reader, Matt was very resourceful at finding books in the library that stimulated his imagination in this area. What he had access to back then was nothing compared to what a teenager can find now on the Internet.

His sexual activity continued for years through camping and locker room opportunities. His parents never knew. When he was about 16, his family moved, and Matt lost touch with the network of boys with whom he had opportunity for sexual contact. He was a loner at his new high school, and concentrated more on developing his intellect. He had some female friends, but there was no attraction.

Matt read a lot of spiritual books during those years, such as the biographies of Wesley and Luther. He went to church and believed in Jesus. This part was hard for me to understand, but Matt told me that he didn't know his homosexual activity was wrong according to the Bible. For a long time, he was able to separate his sexual life from his spiritual life, and kept them in separate compartments of his soul. He told me he continued to love God and prayed to Jesus. It puzzled me that he felt no guilt, only the need for secrecy. However, I knew he was telling me how it really was for him at that point in his life.

One interesting aspect of Matt's extraordinary intellect and spiritual insight was this: by the age of six or seven, he had already realized that the entire Bible was a Jewish book, and that Christianity was built entirely on a Jewish foundation. No one had taught him this, and yet it seemed obvious to him. However, most Christians do not just figure this out by themselves, and certainly not at that young age. This would be the foundation of Matt's future affiliation with the Messianic Jewish movement.

Even with his secret sexual involvement, this young man loved the Lord. For whatever reason, he remained in a relationship with the Lord without his conscience convicting him. I wondered why, but Matt answered that the Lord must have known he wasn't ready to deal with this issue yet. He said the enemy tried to use the strength of his sexual drive to separate him from God, but his love for God remained. He just kept his sexual life in a separate compartment from his love for God. Perhaps some readers will be able to identify with the idea of compartmentalizing different parts of their life. My soul has always been more integrated, and for me, compartmentalizing is a foreign concept; perhaps this is a left-brain versus right-brain issue, different for boys and girls.

The enemy also tried to separate Matt from God by bringing people into his life who weren't godly, who cursed, and were involved with drugs and alcohol. But his love for God persisted, and Matt has known many others who said that their love for God, and His love for them, won out in the end. Matt never drank or took drugs because he realized that they would lower his inhibitions, and he might accidentally reveal his secret. He needed to be in control, and this kept him from doing drugs.

During college, Matt had an affair for several months, but his partner could not return his feelings of love or commitment. He was only interested in sex. Matt found that in more than one relationship, the other man was promiscuous and was not looking for a committed love relationship, which he was searching for.

In the 1970s, Matt's family was introduced to the Charismatic movement, and they were filled with the Holy Spirit. This was when the Lord began convicting Matt of his sin in this area, and he began to live a celibate life. However, there were several other relationships that ensnared him before he was able to maintain victory in his sexual life.

One of his final snares was a man in his church group. Matt felt guilty about this relationship and realized his partner had a demon of lust. This man did receive deliverance from leaders in the church, but during the course of this deliverance, the man revealed Matt's identity as his partner. Since Matt's own father was part of the prayer team that delivered him, his father finally learned of his son's secret life. However, he never mentioned to his son that he knew. Perhaps this was a gracious response, allowing Matt to work through his own repentance and victory without having to stand before his father in shame.

You Are Not Alone

There are incredible resources available to those who struggle with same-sex attractions, or those active in the gay lifestyle. These ministries also offer support for their family members. This chapter will provide some of these resources for the reader to pursue. These resources will also help people who are struggling with other types of sexual brokenness besides homosexual issues.

Of the many believers who come to the Lord in their sexual brokenness and ask to be set free from these desires, there are varying degrees of healing and deliverance that they might experience. Some people receive a dramatic deliverance from all homosexual feelings upon committing their lives to the Lord or being filled with the Holy Spirit. Some do not and continue to experience varying degrees of struggle and temptation. For many, the healing comes gradually, and the battles become fewer and easier to overcome. Matt told me that for some, the struggle seemed to go on endlessly.

I do not know why some receive instant and miraculous deliverance from all feelings of same-sex attraction, and others have to continue to resist and struggle. It may be a sovereign decision of the Lord. What we do know is that God is Love, and He knows the depths of each heart that comes to Him for healing and deliverance. The Lord knows how much each person can sustain, and He is able to help those who are being tempted (see Heb.

2:18). And the Lord's exquisite ability to deliver us from these temptations is more delicate than any surgeon, so that the dear child He is perfecting is not broken, crushed, or destroyed in the process. God is *worthy* of our trust.

Perhaps for some, the continued battle is actually good training for the onslaughts of temptation that will come upon His people in these last-days' battles with evil. It is different for each one of us, but the Lord is always a great deliverer, who will make a way of escape from the temptation to all who sincerely repent and cry out to Him (see 1 Cor. 10:13).

As a matter of fact, these same principles hold true for heterosexuals who are trapped in equivalent or worse bondage. *We all need to surrender our fleshly cravings and take up our cross.* None of us are permitted to indulge our lusts, whether it is toward a male, a female, or a pornographic fantasy. Even within marriage, the Lord has holy standards and expectations for our behavior. I know that some Christians assume that once a person is married, "anything goes." Actually, anything doesn't go. I do not feel led to give an in-depth teaching on this matter, but we must be humble and prayerful as we consider our sexual expressions within the bounds of marriage. We should never demand our own way with our spouse. We should not use our precious spouse as an object to gratify lust. Our spouse is the Bride of Messiah, more than he or she is our possession. *How would we treat His Bride, before He has consummated His union with her?* As we humbly seek Him about this matter, the Holy Spirit will teach us which attitudes and behaviors please the Lord, and which ones He does not bless.

All people have urges to gratify various "needs," but look at Yeshua's example. *He was tempted in every way as we were, yet without sin* (see Heb. 4:15). Our Lord was a pure and highly disciplined individual, who did not live to please Himself, but to do the will of His Father. You might think no one could ever live this way, but the Lord said, *"Therefore, be perfect as your heavenly Father is perfect"* (Matt. 5:48).

He knew that it is absolutely possible to live a pure and holy life. Otherwise, He would not have told us to do so. However, we can never be complete unless we are genuinely in a bond of love with the One who can perfect us.

Matt was not one of those who received a complete deliverance from these desires and attractions. However, he made up his mind he would obey the Lord and walk in righteousness, and he learned not to follow these urges. *He told me that a secret to his victory was realizing the difference between sex and love.* Soon after he made a life-long decision to walk uprightly, he realized that since he desired to be in a committed relationship and to have children, the Lord would bless him through marriage to a woman.

People will say, "But I didn't choose this; it was not my decision to be this way." Granted, no one chooses how they feel. However, how we act is our decision. Matt's feelings did not disappear, but he exercised self-control and made a decision not to act contrary to the Lord's commands.

When Matt met the precious, believing woman who would become his wife, he was completely honest with her about his history. Knowing that there would be challenges in their marriage, the Lord chose a special bride to love Matt. He gave her a love that was willing to work with him throughout his *progressive walk of purity.* Not every woman could handle this, of course, but the Lord knew the perfect young woman who could more than handle it—she could cover him with loving support without self-pity. Matt's wife knows that she is greatly loved, and that her husband honors and appreciates their sacred covenant. Her heart trusts in his love and commitment to her.

Although his sexual urges still tempt him at times, he realizes that love is more nurturing to his soul than momentary physical gratification. His need for love is greater, and the Lord has provided for him a loving wife and two wonderful and healthy grown sons. He wisely values the love more than the sexual desires, and knows that to gratify the flesh would jeopardize the trust and intimacy of the love relationship the Lord has blessed him with.

Matt does not believe that God made him this way. His personal belief is that same-sex attractions spring from some deficit in patterning or identification with the father figure. He said that in some cases, this deficit only causes improper heterosexual responses; at other times, it creates a need for a healthy male bonding. Without parental patterning, this healthy need becomes sexualized. The individual then attempts to meet that need in a sexual way, with a person of the same sex.

ABUSE

Matt was not abused, but in many cases, this brokenness springs from abuse in the early years. The damage caused by sexual abuse of children and teens is incalculable. The selfish perpetrator does not look at his victim as a human soul, but rather as an object to be used. He does not consider the years of pain, shame, struggle, confusion, and dysfunction that await the little one whose innocence he stole forever. He takes their childhood from them as easily as tossing away an empty pack of cigarettes. In doing so, he is also stealing their future. If we did not have a Savior who has redeemed our future from the pit of torment with His own blood, we would be like those who have no hope.

The child pornography industry is a huge factor in stimulating these sick and unnatural burnings. Everyone will give an account to God for what they have done. Those who do these things, how can they not fear God?

> *Whoever causes one of these little ones who believe in Me to sin, it would be better for him if a millstone were hung around his neck, and he were drowned in the depth of the sea* (Matthew 18:6).

A number of people who were abused as children never acted on their same-sex attraction, but they felt the attraction. Matt spoke to me about a worship leader he knows who was molested as a child by a Christian. This man has struggled all his life with same-sex issues, even to this day. But about the terrible battle that rages within him, Matt told me, "Even in the depth of his brokenness, he still felt a strong love for God that couldn't be denied."

However, he agonizes over why the Lord allowed this to happen to an innocent child. This is a huge question for victims of sexual abuse as children. This precious man writes songs in which he attempts to reconcile what happened to him with the love of God. He asks, "Where were You?"

God's perspective on suffering is more far-reaching than ours. He is indeed there when these things are being done to us; He weeps with us, even when He does not grant us immediate rescue. However, the Lord has provided for a lasting rescue, where no one will ever hurt us again. His view is eternal. Jesus is concerned about how we emerge from the fire, how we bring our pain to Him. *He is looking for how we come out of the suffering.*

Because of these secret wounds and dysfunctions, many beloved Christians struggle on a daily basis with loving God. If these brothers and sisters are afraid of revealing their background within their church environment, they will be unable to testify about the goodness of God. It gives glory to God when we testify of where we came from, and what the Lord did for us. Otherwise, we can't rescue others who are stuck in the same place. If a Christian has been rescued from homosexuality, even if there are still battles to be overcome, he should not fear man's opinion. Rather, for the sake of others who struggle in secret, he should testify of what God has brought him out of.

However, if church leaders reject and fear a testimony of this nature, it will cause people to withhold their life's struggles, victories, and testimonies. Thus, it will promote and prolong the secrecy.

Unlike many who struggle with sexual brokenness, Matt never said, "God, why did You make me this way?" However, he did cry out to the Lord, "Why is this my struggle? Why does my issue have to be such an unacceptable weakness? Why *this*, Lord?"

We don't have the answer to this question, but we know that *"in all these things we are more than conquerors through Him who loved us"* (Rom. 8:37 NIV).

Matt's favorite Bible verse is Isaiah 44:22. "*I have blotted out, like a thick cloud, your transgressions, and like a cloud, your sins. Return to Me, for I have redeemed you.*"

I am grateful to my friend for sharing his story with me so openly, and I bless his family with abundant joy and the peace of Yeshua, which transcends human understanding.

REVIVAL: THE HIGHWAYS AND THE HEDGES

The Lord is about to do a mighty work of revival and restoration, which will involve the gay community. This is a work He has planned for these endtimes, and which will glorify His name. It will astonish, thrill, and in some cases, divide the Christian community.

This revival will also amaze and reach the secular world. As this phenomenon catches the attention of the secular media, many will come to investigate and will receive the Lord's salvation in the process.

The Lord has revealed this coming revival to a number of godly ministers, within both the evangelical and charismatic communities. A time is coming when these men and women of God will speak and write openly about this great harvest, but they know it will be costly to do so; it will draw a firestorm of accusation. Nevertheless, when the appointed time arrives for the Lord to bring them forward, they will take their stand with boldness because they know it is from the Lord's gracious heart.[4]

It will cause much controversy because many Christians have written off the gay and lesbian community as somehow unworthy, closed, or impossible to bring into the Lord's family. The same gift our Lord purchased for us on the cross was also purchased for them. If His love could touch my hopeless brokenness, there is no one on this earth it cannot reach.

The early Jewish believers in Jerusalem found it hard to grasp that the Lord was pouring out His Spirit even on the Gentiles. Although they wanted to criticize the inclusion of this excluded population, they could not argue with His grace. He had indeed poured out the same Holy Spirit on them as He did upon us, and so they opened their hearts and minds and rejoiced.

> If therefore God gave them the same gift as He gave us when we believed on the Lord Jesus Christ, who was I that I could withstand God?" When they heard these things they became silent; and they glorified God, saying, "Then God has also granted to the Gentiles repentance to life" (Acts 11:17-18).

In Romans 11, Paul even says that grafting the Gentiles into Israel's tree is "contrary to nature" (Rom. 11:24). And yet, the Lord wanted to gather these other nations into His covenant of love and inclusion. Likewise, the Lord will pour out a spirit of grace upon the gay community, and many sons and daughters will "come home" to their Creator and their Savior. They will be granted the grace to receive healing, repent of sexual sin, and to walk in uprightness. Some will marry a spouse of the opposite sex, and some will choose to remain celibate, as the Lord Jesus, the apostle Paul, and many others to this day have remained celibate. What is impossible for us in our weakness and brokenness is possible with God.

The Lord Yeshua actually foretold, and even commanded, His people to go to this closed, isolated, rejected community.

> A certain man gave a great supper and invited many, and sent his servant at supper time to say to those who were invited, "Come, for all things are now ready." But they all with one accord began to make excuses....So that servant came and reported these things to his master. Then the master of the house, being angry, said to his servant, "Go out quickly into the streets and lanes of the city, and bring in here the poor and the maimed and the lame and the blind." And the servant said, "Master, it is done as you commanded, and still there is room." Then the master said to the servant, **"Go out into the highways and hedges, and compel them to come in, that my house may be**

filled. *For I say to you that none of those men who were invited*
shall taste my supper" (Luke 14:16-18a; 21-24).

The Lord said, *"Go out into the **highways and hedges**, and compel them to*
come in...in order that My house may be filled." In this parable, the Lord was
very angry at those whom He had invited to His great banquet, in His generosity and love, but who insulted Him and refused to come.

So in His anger, the Lord turned to strangers, outsiders, those whom
society considered wretched and unworthy. His table must not remain empty, with places unclaimed. No, for the King had spent too much effort in
preparing this banquet and had paid too high a price for it to be wasted. He
felt pain and rejection from the favored ones who had been invited, and their
ingratitude infuriated Him.

They were too prideful and distracted by their financial interests, too
busy with the material things of this world and their own personal affairs to
come and sit at His table, to dine with Him in intimacy. And so He turned
to startled outsiders with all His favor and compelled them to come into His
banquet hall, to abundantly bless them with Heaven's riches.

In its original context, this parable was about the Judean leaders' rejection
of Yeshua's invitation to humility, repentance, and salvation. And being hurt
and angered by our rejection, He turned to a people who were *"not a people,"*
the Gentiles, and invited all nations to His banquet (see Rom. 10:19).

But it is also a parable of the last-days' Laodicean church, which has
rejected the Lord's urgent invitation to sit at His table and dine with Him.
And in like manner, He will turn His attention to the least "deserving," the
least honorable, and those who are the most offensive to His lukewarm
church. And the Lord will give seats of honor to those He knows we will
not accept.

> *And I say to you that many will come from east and west, and*
> *sit down with Abraham, Isaac, and Jacob in the kingdom of*
> *heaven. **But the sons of the kingdom will be cast out into***

outer darkness. *There will be weeping and gnashing of teeth* (Matthew 8:11-12).

And where will He find these guests? First, He searches in the "streets and the lanes"; then, when there are still empty places, He searches out among the "*highways and the hedges.*" In English, a hedge is "a fence or boundary of dense bushes or shrubs."[5] The Greek word for hedges is *phragmos*, meaning a hedge of shrubbery, a wall or a partition, which keeps two parties from ever meeting.[6]

In this passage, it refers to hedged communities, for the word *hedges* is plural. A true shrubbery hedge in England is so thick and confining, that even the smallest animal cannot get through it. Anything walled in there is trapped, cut off, and isolated from contact with the outside world.

There are a number of hedged communities on the earth: lepers; the "untouchables" in India's caste system; the mentally impaired; slaves of human trafficking; prisoners; and the gay community, to a large degree. When the Church prays for the harvest to come in, she must be prepared to embrace these unwanted people groups as those the Lord has deliberately compelled to come into the household of God.

This might connect to the dream I shared in the last chapter, where I stumbled upon the unwanted people on my search to find a good church meeting. I found these wretched ones hedged in behind closed doors. Upon seeing their disgusting condition, I quietly closed the door and backed out.

We must participate with the Lord in the great coming harvest of souls among the gay community. We will see it with our eyes, and this must not offend us, but should cause us great rejoicing.

There are some awesome ministries who are reaching out in radically loving and creative ways to the gay communities. I will cite some of them in the section on Help and Resources.

THE MARRIAGE ISSUE

I understand that many gay people feel that if we cannot support the legalization of gay marriage, we are the enemy. They feel that the only practical way we can prove that we love them is to support their "civil right" to marry their same-sex partner.

Before addressing civil rights, let us first look at the bigger picture. In one sense, it would be more beneficial to people's eternal souls if we address the fact that all of us have sinned, and we all need Yeshua's sacrifice to enter the Kingdom of God.

If a government or society legalizes gay marriage, it might make some people relieved and happy for the brief season that they have on this earth. *But life is very short, and soon, we will all be standing before the judgment seat of Christ, giving an account for our lives.* On that day it will not matter if we had a happy marriage, or if we were a persecuted minority, or if we received what we thought were our rights or didn't receive them. No matter what real or perceived injustices were done to us on this earth, none of that will matter when we stand before His throne.

The only thing that will matter is:

"Did you love Me with all your heart and all your soul and all your strength?"

"Did you know that I suffered an agonizing death, nailed to a tree, to completely pay for and blot out all your sins?"

"Did you forgive those who abused you, even as I forgave you your trespasses?"

"Did you appreciate the price I paid to cleanse your filth, and did you put away those things from your life?"

"Did you thank Me, and were you willing to take up your cross and follow Me?"

"Were your own sexual or emotional needs greater than the price I paid to make you a holy and perfect child before My Father?"

"Did you put My Father's will ahead of your own will and rights?"

As for the legalization of gay marriage, this is the Lord's heart as He has expressed it through Scripture:

If marriage were merely a social contract, conferring particular legal or financial benefits to the married couple, which would not be available to unmarried couples...

If there were no Creator who made us...

If we were here on this planet by reason of a series of genetic accidents, with no purposeful, intentional, intelligent design...

If all social conventions and arrangements were simply determined by the will of the people...

If individuals and nations did not need to answer to any higher authority...

If there were no medical, emotional, or societal consequences to any particular combination of permanently joined sex-partners...

...then it wouldn't matter if we legalize gay marriage, as well as marriage between any other combination of people, regardless of age, gender, or the number of partners.

But marriage is not a social contract, nor is it a business arrangement. It was not invented by any political group who wanted to gain advantage in their society. Marriage is a covenant created by God at the beginning of life as we know it. *God ordained marriage as a picture of the relationship He desires to have with His people.*

He made us male and female, and our ability to procreate requires one male and one female. Among all the creatures on earth in their natural habitats, the only mating that takes place is between male and female; many of these animals mate with the same partner for life. That is because all creatures have an innate knowledge that this is how they will bear offspring according to their genus and species.

Who or what opposes same-sex marriage? Is it the politics of man, or is it God Himself who opposes the violation of His covenants with mankind?

I feel compassion for same-sex couples who desire to legitimize their love relationship; I truly understand the sense of injustice they must feel. It must seem unfair that they can't enjoy the same benefits as heterosexual married couples.

But if a nation deliberately violates the sacred covenants of God by which we stand or fall, that nation will not stand. There are fixed and eternal spiritual laws in the universe, and it is immaterial whether we like them or not. If we don't like the law of gravity, that's a shame. We will still get hurt if we jump off a bridge. Even if we don't like God's requirements for righteousness, we will still face inevitable consequences if we violate them. They are not subjective, nor are they determined by the wishes of the majority population. God never changes to match our desires. We must change to line up with His standards. All of us must bend our will to His, not merely one population.

Therefore, He has extended mercy and tender compassions to all who struggle with urges that don't line up with His standards. We are all impure and bent, both heterosexuals and homosexuals, and we all have to surrender our rights and our wills to be pleasing to Him. There are many who have overcome in this area. I will now include some wonderful and compassionate sources of help and healing.

HELPS AND RESOURCES

Here are a few of the best sources I have found, which offer compassionate help to those desiring healing and freedom in any area of sexual brokenness, including same-sex attraction and other gender issues.

Exodus International:[7] This nonprofit, interdenominational organization is "the largest information and referral ministry in the world addressing homosexual issues" (www.exodus-international.org). On the Web site, you can find all types of counseling referrals, true testimonies of those who have found freedom, books and CDs, and many links to other resources. If you or anyone you know desires help without condemnation, this is the perfect place to begin your journey.

There is an amazing conference series called "Love Won Out," which is a joint venture between Exodus International and Focus on the Family.[8] Here is a brief description of this ministry, as it appears on the Love Won Out Web site:

> Focus on the Family's Love Won Out ministry exhorts and equips the Church to respond in a Christ-like way to the issue of homosexuality. And to those who struggle with unwanted same-sex attractions, we offer the Gospel hope that these desires can be overcome.
>
> By offering conferences, education, counseling, and research, the Love Won Out team strives to uphold God's design for sexuality in a way that transforms lives.
>
> Whether you're a parent, friend, family member, or ministry leader who wants to lovingly reach out with uncompromised faith—in compassion and grace—to a loved one who deals with homosexuality, Love Won Out has the resources to help.

I have watched portions of a Love Won Out conference on God TV's Web site.[9] The speakers gave compelling, intelligent, and heart-rending testimonies. I was astonished that this level of transparency and genuine compassion was available to those who struggle, as well as to their families and friends.

Another resource is the Web site of Chad Thompson, who is the author of the book *Loving Homosexuals as Jesus Would*.[10] He presents the need for radical, self-sacrificing love as the most genuine demonstration of our love for the gay community. On his Web site, Chad discusses some of the tensions caused by involvement in political issues, and how we can approach these tensions without compromising God's standards.

One last resource I will mention is the Web site of international speaker Sy Rogers.[11] Sy is a brilliant, funny, transparent speaker whose wit and raw honesty are stunning. He has come out of terrible brokenness and abuse and shares in such a way that even the most jaded heart can thaw before him.

THE LORD'S HEART FOR GAY PEOPLE

I would like to share with you now the word the Lord gave me for those who struggle with this issue. When I received this word, it seemed to be coming from my own heart, as one who is twisted and broken (which I am). But at the same time, I didn't feel that I was creating this word, but was hearing it in my heart from the Holy Spirit. It has a very "existential" feeling to it. I pray it blesses you.

> *Beloved child: We all have things we didn't ask for. We have hard things that obsess us. Some of us have illness, chronic pain, or deformities. Some of us feel lonely and abandoned from the womb. Some of our mothers never held us, and we have a huge hole in our heart. Some of our fathers treated us like objects on whom to try social, spiritual, or sexual experimentation.*

Some of our parents used us for evil rituals, and we were help-less and terrified. Some were selfish alcoholics and drug addicts. Some of us had mentally ill siblings, whose problems kept our parents screaming in frustration and anger.

Some of us weren't accepted by the popular girls and were tor-mented by rejection. Some of us were nerdy, artistic, or scholarly boys who were too smart and sensitive, and the bullies at school made a meal of us. We wanted to be sick, to plead with our moms not to send us to school, but we knew we had to go and face another day of torment. We were mocked and beaten.

Some of us dreaded every Tuesday in gym class, when we all had to stand naked in front of our heartless gym teacher, feeling so ashamed and exposed in our undeveloped puberty. Some of us were fat in a sea of athletic and sculpted bodies. Every Tues-day, there was nowhere to hide.

Some of us heard voices that weren't there and wondered why they wouldn't stop. Some of us felt compelled to steal things, and others, to look at secret, shameful pictures in magazines or computers. Some of us had a friend who gave us one book early in our puberty, which we wish to God we had never read, for it forever altered our psychological and sexual chemistry and ruined all of our future relationships.

And some of us harbored secret and shameful thoughts of same-sex attraction and fantasies. Under our bed covers of darkness, we gratified ourselves, feeling pleasure and shame. And for some, the shame and torment were so unbearable, that we took a sickening overdose or hung ourselves, thinking the pain would finally stop.

*O, beloved child of God, we are all bent! Without Jesus, we are all broken, ill, slaves to diseases, impulses, histories, and environmental damages we **never** asked for! Do you think heterosexuals are not enslaved and tormented? Do you think straight people are any more normal or less broken, or any more righteous than you?*

We all need a Savior, a kind and tender teacher and gentle shepherd who will lead us by the hand out of our shame and bent-ness.

We never asked for these feelings, diseases, shames, and torments, but He died to rescue, redeem, and restore us from our brokenness. We are just like you, and you are just like us!

We don't need to embrace our sick desires. We can run into the arms of a powerful God, a lover, who is beckoning us out of our shame, our inability to be "good" and fix ourselves, and into grace, acceptance, and supernatural transformation from an earth-crawler into a beautiful butterfly. Fly into Yeshua's arms, child of God, and your shame will be remembered no more!

Let him who is without sin cast the first stone! **Amen.**

ENDNOTES

1. One can read the story of this brutal murder at www.en.wikipedia.org/wiki/Matthew_Shepard.

2. See http://strongsnumbers.com/hebrew/7901.htm.

3. See http://www.studylight.org/lex/heb/view.cgi?number=08441.

4. The insights and prophetic understanding in this section were graciously given to me by my dear friend, David Michael in Hemet, California. He

is one to whom the Lord has revealed this end-times work, and I am so grateful to him.

5. Frank Abate, ed., *The Oxford Desk Dictionary and Thesaurus* (New York: Oxford University Press, 1997).

6. See http://www.studylight.org/lex/grk/view.cgi?number=5418.

7. See www.exodus-international.org, or call 888-264-0877.

8. See www.lovewonout.com, or e-mail lovewonout@family.org.

9. See www.god.tv. You can sign up for a free subscription; then click on "God On Demand," and look on the left menu for "Love Won Out."

10. See www.lovinghomosexuals.com.

11. See www.syrogers.com.

Part 2

Worship and Strange Fire

Chapter 8

The Fear of the Lord

I N Genesis 22, we read the terrible account of Abraham's greatest test: would he obey the Lord's word and sacrifice his beloved son Isaac, although he was the promised son through whom all of Abraham's descendants were to come?

> *As the two of them went on together, Isaac spoke up and said to his father, Abraham, "Father?" "Yes, my son," Abraham replied. "The fire and the wood are here," Isaac said, "but where is the lamb for the burnt offering?" Abraham answered, "God Himself will provide the lamb, for the burnt offering, my son." And the two of them went on together. When they reached the place God had told him about, Abraham built an altar there and arranged the wood on it. He bound his son, Isaac and laid him on the altar, on top of the wood. Then he reached out his hand and took the knife to slay his son (Genesis 22:6b-10 NIV).*

We know that the angel of the Lord stopped Abraham at the last second. This was as close as he could have come to slaying his own son. We learn in further accounts that the fear of this event stayed with Isaac for the rest of his life.

"THE FEAR OF ISAAC"

In time, we see Isaac's son Jacob, who worked for 20 years for his unscrupulous uncle Laban. Jacob had been cheated out of his wife and his wages, and had been living in unkind conditions of deprivation. After fleeing from Laban and getting caught, the two men made a covenant together. Notice Jacob's titles for God in his argument with his uncle:

> If the God of my father, the **God of Abraham** and the **Fear of Isaac** had not been with me, you would surely have sent me away empty-handed (Genesis 31:42a NIV).

When Laban and Jacob took an oath together, we read that *"Jacob swore by the Fear of his father Isaac"* (Gen. 31:53).

We've frequently heard the Lord define Himself as "the God of Abraham, Isaac, and Jacob." But notice that Abraham's grandson Jacob did not say, "The God of Abraham and Isaac," but rather, *"the God of Abraham and the Fear of Isaac"* (Gen. 31:42). To make sure we know that this was not just a random slip of the tongue, we see Jacob repeat it a few moments later: *"So Jacob took an oath in the name of the Fear of his father, Isaac"* (Gen. 31:53 NIV).

Although the Lord has many titles that He is called in Scripture, nowhere else does He call Himself the "Fear of" any other patriarch or prophet. Why did Jacob refer to God this way, using a different title for Abraham's God than for Isaac's God?

Once I was listening to a prophet speak about the fear of the Lord and how most Christians are not prepared for His second coming. As I was praying about this, the Lord showed me Isaac and began to teach me why Jacob used this expression.

The Lord showed me that Isaac's fear stayed with him his entire life, since the day his father lifted up the knife against him. Isaac was seconds away from slaughter. He lay bound on a pile of wood, about to become a burnt offering. Isaac had seen his father lay sheep on the altar many times.

He had seen his father cut their throats and spill their blood; he had seen his father set fire to the wood and had watched that entire sheep disappear in licks of flame and a cloud of smoke. He was a split-second away from being that sheep. Would you say this was a traumatic experience?

We could never judge Abraham for this act, since he was simply obeying God, no matter how "unethical" the command may seem to us. Even so, if you have been snatched from the jaws of death, you live the rest of your life differently. If you narrowly escaped being slaughtered by your father, the one you loved and trusted, you live as a rescued one, saved from slaughter at the last second. Your priorities are different when you have been under the knife.

In addition to this, you know that your father was not a twisted psychopath; rather, this gentle and righteous man was *obeying God* when he bound you, laid you on the wood, and lifted up the knife to slay you. So in a sense, you were almost slaughtered by God!

And so Isaac walked into his old age from that early moment in the fear of the Lord. In God's mercy, a ram suddenly appeared in the thickets to save his life. It seems odd that Abraham hadn't noticed the struggling, bleating ram moments before, as he was preparing the altar and his son for sacrifice. I wonder if Abraham meant what he said when he told his son, "*God will provide the lamb.*" Perhaps the Creator did indeed provide a ram that wasn't there moments before; He created it at that moment for this purpose, to rescue Isaac from death.

Isaac was redeemed by a ram, caught by his horns. If God rescued you at the last second from literal death, would you walk for the rest of your life in the fear of the Lord? Wouldn't our petty offenses and selfishness fade away, under the shadow of death and the haven of rescue?

But we are also rescued ones. We were under the death sentence of eternity in torment, where our worms would never die and our flames would never be quenched (see Isa. 66:24). We were one breath away from slaughter, but God provided a Lamb to die in our place, to save our life. Do we understand what the Lord did for us, and do we walk like Isaac?

THE FEAR OF THE LORD

There are many Scriptural references to people who "feared the Lord." Although we barely ever hear this term in Christian circles today, the Bible used this description frequently when referring to people who found favor with the Lord.

It is used of both Jews and non-Jews, among men and women of all ranks in society: Job feared the Lord, as did the Roman centurion, Cornelius.

The books of Moses, as well as the prophetic and historic writings of the Bible continually command the people to fear the Lord. There are at least 58 references to the fear of the Lord in the Psalms alone.

In Malachi 3:16-18, we read that those who feared the Lord would be spared in the day of trouble, whereas those who did not fear Him would not be spared.

The humble thief on the cross rebuked the insulting thief by saying, *"Don't you fear God?"*(See Luke 23:40.)

Even the angels in the Book of Revelation warn the last-days inhabitants of the earth to *"Fear God and give Him glory, because the hour of His judgment has come"* (Rev. 14:7).

Isaiah prophesied that the coming Messiah would be filled with the seven Spirits of God, which represent the fullest expression of God's divine attributes abiding in Him. One of these Spirits is the Fear of the Lord:

> There shall come forth a Rod from the stem of Jesse, and a Branch shall grow out of his roots. The **Spirit of the Lord** shall rest upon Him, the Spirit of **wisdom** and **understanding**, the Spirit of **counsel** and **might**, the Spirit of **knowledge** and of the

fear of the Lord. *His delight is in the fear of the Lord* (Isaiah 11:1-3a).

These are not seven different Spirits, but rather can be viewed as seven streams of the Holy Spirit, which proceed from the Father (see Rev. 1:4; 3:1; 4:5; 5:6). In Revelation 4:5, we are told that these seven Spirits appear as seven blazing torches before God's throne.

We know that the Holy Spirit can divide and distribute Himself among many individual believers, as we read in Acts 2:3. It is like the same Pillar of Fire that appeared to the children of Israel, now divided Himself into many little torches, which rested on each believer!

Throughout the Lord Yeshua's ministry on earth, we could find examples of each of these seven Spirits demonstrated in His words and acts. But above all miracles, wisdom and prophetic knowledge, the Lord was consumed with a *desire to obey His Father* at all costs. The Lord said He had come only to do His Father's will. His words and deeds were not of His own initiative, for He did only what He saw and heard the Father doing.

Beloved, this is the fear of the Lord! *Yeshua's lovesick, costly desire to please the Father at every moment was the fear of the Lord in action.* He couldn't bear to hurt His Father by walking in disobedience, independence, or selfish desires.

Speaking about the fear of the Lord in Yeshua's life, the writer of Hebrews says,

> *Who, in the days of His flesh, when He had offered up prayers and supplications, with vehement cries and tears to Him who was able to save Him from death,* **and was heard because of His godly fear** (Hebrews 5:7).

A better translation of this last phrase would be, **"He was heard because of the fear of God which was in Him."**

They Died as a Warning to Us

Paul warned the Church that the punishments that befell Israel were written down as a warning and example to the New Covenant believers (see 1 Cor. 10:6). These should give us a healthy fear of the Lord, knowing He is the same yesterday, today, and forever.

Here are four Scriptural examples that serve as warnings to the Church. Two of them are connected to the theme of holiness and will be detailed in Chapter 10. The other two examples are about disobedience and hypocrisy. I will cover these in chronological order.

> *Then Nadab and Abihu, the sons of Aaron, each took his censer and put fire in it, put incense on it, and offered **profane fire** before the Lord, **which He had not commanded them.** So fire went out from the Lord and devoured them, and they died before the Lord* (Leviticus 10:1-2).

This offering of "strange fire" or unauthorized, profane, common, and unholy fire, serves as an urgent warning to the Church. The fiery and unexpected death that fell upon the two sons of Aaron brought tremendous fear to Moses, Aaron, the Levites, and all the people of Israel.

The High Priest in particular was under a much higher accountability before the Lord than were the Levites. The Lord had laid out very specific guidelines about the burning of incense. These two sons of the High Priest went presumptuously into the Holy Place and offered fire that was not authorized or prescribed by the Lord to His servant Moses.

The second example is the harsh punishment that befell Israel, due to unbelief, grumbling, and disobedience. Frankly, many in the Church have been equally guilty of these behaviors.

> *Because all these men who have seen My glory and the signs which I did in Egypt and in the wilderness, and have put Me to*

the test now these ten times, and have not heeded My voice, they certainly shall not see the land of which I swore to their fathers, nor shall any of those who rejected Me see it.... ***The carcasses of those who have complained against Me shall fall in this wilderness*** (Numbers 14:22-23, 29a).

The Lord brought the children of Israel into the desert and placed them in a number of "trying" circumstances. Some of the tests that they failed were:

+ Impatience and unbelief as Moses tarried too long on the mountain, and then committing idolatry with the golden calf at the foot of the holy mountain;

+ Fear and lack of trust concerning food and water issues;

+ Unwillingness to go into a new place and do battle with gigantic inhabitants;

+ Rebellion against God's chosen leadership;

+ Murmuring and complaining about the hardships of the desert;

+ Ingratitude and forgetting all that the Lord had done to bring them out of bondage.

We should not think that these issues are less deadly to us than they were for the Israelites in the desert. Paul says that these very punishments were written to warn us not to provoke the Lord to anger, lest we fail to enter the full inheritance He has prepared for His last-days' Church. I believe I have been guilty of all of the above at various times in my life. This instills the fear of the Lord in me, knowing that I have behaved as badly as my ancestors.

The Western Church has not crossed over from the wilderness into her spiritual Promised Land. Like Israel, we have remained immature and have not yet passed our wilderness tests. Those who qualify, like Joshua and

Caleb, become the sons of God and inherit the promise (see Rom. 8:17-19). The sons of God have grown up into the full measure of Messiah's stature (see Eph. 4:11-13). If we fail our wilderness tests, like our forefathers, we will drop away in obscurity and never taste the good fruits of sonship, walking in the fear of the Lord as Yeshua did.

The third example involves treating the holy Presence of God in a casual and flippant manner.

> *They set the ark of God on a new cart and brought it from the house of Abinadab, which was on the hill. Uzzah and Ahio, sons of Abinadab, were guiding the new cart with the ark of God on it, and Ahio was walking in front of it. David and the whole house of Israel were celebrating with all their might before the Lord, with songs and with harps, lyres, tambourines, sistrums and cymbals. When they came to the threshing floor of Nacon, Uzzah reached out and took hold of the ark of God, because the oxen stumbled.* **The Lord's anger burned against Uzzah because of his irreverent act;** *therefore God struck him down and he died there beside the ark of God* (2 Samuel 6:3-7 NIV).

The Lord's swift punishment upon Uzzah frightened and angered David so much that he refused to bring the ark up to Jerusalem. He did not understand God's requirements for transporting the holy Ark of the Covenant, which was the dwelling place of His glory.

It is very important that we handle God's glory with reverence and in His prescribed way. We cannot administer the things of God with our own man-made ideas and experiments. We will explore more about the practical applications of this warning in Chapter 10.

The fourth example is from the New Testament and involves the hypocrisy of a believing couple in the earliest days of the church in Jerusalem.

> *Now a man named Ananias, together with his wife Sapphira, also sold a piece of property. With his wife's full knowledge he kept back part of the money for himself, but brought the rest and put it at the apostles' feet. Then Peter said, "Ananias, how is it that Satan has so filled your heart that you have lied to the Holy Spirit and have kept for yourself some of the money you received for the land? Didn't it belong to you before it was sold? And after it was sold, wasn't the money at your disposal? What made you think of doing such a thing? **You have not lied to men but to God.**" When Ananias heard this, he fell down and died. And **great fear seized all who heard** what had happened* (Acts 5:1-5 NIV).

Several hours later, Sapphira came in, not knowing what had happened to her husband. Peter asked her, *"Tell me, is this the price you and Ananias got for the land?"* (Acts 5:8 NIV). In asking this question, the Lord was giving her one more chance to repent and tell the truth. However, she lied to Peter and was struck dead immediately. *And the fear of the Lord came upon the church.*

Peter was operating in a gift of knowledge when he saw through Ananias' lie. He could not have known the price they had been paid unless the Holy Spirit revealed it to him. We need to be mindful that no matter how deep a secret sin is hidden in our hearts, the Holy Spirit could reveal it to a prophet at any time He desires, including in a public meeting. He does this not to humiliate us, but to save us from hell, which is where hypocrites will end up.

> *The master of that servant will come on a day when he is not looking for him and at an hour that he is not aware of, and will cut him in two and **appoint him his portion with the hypocrites.** There shall be weeping and gnashing of teeth* (Matthew 24:50-51).

THERE IS A HEALTHY FEAR

This warning gives me a profound fear of the Lord, and a powerful determination to never lie or walk in any form of hypocrisy. When we speak to people, we never know to whom the Lord might reveal the secrets of our heart. I am terrified of hypocrisy in my life, and I ask the Lord to search my heart from time to time, to make sure I am truly transparent in public and in private. If we will repent before Him privately, the Lord is so gracious never to humiliate us publicly.

> *The heart is deceitful above all things, and desperately wicked; who can know it?* (Jeremiah 17:9)

I heard Sadhu Sundar Selvaraj preach on Ananias and Sapphira. He shared that once he was waiting to speak at a large meeting where the people were joyfully dancing and worshiping. One woman in particular seemed the most vocal and exuberant in her zeal for the Lord.

While he was speaking, Sadhu saw the Lord Jesus walked down the aisle toward that woman, and He reached His hand into her chest and pulled out her heart (her spiritual heart) for Sadhu to behold. It was black with sin, and the Lord instantly showed him five secret sins in her life. He was astonished, since this woman looked so joyful in her worship. *Then the Lord required him to publicly expose her sins in front of everyone.* The woman fell down and wept tears of repentance on the spot, as her secrets were laid bare in front of everyone. Can you imagine?

> *For nothing is secret that will not be revealed, nor anything hidden that will not be known and come to light....Therefore whatever you have spoken in the dark will be heard in the light, and what you have spoken in the ear in inner rooms will be proclaimed on the housetops* (Luke 8:17; 12:3).

Although I had read the account of Ananias and Sapphira many times, the tangible fear of the Lord fell upon the audience that night as Sadhu preached in the power of the Spirit. I had been a believer for 34 years, yet I had never felt this fear before. I was afraid of the Lord and even questioned my salvation. I didn't fully doubt that I was saved, but I felt completely vulnerable and undone. I felt like the ceiling was gone, the sky was rolled back, and I was exposed before a righteous and holy God. I felt like His glance was penetrating every secret thought, act, and private crevice of my heart.

I didn't feel convicted of any particular hypocrisy in my life. But I felt a general sense of anxiety and wondered who could stand under this kind of scrutiny. My body trembled; my soul wanted to run away and hide.

Even though I know and love the Lord, I wanted to crawl away somewhere. That is what the fear of the Lord feels like, but of course there is nowhere to go. You know it won't do any good to run away, and you also know that in Heaven you won't be able to go anywhere. You will just stand there and take it, or you will lie on your face and take it, because there is no option.

In a way, the fear of the Lord is a terrible feeling, but it's not the same thing as the condemnation of the enemy.

They both feel uncomfortable, but the difference is this. One feels like, "I hate you, you revolting piece of slime. I remember every vile thing you ever thought or said, and I'm playing them back before the throne of God every day, so that He realizes how repulsive you are."

The other feels like, "*Yes, you are naked; yes, you are dust; yes, you are vulnerable; yes, you don't deserve to be here. But I love you, and I will make you acceptable; I am able to present you blameless.*"

As I waited for Sadhu to bring us to the reassurance we all needed, I thought, "What if there is still hypocrisy in my heart and I haven't discovered it?" I knew that deception is deceptive.

Sadhu did not require everyone to kneel down as he brought us to a place of public repentance and soul-searching. Rather, he said, "Those of you who want to kneel down and search your hearts, do so now."

While we were kneeling for quite some time, Sadhu announced, "This is the word that the Lord Jesus is speaking to me right now: *"Hypocrites will be judged...hypocrites will be judged."* We were all thinking, "O Lord, please don't let it be me!"

I became so worried that something bad was in my heart that the Lord finally said to me, *"Trust Me."*

Then I felt reassured and just rested in His presence, knowing He would certainly convict me if something needed to be addressed. So, there is a balance in our response to this warning. The Lord loves us! He is able to keep us from stumbling and to present us blameless before the Father on that day! (See Jude 24.)

WHO WILL BE INVITED?

The Lord wants to impart the fear of the Lord to His Church. Many Christians think that because they are saved, there is no need to repent. *They tend to coast on automatic grace, which requires no scrutiny or repentance.* The Lord's people often take their salvation for granted, and this is a dangerous mistake. It was costly to Yeshua, and it will be costly to us, or it isn't real.

In "The Way of the Master," an evangelism training resource by Ray Comfort and Kirk Cameron, we learn that there are millions of false converts among the churches.[1] We also read in the parable of the ten virgins that only five of the ten virgins were prepared for the wedding banquet. This implies that only half of all professing Christians will be ready for the Lord's return.

> *At that time the kingdom of heaven will be like ten virgins who took their lamps and went out to meet the bridegroom (Matthew 25:1 NIV).*

All of the ten were actively awaiting the Bridegroom, and all had lamps. The three characteristics that identify them as professing Christians in the last days are these: they were virgins; they had a source of light; and they were expectantly waiting for the Bridegroom.

> *Five of them were foolish and five were wise. The foolish ones took their lamps but did not take any oil with them. The wise, however, took oil in jars along with their lamps. The bridegroom was a long time in coming, and they all became drowsy and fell asleep* (Matthew 25:2-5 NIV).

The only difference given between the wise and the foolish was that the wise had extra oil in jars, in addition to the supply in their lamps. Notice that even the wise ones became drowsy.

> *At midnight the cry rang out: "Here's the bridegroom! Come out to meet him!" Then all the virgins woke up and trimmed their lamps. The foolish ones said to the wise, "Give us some of your oil; our lamps are going out." "No," they replied. "There may not be enough for both us and you...go...and buy some for yourselves." But while they were on their way to buy the oil, the bridegroom arrived. The virgins who were ready went in with him to the wedding banquet and the door was shut* (Matthew 25:6-10 NIV).

When the midnight cry rang out, the lamps of the unprepared virgins began to flicker and grow dim; their oil was insufficient. Notice that they could not meet the Bridegroom using other people's light, but needed their own source of light. As they rapidly found themselves in darkness, they begged for oil from their well-prepared companions.

The secret treasures we have stored in our hearts for our own final battles against evil, seduction, or martyrdom cannot be squandered on those who did not care enough to prepare. We will need *all* of what we have stored, and we will simply not have any oil to spare. All have received the same warning from this parable, and all are equally accountable for preparedness.

> Later the others also came. "Sir! Sir!" they said. "Open the door for us!" But he replied, "I tell you the truth, **I don't know you.**" Therefore keep watch, because you do not know the day or the hour (Matthew 25:11-13 NIV).

Five out of ten virgins were shut out of the Wedding Banquet. Those who are wise will stay connected to an inexhaustible source of oil. They are continually being filled with the oil that is only found in the secret place of waiting on the Lord and spending time communing with Him.

Knowing *about* the Lord is head knowledge and does not transform our deepest motives. Spending private, intimate time with the Lord allows us to know His heart and allows Him to know our heart. This changes us from the inside out, and we become transformed into His likeness.

> For the wedding of the Lamb has come, and His bride has made herself ready. Fine linen, bright and clean, was given her to wear...."Blessed are those who are invited to the wedding supper of the Lamb!" (Revelation 19:7-9 NIV)

To attend a wedding, one must be invited. It is not an automatic privilege to be the Bride of Jesus Christ. Blessed are those who are invited to the wedding supper of the Lamb.

The Bride must make herself ready *before* the midnight cry rings out. We must purify our hearts and put away every unclean thing from before our eyes and ears. *Our eyes, ears, and mouth are the gates to our body. We must vigilantly ensure that our gates are not defiled with impurity, for our bodies are the temple of the Holy Spirit.*

THE PURE IN HEART

Blessed are the pure in heart, for they shall see God (Matthew 5:8).

Who may ascend into the hill of the Lord? Or who may stand in His holy place? He who has clean hands and a pure heart (Psalm 24:3-4a).

The fear of the Lord brings a pure heart. Although we cannot stop impure thoughts from springing up momentarily, we do not have to stay focused on them. Sometimes, when I am unable to sleep for hours during the night, I start drifting into scenes from a clever sitcom I used to watch. Many of these witty lines and scenes had a strong sexual undercurrent, which is often what made it funny. Of course, it was always sex outside of marriage, as is the basis of almost all sophisticated programs.

To be honest with you, if I dwell on these situations, I still find them funny and could laugh over them right now. The problem is, at this point in my walk, I am in the presence of the Lord every second of every day, and I am not permitted to indulge in things that seemed innocuous in the past.

The closer we walk with Yeshua, the more accountable we are for every stray word or thought. So, I will be lying there unaware of what I am thinking and suddenly realize that for some minutes, I have been replaying a scene from this show. Then I have a choice, and I need to make it *fast*. I can either deliberately "finish up" the scene because it is enjoyable, or I can hit the delete button fast. The Lord's angel is (figuratively) holding a stopwatch to see how long it will take me to hit "delete" once I become aware of my mental activity.

Sometimes I like the scene and finish it out. This is a bad choice, and it hurts the Lord. This may seem like a tiny impurity for a tiny fraction of my mental life, but every second and every choice counts with a holy God. If I am not pure in heart, I will not see God. If I fear the Lord, I will not indulge that scene for one more second. The fear of the Lord will keep my wayward heart pure.

Everything we say and think is broadcast 24-7, streamed live into Heaven before God, as well as His angels and saints. Our thoughts are just as loud as if we said them. Nothing is hidden, but all is laid bare before Him with whom we have to give an account (see Heb. 4:13). That puts the fear of the Lord in me. He hears everything, and hypocrites will be judged.

If you know someone who claims to be OK with God, but is practicing certain sins in a deliberate, ongoing way, here are a few passages that should rock his (or her) complacency. If these verses do not provoke him to repentance and holiness, I wonder if he ever really knew the Lord. The first one is so frightening that one would be a fool to ignore it.

> *If we deliberately keep on sinning after we have received the knowledge of the truth, **no sacrifice for sins is left**, but only a fearful expectation of judgment and of raging fire that will consume the enemies of God (Hebrews 10:26-27 NIV).*

> *A man is a slave to whatever has mastered him. If they have escaped the corruption of the world by knowing our Lord and Savior Jesus Christ, and are again entangled in it and overcome, **they are worse off at the end than they were at the beginning**. It would have been better for them not to have known the way of righteousness than to have known it and then to turn their backs on the sacred command that was passed on to them (2 Peter 2:19b-21 NIV).*

> *Dear friends, I urge you, as aliens and strangers in the world, to abstain from sinful desires, which war against your soul....For it is time for judgment to begin with the family of God; and if it begins with us, what will be the outcome be for those who do not*

*obey the gospel of God? And, **if it is hard for the righteous to be saved**, what will become of the ungodly and sinner?* (1 Peter 2:11; 4:17-18 NIV)

*The acts of the sinful nature are obvious: sexual immorality, impurity and debauchery...I warn you as I did before, **those who live like this will not inherit the kingdom of God....** God cannot be mocked. A man reaps what he sows. The one who sows to please his sinful nature, from that nature will reap destruction; the one who sows to please the Spirit, from the Spirit will reap eternal life* (Galatians 5:19-21; 6:7-8 NIV).

*No one who is born of God will continue to sin, because God's seed remains in him; **he cannot go on sinning, because he has been born of God.** This is how we know who the children of God are and who the children of the devil are: Anyone who does not do what is right is not a child of God; nor is anyone who does not love his brother* (1 John 3:9-10 NIV).

ARE WE PHARISEES?

The Church is full of condemnation for the Pharisees because of their hypocrisy. These men were Israel's spiritual leaders, and it was their responsibility to teach the people how to apply the Law of Moses to everyday life. The Lord Himself had prescribed these righteous commandments through His servant Moses, and yet the Pharisees didn't have Moses' love for His people. They had added many human traditions to the laws of God, thus making God's commandments more burdensome. And they considered themselves to be superior and righteous men.

In the good things that they did, they were often seeking human recognition and admiration, rather than private approval of God. Can any of us say we have never had motives like that? Our deeds of kindness and charity are very important to the Lord, but He is more interested in the motives of our hearts. The Pharisees also imposed such rigorous spiritual requirements on the people, standards that they themselves could not live up to. The average Israeli felt that he or she could never be religious enough to win God's approval.

Yeshua of Nazareth came as a truly righteous and devout Jew, but He came with a heart of mercy and grace toward Israel. He saw them as harassed and helpless, like sheep without a shepherd (see Matt. 9:36). This is because their shepherds had not cared for the flock.

> Woe to the shepherds of Israel who feed themselves! Should not the shepherds feed the flocks?...The weak you have not strengthened, nor have you healed those who were sick, nor bound up the broken, nor brought back what was driven away, nor sought what was lost (Ezekiel 34:2b,4).

The Lord rebuked the Pharisees because they should have known better! Those who knew God's law should have lived it out as good shepherds over His flock. To him to whom much is given, much will be required (see Luke 12:48). The leaders had been given much, and the Lord held them to a high accountability.

I tell you the truth: the Western Church has a higher accountability to God than the Pharisees had in the first century. The Lord told us that unless our righteousness surpasses that of the Pharisees, we will not enter the Kingdom of Heaven (see Matt. 5:20). The Church has been given more revelation and truth, more grace and access to God's throne, more resources to help people, and more spiritual power to overcome our sin nature. We have been given much more than the Pharisees, and so if we also walk in hypocrisy, it will be judged more severely than theirs.

Each believer and those in leadership must ask the Lord to search his heart. A good time to do this is when we take communion privately with the Lord. When we take it in church, there is no time to do the private soul-searching and cleansing that we all need.

Ask the Lord to take His bright searchlight and shine it into your heart. He waits for us to ask. Sometimes we avoid the Lord because we are afraid of what we'll see. We must not hide from Him. We have a gentle, merciful High Priest who is sympathetic to our weaknesses, even our sins, if we bring them to Him. *The key is repentance.* We examine our hearts and repent before the Lord; we partake of His blood and His flesh and are cleansed and made new again.

The antidote for hypocrisy is complete transparency before the Lord in our private prayer closets. If we do this, we will never be assigned a portion with the hypocrites. Amen.

ENDNOTE

1. Kirk Cameron and Ray Comfort. "The Way of the Master." To learn more about this resource, please visit www.wayofthemaster.com.

Chapter 9

A Soothing Aroma

MANY Christians have difficulty grasping the many types of sacrificial offerings found in the Book of Leviticus, and they wonder how these complex rituals can be relevant to their walk with Jesus. Many people just avoid Leviticus altogether, but you'd be surprised how interesting it actually is. The Lord wants us to understand what was in His heart when He designed the sacrificial system and how it relates to our lives.

As I began to study the Old Testament offerings, the Lord said to me, *"Each offering is expressing one of the languages that I expect from My people's hearts."* This is the key to our understanding.

The Lord was gracious to show me that the four or five main offerings described in the first seven chapters of Leviticus represent these four languages or qualities of the believer's heart:

1. Humility

2. Righteousness

3. Repentance

4. Intimacy

WHERE GOD MEETS WITH MAN

Before we study the offerings, let's look at the tabernacle that the Lord designed for His glory to dwell in the midst of His people Israel. We learn much about the Lord's holiness from the structures in the tabernacle.

> *Set up the tabernacle, the Tent of Meeting, on the first day of the first month. Place the ark of the Testimony in it and shield the ark with a curtain. Bring in the table and set out what belongs on it. Then bring in the lampstand and set up its lamps. Place the gold altar of incense in front of the ark of the Testimony and put the curtain at the entrance to the tabernacle. Place the altar of burnt offering in front of the entrance to the tabernacle, the Tent of Meeting; place the basin between the Tent of Meeting and the altar and put water in it. Set up the courtyard around it, and put the curtain at the entrance of the courtyard....**Then the cloud covered the Tent of Meeting, and the glory of the Lord filled the tabernacle. Moses could not enter the Tent of Meeting because the cloud had settled upon it, and the glory of the Lord filled the tabernacle** (Exodus 40:1-8;34-35 NIV).*

The Lord defined the environment in which He desired to be worshiped by giving Moses precise instructions for the construction and furnishings of the tabernacle in the wilderness. Moses was shown every detail in a vision of the heavenly tabernacle, which he saw on the mountain with God in the Sinai desert. We learn this in Hebrews 8.

> *[Jesus is] a Minister of the sanctuary and of the true tabernacle which the Lord erected, and not man....there are priests who offer the gifts according to the law; who serve the copy and shadow of the heavenly things, as Moses was divinely instructed when he was about to make the tabernacle. For He said, "See*

that you make all things according to the pattern shown you on the mountain" (Hebrews 8:2, 4b-5).

So we see that earthly worship is an imitation or a shadow of the worship that goes on in Heaven eternally. For example, there is a heavenly tabernacle, a heavenly lampstand, and a heavenly altar. Moses needed to build it exactly as he saw it in Heaven. Even the Garden of Eden on earth was an imitation of the garden in Heaven. In Hebrew, *eden* means "paradise."[1] God named His earthly garden after His vast heavenly garden of delights.

And what was the Lord's lofty purpose in setting up both the tabernacle and the sacrificial system? *We were made for love.* In the Father's heart is a great yearning to draw His children close to Him. His desire has always been to share intimate, sweet fellowship with His people. How He enjoyed walking with Adam and Eve in the cool of the day, while they were still innocent and obedient children.

But once we broke covenant and chose satan's seduction over the Creator's plan, there was no way for a holy God to have relationship with His people without the altar of sacrifice.

He is the Alpha and the Omega, the First and the Last.

The Lord was required to offer the first sacrifice to cover our first parents' nakedness.

The Lord was required to offer the last sacrifice (the cross) to restore us to purity and innocence.

The first Adam (man) separated us from our Maker.

The last Adam (Son of Man) restored us to relationship with the Father.

His final Passover table became an altar of sacrifice.

The wood of His cross became the table of communion.

The tabernacle contained an altar in the outer place and a table in the inner place. After the sacrifice came intimate dining, a Father with His beloved children like olive shoots around His table. Our God is a God of sacrifice. He has proven this in the most costly way imaginable. When you lay your heart on the altar, He will come in and dine with you.

We need to be able to approach God in order to know Him. We cannot know His character if He is unapproachable. There is nothing more important in this life than knowing God intimately and being known by God. How does the Father define Himself?

> And the Lord passed before him and proclaimed, **"The Lord, the Lord God, merciful and gracious, longsuffering, and abounding in goodness and truth, keeping mercy for thousands, forgiving iniquity and transgression and sin"** (Exodus 34:6-7a).

> Thus says the Lord: "Let not the wise man glory in his wisdom, let not the mighty man glory in his might, nor let the rich man glory in his riches; but **let him who glories glory in this, that he understands and knows Me"** (Jeremiah 9:23-24a).

The Father's heart was always gracious and compassionate, longsuffering, and showing mercy to thousands. He had to make a provision for our sinfulness so that we could be together. All of the sacrifices were required so that the Lord could be with His people.

The Burnt Offering

The most common offering found throughout the Bible is the whole burnt offering. This offering expresses the language of *Humility, Submission, and Yieldedness.* A burnt offering is a wholly consumed thing, burned with fire. The Hebrew word for this offering is *olah*—"that which ascends to God."[2]

After the blood was poured out, the entire sacrifice was burned before the Lord on the bronze altar. None of the meat was eaten by the priests or the people. It was completely devoted to the Lord and was not for human consumption.

There are so many biblical examples of burnt offerings. We see the first one as early as Adam's children. And even Job, a non-Israelite who was likely a contemporary of Abraham, offered burnt offerings regularly to sanctify his grown children (see Job 1:4-5). When the Lord establishes a principle from the earliest moments of the human race, we know it has relevance for all people and not for the Jews only. Let us now examine some of the key examples of this offering found in Scripture.

ABEL

Abel brought the Lord the fat of the flock. As far back as Cain and Abel, we see the Lord's pleasure in the burnt offering. This helps us to know that these sacrifices were initiated long before the giving of the law at Mount Sinai.

> *Abel also brought of the firstborn of his flock and of their fat. And the Lord respected Abel and his offering, but He did not respect Cain and his offering. And Cain was very angry and his countenance fell* (Genesis 4:4-5).

Many people think that Cain's sacrifice was rejected because he brought the fruit of the field, rather than an animal. I don't believe the Lord's displeasure was exactly due to the offering of vegetables or grain because later we see that Leviticus did permit a grain offering under certain, limited conditions.

I think it was because Cain did not ask the Lord what kind of offering He desired, but was presumptuous in offering what he thought was "his best work." It is likely that Cain's attitude was one of taking pride in the work of his hands, since he was a skillful farmer of the land. He knew what he wanted to offer to the Lord and felt that the Lord should appreciate his offering. Cain and Abel's parents would have taught them that the Lord God had to kill innocent animals to clothe their nakedness after they disobeyed Him. These two sons both knew that a sacrifice was involved in the covering of their parents' sin. We have a large clue that Cain knew that a man cannot just offer God whatever he wishes to give, but must seek what will please the Lord. This is just as true today as it was in the early days of mankind.

> So the Lord said to Cain, "Why are you angry? And why has your countenance fallen? If you do well, will you not be accepted?" (Genesis 4:6-7a)

This question shows us that Cain had no cause to be angry at the Lord. He knew what God meant when He said, "If you do well." The Lord was willing to give Cain a chance to offer what would be accepted, just as his brother's offering was accepted.

I believe that Cain, being the older brother, did not wish to humble himself before his younger brother who was a shepherd. He did not want to admit that Abel had what he needed to find favor with God, and that he would have to purchase a young lamb or goat from his little brother. I believe there was a factor of pride and jealousy of Abel's favored position with God.

Christians sometimes feel jealous of one another if the Lord raises up another believer to a position they desire. This must never be found in the household of God. Each one must humble himself before his favored "little brother." If we do well, will we not also be favored and accepted? Yes, we will, for the Lord shows no favoritism, but He does show favor to those who offer Him what He desires, rather than what they want to bring Him.

The Lord warned Cain that if he did not humble himself, sin was crouching at his door. This sin was pride and jealousy, and it quickly morphed into murderous intentions. Sin gave birth to death, and a righteous man was murdered without a cause. In speaking about false Christians in the last days, Jude warns us: *"Woe to them! For they have gone in the way of Cain"* (Jude 11).

We must always ask the Lord how He desires to be worshiped and what offerings would please Him. It is vital that we do not presume to define worship according to our abilities and then assume that the Lord must respect our offerings.

NOAH

Then Noah built an altar to the Lord, and took of every clean animal and of every clean bird, and offered burnt offerings on the altar. And the Lord smelled a soothing aroma (Genesis 8:20-21a).

Noah offered a burnt offering after coming out of the ark. Noah's name means "comfort" or "rest."[3] He needed comforting after such agony, destruction, and distress upon the waters. And the Lord comforted him with a rainbow.

But the Lord also needed comfort. We cannot imagine the pain and grief it caused His fatherly heart to have to drown every single creature on the earth, except for eight people and the creatures who would repopulate the earth. When Noah offered the Lord a burnt offering, He received it as "a soothing aroma." The Hebrew word for "soothing" is the same root as Noah's name.[4] His broken heart was comforted by Noah's love, thankfulness, and submission to God.

In the days of the tabernacle, this type of offering was voluntary. An individual worshiper could decide to bring a burnt offering when he wanted to show God his consecration unto Him, or to restore a sense of communion with God. Perhaps you have sometimes felt a bit separated from God, but you weren't sure why. You couldn't identify anything you had done, but you felt uneasy. The ancient Israelites were people exactly like us, with the same anxieties in their hearts. This offering restored the sense of being accepted. It was an act of complete devotion.

The Israelite would bring his animal up to the temple and present it before the priest. The individual worshiper was required to place his hand on the animal's forehead, between its horns, and identify with the sacrifice. Notice that it is the worshiper, not the priest, who must kill the innocent animal, thus feeling the costliness of his own uncleanness.

> *He is to lay his hand on the head of the burnt offering, and it will be accepted on his behalf to make atonement for him. He is to slaughter the young bull before the Lord, and then Aaron's sons the priests shall bring the blood and sprinkle it against the altar on all sides at the entrance to the Tent of Meeting* (Leviticus 1:4-5 NIV).

ABRAHAM

The most terrible example of a burnt offering is Abraham and Isaac. The Lord had commanded Abraham to do the unthinkable, to offer the son of God's promise, through whom his descendents would come. This heartbreaking act of obedience is a foreshadowing of the Father sacrificing His only Son for the world.

> *Then He said, "Take now your son, your only son Isaac, whom you love, and go to the land of Moriah, and offer him there as a burnt offering on one of the mountains of which I shall tell you"* (Genesis 22:2).

Abraham's faith in God's goodness was so strong that even as he took the boy up to Mount Moriah to slay him, he told the servants that he and the lad would return. Isaac asked him, *"Father, I see the wood and the fire, but where is the lamb?"* (see Gen. 22:7). Abraham hardly knew how to answer such a question, but he answered from a deep reservoir of trust within him. "*God Himself will provide the lamb, my son*" (see Gen. 22:8).

He could not have known the prophetic significance of this word, as it would apply to the future Son who would also walk up the mountain as a sacrifice. He would not be rescued like His father, Isaac, for He *was* the substitute lamb, and there was no other one who could take His place on the altar of love.

Abraham's burnt offering is called "the binding of Isaac" in rabbinic literature, and it represented his complete yieldedness to God's will, though the cost was unbearable.

Elijah

Next, we see a supernatural burnt offering in Elijah's showdown with the false prophets on Mount Carmel. The God who answered by fire and consumed the sacrifice would be proven to be the one true God, the only One worthy of worship.

> *And it came to pass, at the time of the offering of the evening sacrifice, that Elijah the prophet came near and said, "Lord God of Abraham, Isaac, and Israel, let it be known this day that You are God in Israel and I am Your servant, and that I have done all these things at Your word*" (1 Kings 18:36-37).

During the days of the tabernacle in the regular priestly service, the priests kept the fire always burning on the altar because these offerings went up morning and evening. However, Elijah lived in a time of great apostasy in northern Israel, and the people did not honor the sacrificial system that God had established in Jerusalem. Elijah knew that God would cause His own fire to fall upon the offering that pleased Him. This demonstration brought revival to Israel, at least to some extent.

SOLOMON

As one final example, we see King Solomon's extravagant dedication of the temple on the Feast of Tabernacles. He offered so many burnt offerings that they could not be counted, and the Lord's glory came down and remained, such that the priests could not even enter (see 2 Chron. 5).

YESHUA

As we will see in this chapter, Yeshua the Messiah lived out and fulfilled each type of Old Testament offering throughout His life, death, and resurrection. His submission to the Father was a burnt offering throughout His life. Yeshua's life was a fragrance that ascended to God as an *olah*.

> *I have come down from heaven, not to do My will but to do the will of Him who sent Me* (John 6:38 NIV).

In everything He did, Jesus was completely submitted to the Father's will, no matter how painful, difficult, or humbling: *"Although He was a son, He learned obedience from what He suffered"* (Heb. 5:8 NIV).

The burnt offering was voluntary, not mandatory. In like manner, this offering of your hearts is completely voluntary. If you don't offer it, the Lord will not take it. When we bring to God our hearts, we must lay down our will and our rights. If we hold onto these ugly attributes, we are not living as a whole burnt offering before the Lord, and we are not walking as our yielded and humble Messiah walked.

I had a vision of a burnt offering about six years ago. A group of us were participating in the very first "Day to Pray for the Peace of Jerusalem," which happened to fall on the first day of Tabernacles that year.[5] We were worshiping and praying fervently for Israel. My eyes were closed, and yet I saw a burnt offering on the altar of the church. I saw a pile of wood that was burning, with much smoke pouring up to God. I noticed that there was no animal on the altar, because Yeshua was our Lamb. This scene was so real to me, I was afraid the church was on fire! When I opened my eyes, I was surprised to see that there was no actual fire burning. I knew that the Lord had found our intercession to be an acceptable burnt offering to Him.

This is an example of a whole burnt offering, translated into the New Covenant realities of today. I never saw another burnt offering in a vision until I was at a repentance conference in 2006; we were repenting with great weeping over abortion. During that meeting, I saw the same whole burnt offering vision once again. The Lord had fully accepted the sacrifice that came out of our hearts during our repentance and intercession.

We are a royal priesthood, and priests offer sacrifices. We do not worship to feel good, nor do we pray merely to receive our wishes. Rather, we worship and pray to give the Lord the whole offering of our heart.

THE GRAIN OFFERING

The language of the heart expressed by the grain and drink offering is *Righteousness, Obedience, Diligence, and Perseverance.* The regular morning and evening sacrifices of the grain and the drink offering are an act of disciplined obedience. It is not something you only do when you feel like it. This speaks of the regular habit of serving God in offering Him our prayers, tithes, time spent in His Word, and in the regular taking of communion.

Taking communion regularly is very important because we live in a polluted world. We can feel defiled very easily in all we are exposed to in our everyday lives. This includes people using irreverent language around us in the workplace, as well as unclean forms of entertainment that we are exposed to through family members. They don't understand what they are inviting into our house or how the Lord feels when He sees such things. When we take communion, we remember the Lord's suffering and His death. It is like we are putting our hand on the Lord's forehead, as with the young bull and saying, "I identify with Your suffering. I don't take lightly what You went through."

The grain offering was also voluntary, just as these disciplined acts of devotion are for us. The grain represents the Word of the Lord, as well as the Lord's broken body, which we eat as our spiritual food. After we have eaten, we share this food with His flock as the Lord grants us opportunity.

In the days of the temple, the grain offering was designated for the priests to eat. But before they could eat their unleavened share, they had to burn a memorial portion to the Lord. And so the Israelites would bring grain to the priests in four possible forms:

1. Unleavened bread

2. Crackers or wafers, which are like matzah

3. Pancakes (fried on the griddle)

4. Cooked cereal (like cream of wheat)

These four offerings were brought into the temple as a voluntary act. The people were feeding their leaders. Only a handful of the grain was burned before the Lord, because the priests needed it for nourishment. In the same way, when we bring tithes and offerings into the house of the Lord, we are providing food on the table of those who serve. The Lord would remind His people, *"This is never to be neglected."*

In addition to offering grain every morning and evening, the priests poured out wine into the basin of the altar. I believe that the grain offering was a picture of Yeshua's flesh, which He called the true bread from Heaven; likewise, the wine was a prefiguring of the cup of the New Covenant in His blood. The morning and evening grain and drink offering were to remind us that we need to connect to the Lord's sacrifice every day of our lives.

*I am the living bread that came down from heaven. If any-
one eats this bread, he will live forever. This bread is My flesh,
which I will give for the life of the world....This cup is the new
covenant in My blood, which is poured out for you....Do this
in remembrance of Me....For whenever you eat this bread and
drink this cup, you proclaim the Lord's death until He comes*
(John 6:51; Luke 22:20b,19b; 1 Corinthians 11:26 NIV).

The Lord was speaking to Israelites, who understood the daily grain and
wine offerings from days of old. But now, the Lord was telling them, *"It was
always Me!"*

We read in Psalm 22 a prophetic description of Yeshua's crucifixion:

*I am poured out like water, and all My bones are out of joint.
My heart is like wax; it has melted within Me* (Psalm 22:14).

King David saw the future Messiah poured out like a drink offering.
Likewise, as the apostle Paul waited in prison for his execution, he wrote to
his beloved Timothy: *"For I am already being poured out like a drink offering,
and the time has come for my departure"* (2 Tim. 4:6 NIV).

I Am the Broken Piece!

There is a mysterious practice that has become a part of the traditional
Passover Seder, which did not exist at the time of Yeshua's ministry. Messianic believers are convinced that it was originated by early Jewish believers
in Yeshua the Messiah, due to the symbolism embodied in this ceremony. It
involves one special, broken piece of matzah, called the *afikomen*.

In this ceremony, three large pieces of matzah are wrapped together in
a linen cloth. These three pieces represent God, the mediating priest, and
the people of Israel. Therefore, the middle piece, which is broken represents
Yeshua, the mediating priest, who stands in the gap between God and the
people.

The leader then removes the middle piece of matzah, breaks it in two, and hides one broken half around the house, still wrapped in the cloth. After the meal, the children search for this hidden piece and bring it back to the leader. He makes sure that it fits with its other broken half and declares that the two halves have been made whole again. Then everyone at the table eats a small bit of this broken piece together. It seems obvious that this ceremony originated with the Jewish disciples, following Yeshua's death and resurrection. They incorporated the symbol of His broken body into their Passover Seders, just as Yeshua had connected the breaking of bread with His broken body.

During the final Passover meal that the Lord ate with His disciples, He broke bread and gave it to them, saying, *"Take and eat. This is My body, broken for you"* (see 1 Cor. 11:24).

He was broken as a sacrificed lamb; His body was wrapped in a linen cloth and hidden away. After some time has elapsed, He is found and made whole again, He is raised to life. This broken one has ransomed back many from their brokenness, and we are also made whole, along with Him (see Heb. 9:15).

Something amazing happened during my family's Passover Seder on April 19, 2008. This occurred during the period that I was writing my second book, *A Prophetic Calendar: The Feasts of Israel* (Destiny Image Publishers, 2009). In the course of writing the Passover chapter, the Lord had given me a word from His heart about the *afikomen*. I will share this word as it appears in the book, and then I will share the "miracle" we saw.

> *I AM the hidden treasure, buried in the folds of cloth and the layers of Matzah. I AM hidden; though they eat My body; I AM hidden from their eyes. I AM the pearl, the treasure, the One broken and waiting to be discovered by the youngest child. This signifies that only one with the heart of a child can find Me and recognize Me, hidden in the room.*

It is a surprise party. Normally, the guest of honor is surprised when the other guests jump out and greet him. I AM the guest of honor in the ceremony of the Afikomen, and when I jump out, they will all be surprised. I was here all along, waiting, in their very Passover. It was always Me, broken, buried, raised to life, but waiting to be discovered by the leaders of My banquets, by the leaders of My Jewish people, even their Sanhedrin.

When they find the Afikomen, they find Me. Then that which was broken will be made whole. They will hold up the whole piece with the missing half restored, restored and whole again. How can they find God without Me? I AM the missing piece, the broken piece, the hidden piece, the discovered piece, the redeemed-by-a-child piece, and the reconnected piece to the original piece from which I was broken off.

We will be made whole again; do not fear. This is My heart for the story of the Afikomen. Tell My flock what I have told you.

OUR PASSOVER MIRACLE

On April 19, 2008, our family conducted our yearly Seder. At the table were my three grown children, as well as my son Raviv's wife, Amber, and another guest. After breaking the *afikomen*, my husband has a custom of putting the broken half up his sleeve so he can hide it later when we are not looking.

During dinner, he accidentally leaned on the piece in his sleeve and broke it, although we didn't know this. He then felt this crumbled piece was not suitable for hiding, so he replaced it with a new piece of matzah without letting us know. I also didn't know that he quietly ate the shattered piece with his dinner.

After dinner, we all went into the kitchen to hide our eyes while my husband hid his new piece somewhere in the living room/dining room. No matter how old my children get, they act like "kids" when it comes to scrambling to find the *afikomen*. And so they and the other two guests raced off, in great competition, to find the hidden piece. My daughter-in-law Amber quickly went to a corner cupboard and found it, wrapped in a napkin in plain view behind the glass door.

She was very excited to find it, but when she handed it to my husband, he would not accept it. He said that it was not the "real" *afikomen*, but that it was a "decoy." We didn't understand what he meant by "decoy," since he was the only person hiding it, and no one else had hidden another piece. I checked with him to see if he had hidden a second piece, but he said he had only hidden the "real" piece in a different spot from where Amber had found the "decoy."

Within a few minutes, my daughter Ariela found "the real *afikomen*" in the living room. She always seems to be the one who finds it every year. She then gave the "real" one to her father, who declared it to be real. We were perplexed and felt bad for Amber, who had legitimately found it first. I was puzzled about the extra piece she had found, and where it had come from. I began to question everyone at the table, and it became clear than none of us had put this other piece in the corner cupboard.

Moreover, my husband and I had pulled out many dishes and casseroles from that cupboard just before the meal began, and we would have seen this piece wrapped in a white napkin, which was in plain view. When did it appear there, and who put it there?

We then shared and ate the "real" piece, using it as a symbol of the Lord's broken body. But Amber's piece remained on our table, still a mystery. At this time, we also drank the third cup of wine, which is traditionally called "the cup of personal redemption." Messianic Jews believe that it was this redemptive cup that the Lord Yeshua identified as the New Covenant in His blood.

No one in our house had hidden that piece that Amber found in the cupboard, and we had no explanation. The girls and I were excited as we began to wonder, "Could this be a genuine miracle in our midst?"

The next morning, I felt the Lord show me that it was indeed a miracle, and that Amber had found His true piece. This was the piece that was hidden in my husband's sleeve, which we had already blessed and consecrated as the Lord's broken body; He was honoring that original piece. Although my husband ate the shattered pieces, I believe that before he could eat them and when he wasn't paying attention, an angel stole away one of the broken pieces, wrapped it in a napkin and hid it in the cupboard. Even though it was shattered, we should have honored it and eaten it as the "communion" piece, rather than replacing it with a new piece that was not consecrated. You can believe it or not, but there is no logical way this extra piece appeared there.

The Lord wanted to honor Amber by having her find it for the first time in her life; this would make her feel like a truly connected and beloved member of our family. Of course, I have always loved her and treated her as a family member, but sometimes, a person who marries into a Jewish family can feel like an "outsider." The Lord was going to great lengths to grant her honor and inclusion in our family tradition.

He gave me special instructions to "reward" her for finding the true piece that He had already blessed. Normally, the child who finds it receives a reward, and the Lord wanted me to give her the privileged child's reward. The Lord filled me with joy as I understood what He had done for all of us and for my precious daughter-in-law in particular.

Then on Monday morning I was having a Coffee Talk, and the Lord began to speak to me. I can only share a portion of what He shared with me, as some of it is personal.

> *It was Me, Coffee Girl. Didn't I tell you that I AM the Missing Piece? If I put Myself into that broken half so that My people can eat My body later when I AM found, don't you think I*

wanted My piece to be treated with respect and honor? Don't you think I would care about that little piece of matzah that had already been sanctified and prophesied over in your Haggadah the night before?[6] I did that! I also had something up My sleeve, and it was a sign to your family, who knew and watched the whole thing unfold, wondering at the mystery.

We all need a good mystery now and then…a good caper. This one is "The Case of the Extra Matzah!"

I told you that he who finds the afikomen finds Me! Amber found Me, and she found My love in your gesture to her. She found My welcome.

I became the New Covenant, the Lamb, the Pesach, the Afikomen, the Missing, Broken Piece, the Third Cup of Personal Redemption. It was always My mo'ed,[7] My banquet, and the matzah is Mine; in fact, it is Me.

You have discerned correctly, and I blessed your Seder on Erev Shabbat[8] because you honored Me. For that honor, I gave you the mystery of the extra matzah the next night. I was the surprise guest of honor, and everyone was surprised when I jumped out! You were not expecting it or looking for a Passover sign and wonder. That is why I surprised you, like a guest popping in, just when your family had it "all wrapped up."

You have a Father who loves you!

THE SIN AND GUILT OFFERINGS

The language expressed by the mandatory sin and guilt offerings is *Repentance, Atonement, Cleansing, and Restitution.* These two offerings were required any time a person's conscience registered that he had inadvertently sinned. If he knew what particular sin he had committed, he would go, take a sin offering to the priest, and confess his sin. We know that it is important to the Lord that we confess our sins and not presume on the grace of automatic forgiveness.

> *If we confess our sins, He is faithful and just to forgive us our sins and to cleanse us from all unrighteousness. If we say that we have not sinned, we make Him a liar, and His word is not in us* (1 John 1:9-10).

The sin offering and the guilt offering are very similar, and we will cover them together. The Scripture defines both as the sacrifice required for "unintentional sin." They were not designed to cover premeditated sin. A person could not say in his heart, "I'm going to sin today because I can always kill an animal tomorrow." The Lord was not likely to cover that type of attitude.

The sin offering was for a variety of unintentional sins, as the Law of Moses defined sin. The guilt offering, also called the "trespass offering," was specifically for the types of sin that required restitution. In cases of theft, neglectful property loss or destruction, cheating someone or misappropriating something devoted to the Lord, the person was required not only to bring a guilt offering, but also *to make restitution to the one he had wronged.*

To help make this practical, let's think of a few modern-day examples, where the Lord's standards of righteousness would still be the same as those He held in biblical times.

If you borrowed someone's car and damaged it, you are required to make full restitution, and the Lord required an additional 20 percent of the value as a sign of genuine repentance. We see that the Lord Jesus totally upheld this law when He met a wealthy tax collector named Zacchaeus. Tax collectors had a reputation for cheating their fellow Israelis by extorting money or taking extra for themselves. This man was desperate to see the Lord but was too short to see Him through the crowds, so he climbed a tree to get a glimpse of Him as He passed by.

> And when Jesus came to the place, He looked up and saw him, and said to him, "Zacchaeus, make haste and come down, for today I must stay at your house." So he made haste and came down, and received Him joyfully....Then Zacchaeus stood and said to the Lord, "Look, Lord, I give half of my goods to the poor; and *if I have taken anything from anyone by false accusation, I restore fourfold*" (Luke 19:5-6, 8).

The Lord commends him for his obedience, and says, "*Today salvation has come to this house*" (Luke 19:9). We can see how highly the Lord values one who is willing to make painful restitution.

Here is an example of misappropriating something devoted to the Lord. Perhaps we planned to give the Lord our tithe in a certain week or month, but our bills seemed so crushing, that we decided to just pay the bills and get the burden off of us. This tithe was devoted to the house of the Lord, but we used it for our own needs. However, we didn't do it in a defiant or selfish way; in fact, we felt bad about it. We did it out of fear or desperation. Many of us can relate to this.

Beloved, the gracious Lord knows your heart and your burdens. He does not condemn us at any time. But He is also a righteous God, who would be pleased if we repent before Him for withholding what was due Him. At other times, we might simply have forgotten to give a gift to the Lord that we had intended to give.

These types of inadvertent sin would normally require restitution, unless it is impossible. In these cases, we should repent, and He might graciously release us from further restitution. He has dealt with me very kindly in some of these cases, far more generously than I deserved. But it was important to Him that I repent and ask Him sincerely if He required me to make restitution. *If we repent now, we will not have to hear the Lord call us a thief when we stand before His throne of judgment.*

Another example is if someone lent us something, and we never gave it back. When the Lord reminds us of this neglect, we need to make restitution, not make excuses.

If we have stolen something or cheated anyone in any way, and the Lord graciously reminds our conscience of this painful reality, we should try our best to make some form of restitution if such a thing is possible. I know from my own sins that sometimes it is not possible to go back and make things right. But again, I need to be brutally honest with the Lord, to review with Him exactly what I've done, and ask Him sincerely what He requires me to do about it, to be in right standing with Him. This is hard, painful work.

In His mercy, there have been times when I have repented before the Lord for some form of theft or cheating, and have asked Him what He would want me to do at this point. The Lord has at times chosen to release me from any guilt or further obligations. There is a balance between the sternness and the forgiveness of God. Our broken heart over our own sin releases much tender forgiveness from His fatherly heart.

When an Israelite sinned, he brought a sin offering to the temple. The priest would always pour out the blood and burn the fat. It was forbidden to eat any flesh that still had the blood in it, and the fat was never to be eaten, for it was the Lord's portion.

> *For the life of the flesh is in the blood, and I have given it to you upon the altar to make atonement for your souls...Therefore I said to the children of Israel, "No one among you shall eat blood, nor shall any stranger who dwells among you eat blood"* (Leviticus 17:11-12).

Once this had been done, Aaron's descendants were allowed to eat part of the flesh of the sin or guilt offerings. However, *when the priest sinned*, he was not allowed to eat any of it; it was burned, and the rest of it was taken out of the camp. This was because the priest was a leader in high accountability, and he was not allowed to benefit from the sacrifice for his own sin.

Once a year on the Day of Atonement, the high priest would go into the Most Holy Place. Here, he sprinkled the blood of bulls and goats on the Mercy Seat, to atone for his own sin and those of the people. His priestly duties were very exacting, and any disobedience would mean that Israel's sins were not pardoned, and the people would die in their sins. The very lives of the people hung on the obedience of the high priest.

The Lord Jesus Christ was a high priest of a higher order than the Levitical priesthood; He carried a level of accountability we cannot fathom. The priest had to obey perfectly for 24 hours. The Lord Yeshua could not sin once during His entire lifetime, or our sins could have never been pardoned. We would be damned eternally if this Man had sinned once in His whole life. So high were the stakes, it makes me shudder. That is why the enemy threw every possible enticement at Him continually, knowing that if he could cause Yeshua to slip up once, all of humanity's souls would be with him forever in the lake of fire.

> *When Christ came as high priest…He did not enter by means of the blood of goats and calves; but He entered the Most Holy Place once and for all by His own blood, having obtained eternal redemption….For Christ did not enter a man-made sanctuary that was only a copy of the true one; He entered heaven itself, now to appear for us in God's presence* (Hebrews 9:11a,12,24 NIV).

Seven hundred years before the birth of Jesus, the prophet Isaiah wrote of a scapegoat who would come and bear the iniquities of the people, one who would give His life as a guilt offering in exchange for the punishment that we deserved.

> *Surely He has borne our griefs and carried our sorrows; yet we esteemed Him stricken, smitten by God, and afflicted. But He was wounded for our transgressions, He was bruised for our iniquities; the chastisement for our peace was upon Him, and by His stripes we are healed. All we like sheep have gone astray; we have turned, every one, to his own way; and the Lord has laid on Him the iniquity of us all (Isaiah 53:4-6).*

Through Yeshua's sin offering, we can approach the Father's presence without fear or shame, for the blood of His sin offering has made us clean and holy children in God's sight. Hallelujah!

> *Therefore, brothers, since we have confidence to enter the Most Holy Place by the blood of Jesus…let us draw near to God with a sincere heart in full assurance of faith, having our hearts sprinkled to cleanse us from a guilty conscience* (Hebrews 10:19,22 NIV).

THE FELLOWSHIP OFFERING

The final offering is the fellowship offering, which was the only offering that the people of Israel were allowed to eat with the priests and with each other. It was a very holy meal eaten in a very holy place. The language expressed by this type of offering is *Intimacy, Extravagant Love, Thankfulness, and Generosity.* The Hebrew word is *sh'lemim,* which comes from the word *shalom,* which means peace, wholeness, or integrity.[9] These offerings were voluntary and were offered in these cases:

1. Fulfilling a vow

2. Thanksgiving

3. A free-will offering (just because your heart desires to give it)

If we make a vow to God, it is important to keep it. For example, you might tell the Lord, "If You heal me of this disease, I'll serve You for the rest of my life." Or, "If You get me out of this horrible debt, I'll give a certain amount of money to a certain ministry." Or, "If You will rescue my son from drug addiction and prison, I'll give this particular offering."

In times of great trouble people often make vows to God; then when God comes through, the person forgets all about his promise. This is a very serious infraction indeed. Did you know that when you make a vow to the Lord, He hears it, and it is recorded in Heaven? It is a voluntary offering, but once you have promised Him, you must fulfill your vow.

In the case of thanksgiving, it is not something you promised ahead of time. You just are so grateful for something special the Lord did for you that you want to thank Him. And so you give a special offering to any person or ministry that you feel would bless Him, or where your heart is inclined.

In the case of a freewill offering, it is just what it says: freewill. You bring it of your own free will, not compelled, not pressured, not harassed. You truly desire to give a gift that you alone decided upon, from your own heart of love and generosity.

We see at least two examples of these offerings in the New Testament. The first case, which we have read many times, puts the fear of the Lord in all of us!

In the first weeks and months after the Lord's ascension, the Holy Spirit was granting great power and boldness to the Jewish believers in Jerusalem. They were so unified in purpose that they freely shared their possessions with one another and with the needy among them. Those who had money or properties would sell them and bring the proceeds to the apostles to distribute as needed.

As they brought these monies to the congregation, we see a beautiful example of the freewill offering in operation in a Jerusalem community of believers. No one had pressured them to sell their property or bring these offerings. Each believer chose what he or she wished to give and gave it freely without compunction.

A couple in the congregation named Ananias and Sapphira decided to sell a property, but they agreed between themselves to only give a portion of the proceeds to the apostles. The problem was that they lied about what they had done. They told Peter that they were bringing the entire sale price of the property. The Holy Spirit showed Peter that Ananias was lying when he brought the money in, and the Lord struck him dead instantly. Later, when his unsuspecting wife came in, Peter gave her a chance to tell the truth. But she affirmed the lie and was struck dead as well (see Acts 5:1-10).

The most important point is this: When Peter rebuked Ananias, he said, *"Didn't the property belong to you before it was sold? **And after it was sold, wasn't the money at your disposal?**"* (see Acts 5:4). In saying this, Peter makes it clear that whatever they might have chosen to give would have been acceptable. It was truly up to them. What brought them a swift death sentence was to lie before God's face. Such hypocrisy is an abomination to the Lord.

I know a missionary family who are very poor. They have traveled the world and never owned anything of their own. Several years ago, they met a wealthy Christian who told them he wanted to bless them greatly and was going to give them a very large sum of money. They were very encouraged and began making hopes and plans based on this wonderful offering that was coming.

The man never gave them a cent. He simply, for whatever reasons, did not fulfill his vow to them. No one had forced him to make such a vow. He made it of his own freewill and enthusiastically spoke this promise to these needy people. This unfulfilled promise was hurtful to their hearts, in addition to their other severe troubles.

I cannot know what internal or external circumstances caused this man to renege on his promise. But it would be better not to promise something than to promise it to the Lord and break your promise.

> *I will pay my vows to the Lord now in the presence of all His people....I will offer to You the sacrifice of thanksgiving, and will call upon the name of the Lord* (Psalm 116:14,17).

> *Let them sacrifice the sacrifices of thanksgiving, and declare His works with rejoicing* (Psalm 107:22).

A second case of a freewill offering in the New Testament is found in Acts 21:20-26. In this case, we see the apostle Paul and several other Jewish believers taking what is called a "Nazarite vow," and fulfilling it by sacrificing freewill offerings at the end of the period of consecration (see Num. 6:2-15). Paul chose to take these vows and pay for these offerings because he needed to prove to the Jewish community that he was not teaching Jewish believers to forsake the Law of Moses.

On the biblical calendar, the times of year when the Lord particularly wants to receive freewill offerings are the three pilgrimage feasts, when all Jewish men are required to come up to Jerusalem to celebrate before the Lord. These feasts are Unleavened Bread, Pentecost, and Tabernacles. At these seasons, the Lord instructs us,

> *"Do not come before the Lord empty-handed."*

For years I used to ask the Lord, "How much do You want me to give to such-and-such?" I was often disappointed that I could not sense His voice telling me an amount to give. Finally, a few years ago, the Lord said to me, *"Why do you think they call it a freewill offering? It is voluntary. I'm watching your heart to see how much you **want** to give."*

The Lord just loves to look at our hearts. He doesn't want to be a dictator and watch us obey in stiff or grudging compliance. He loves to see a heart that actually desires to give, and He gives each child free will to choose what they desire to happily give, without pressure or resentment. I wish I had understood this sooner.

There are many practical ways believers can give freewill offerings, too many to describe in this book. I know each reader can think of special ways you have given to the Lord and felt His delight in them. He sees every sacrifice, and He will reward each one (see Matt. 16:27). I will give one case that the Lord showed me was a good example of a fellowship offering, although this is only one of many variations.

For Pentecost 2008, many believers from 22 nations traveled to Jerusalem to attend a prophetic conference. The trip was expensive, and some had used up their savings accounts to come. This was not a vacation in any sense of the word. For five days, they fellowshipped and prayed together in a tent on the Mount of Olives, whose temperature was often over 100 degrees. They ate their meals together and worshiped together. They repented for the sins of their nations, including anti-Semitism, and prayed for the peace and salvation of Israel, which was facing the threat of imminent war at that time. (That threat is not reduced as of this writing, so there is much need for prayer for Israel's protection.) These pilgrims put the Lord's interests ahead of their own personal needs. This was a sacrifice, but it was also joyful because of the unity of purpose they felt.

OUR MOTIVES

Our offerings can come in many forms. It can be something very private, just between the Lord and us. Every one of our sacrifices, large and small, private or public, is precious to the Lord. He knows the motives of our hearts, and when we say in our secret place, "I could have spent this money on such and such, but there is someone with a greater need..."—that is stored up in Heaven and waiting for us.

Our God was approached through sacrifice in the Old Testament, and He is approached through sacrifice in the New Testament. It is true that we cannot sacrifice to make atonement for our own sins; Jesus' blood did that, and there is nothing we could ever do to add to that.

But walking with Yeshua is a sacrificial life. We have to take up our cross daily and follow Him, a Man of sorrows and acquainted with grief.

It is not about us. It is about putting the interests of the Lord's Kingdom above what we eat, drink, own, and enjoy, and we should not be entertaining ourselves in our spare time. We should be devoting these last critical hours before His return to fasting, praying, and repenting on behalf of the wickedness of our nation and praying for the peace of Jerusalem. He will reward these sacrifices greatly. Prayer is a great sacrifice. It is not easy work, and at times it is exhausting, but He will reward us.

Always remember that the most important thing to the Lord is the *motive* with which you give the offering. If you remember this, you will find great favor with God, and your reward in Heaven will be beyond what you can imagine right now.

A Kingdom of Priests

And so it was, when those bearing the ark of the Lord had gone six paces, that he sacrificed oxen and fatted sheep. Then David danced before the Lord with all his might; and David was wearing a linen ephod (2 Samuel 6:13-14).

When King David brought the ark up to Jerusalem, he danced with joy before the Lord, for he was carrying the very glory of God. But after six paces, he offered burnt offerings. David was a king, but he wore the linen ephod of a priest. He danced like a worshiper, but he sacrificed oxen like a priest. Although he was a king, his service to God was also priestly. This was a foreshadowing of the priesthood of all believers, and not only one particular tribal entity.

Moses had declared Israel to be a kingdom of priests. In some sense, they were all priests, despite the separation of Aaron's descendants to perform the most holy sanctuary functions.

> *And you shall be to Me a kingdom of priests and a holy nation* (Exodus 19:6).

Peter speaks this same astonishing reality to the New Covenant believers, telling us that our primary role is to offer spiritual sacrifices to God as His holy priesthood.

> *You also, as living stones, are being built up a spiritual house, a holy priesthood, to offer up spiritual sacrifices acceptable to God through Jesus Christ* (1 Peter 2:5).

Yeshua Is the Ark of Glory

The overcomers, who are granted to reign with Messiah during the millennial kingdom, are appointed to be priests before God, offering sacrifices before Him for a thousand years.

> *Over such the second death has no power, but **they shall be priests of God** and of Christ, and shall reign with Him a thousand years* (Revelation 20:6).

First and foremost, now and into the age to come, we offer the sacrifices of praise, prayers, and service to God. The Lord Yeshua is the ark of God's glory, shining out from the innermost place in our temple. *He is the power and glory of Heaven which we carry in our mortal tents.*

After 40 years in the wilderness, the Lord took the Levites out ahead of Israel, carrying the ark of God's glory two thousand cubits ahead of them into the Jordan. When their feet touched the water's edge, the river parted, and all the people crossed over on dry land, as the Levites held the ark in the middle of the riverbed. The glory of God made a way for the people to leave the desert experience and enter their Promised Land.

In like manner, Yeshua is the ark of God's glory and has gone ahead of us by 2,000 years, making a way where there was no way. He is our high priest, He is the glory of the Father, and He has walked through the wilderness and through the floodwaters of death ahead of us. Now, we need only to follow Him implicitly and without deviation, in order to finally leave our wilderness time and enter the fullness of the Promised Land.

We have not yet tasted more than a few small tokens of the fruits of the land, which is perfect union with Messiah. While yet in this present age, those who desire the Lord fervently will be granted to cross the Jordan and enter the *full measure of Messiah's stature and maturity* (see Eph. 4:13).

This company of believers, who have followed the Lamb and forsaken all, will qualify to become the mature sons of God, which the Lord Yeshua, the prophet Daniel, and the apostle Paul foresaw in this last generation.

> *But I say to you, love your enemies...**that you may be sons of your Father in heaven*** (Matthew 5:44a,45a).

> *Therefore **you shall be perfect**, just as your Father in heaven is perfect* (Matthew 5:48).

> *For the earnest expectation of the creation eagerly waits for **the revealing of the sons of God*** (Romans 8:19).

> *Therefore, leaving the discussion of the elementary principles of Christ, **let us go on to perfection*** (Hebrews 6:1a).

*Those who are wise shall **shine like the brightness of the firmament**, and those who turn many to righteousness like the stars forever and ever* (Daniel 12:3).

This maturity, perfection, and brightness are available to every single believer on the earth, from the least of us to the greatest. *The Lord is not withholding it from us.* The decision is ours, as to how closely we will walk with Him before He returns. How much do you desire to walk as a son of the Kingdom? *He is worth it all!* Amen.

ENDNOTES

1. See http://www.studylight.org/lex/heb/view.cgi?number=05731.

2. See http://www.studylight.org/lex/heb/view.cgi?number=05930.

3. See http://www.studylight.org/lex/heb/view.cgi?number=05146.

4. See http://www.studylight.org/lex/heb/view.cgi?number=05207.

5. These special meetings occur on the first Sunday of October each year and are sponsored by Eagles' Wings Ministries, under the direction of Robert Stearns. See www.daytopray.com or call 1-800-51-WINGS.

6. The night before our family seder, I had led a church seder, using a new Passover Haggadah which I had just written a few weeks before. In this new Haggadah was the prophetic word where the Lord said, "I AM the Broken Piece. When you find the Afikomen, you find Me."

7. *Mo'ed* is the Hebrew for "appointed time or season." More on this is found in *A Prophetic Calendar: The Feasts of Israel*, Chapter 1.

8. *Erev Shabbat* means the Eve of the Sabbath, or Friday night. The night before this family seder was Friday night, when I had led the large church seder, where the Lord was greatly honored.

9. See http://www.studylight.org/lex/heb/view.cgi?number=7965.

Chapter 10

Be Holy as I Am Holy

Then the children of Israel, the whole congregation, came into the Wilderness of Zin in the first month, and the people stayed in Kadesh; and Miriam died there and was buried there (Numbers 20:1).

THIS passage is referring to the first month of Israel's fortieth year in the desert. As I was reading this during the summer of 2007, the Lord spoke to my heart that we were currently in the first month of our fortieth year since Jerusalem came back into Jewish hands in 1967. I quickly thought through this time calculation and realized that since June 1967, both Israel and the Church have been through a biblical generation of "wandering." I sensed the Lord was showing me that we now stand at the brink of crossing into a spiritual "Promised Land," such as the Church has not yet experienced during the charismatic renewal or other significant moves of God that have transpired.

Within a few months after receiving this insight from the Lord, I was very encouraged to begin to receive e-mails and hear teachings from prophetic men and women whom I respect, saying that the Church stands at a moment of unprecedented opportunity to "cross the Jordan." This will take us into a place of radical holiness and purity, which will allow us to experience the manifest presence of the Lord. As we yield all of our wills and rights to Yeshua, we will be transformed into His likeness, as one looking into a mirror and being changed into His image, looking back at us (see 2 Cor. 3:18).

This move of God will be accompanied by the power of God to do exploits, exceeding even those found in the Book of Acts.

> *Most assuredly, I say to you, he who believes in Me, the works that I do he will do also; and **greater works than these he will do**, because I go to My Father* (John 14:12).

On the one hand, we stand at the place of crossing over. On the other hand, we are not in a place that qualifies us to cross over. There are two biblical qualifications that the Church has not yet met: *sanctification and circumcision of the heart.* Sanctification refers to being set apart and holy unto the Lord. Circumcision of the heart refers to the cutting away of defilement and unrighteous thought patterns and behaviors from our innermost being.

> *When you see the ark of the covenant of the Lord your God... then you shall set out from your place and go after it....**Sanctify yourselves**, for tomorrow the Lord will do wonders among you.... Make flint knives for yourself, and **circumcise the sons of Israel** again the second time* (Joshua 3:3,5a; 5:2).

To be sanctified or holy means to be separate and set apart unto the Lord. It is a state of unadulterated devotion only to the Lord. Many Christians think that we are already a holy people who are devoted to the Lord, but our thought life and lifestyle choices expose this belief as delusional. How far we have fallen from holiness!

To be circumcised of heart means that the following "works of the flesh" have been surgically removed from our hearts by the Spirit of the Lord: adultery, fornication, lewdness, unclean language and behavior, idolatry, sorcery, hatred, contentions, jealousies, outbursts of wrath, selfish ambitions, dissensions, resentment, heresies, envy, murders, drunkenness, revelries, evil and bitter thoughts, thefts, false witness, and blasphemies (see Gal. 5:19-21a; Matt. 15:19). The opposite of these are humility, gentleness, holiness, and self-control.

Those who cross over will be trusted with great authority. The words they speak will be endued with such power that they will become reality, whether spoken for good or for evil. How can the Lord trust His people with such great authority if they are not set apart unto Him, or are defiled from within by evil words, motivations, and attitudes?

"You Did Not Make Me Holy"

> *Now there was no water for the congregation* (Numbers 20:2).

The Lord brought the Israelites into the desert to humble them and test their hearts. Surely, being in a vast desert without water would test the hearts of this crowd of 600,000 men, as well as women, children, and livestock. Forty years earlier, they had faced this test of thirst and had quarreled with Moses. He had struck the rock at the Lord's instructions, and water miraculously gushed out. Now they were back to where they had started, and again, there was no water.

At this point, it is hard to picture *not* complaining. However, the Lord expected them to pass the same test they had failed one generation ago. What would we have done or said under these same conditions? Moses and Aaron went and fell facedown in the tent of meeting and the glory of the Lord appeared to them.

> *Take the staff, you and your brother Aaron gather the assembly together. **Speak to that rock before their eyes** and it will pour out its water* (Numbers 20:8 NIV).

But Moses was frustrated with the complaints and unbelief of this enormous community under his leadership, and he vented his feelings, saying, "Listen you rebels, must we bring you water out of this rock?" Forty years of exasperation had built up to a point where he transgressed and trespassed over the will of God.

He had struck the rock 40 years ago in obedience, but now, in disobedience to the Lord's new commandment, he struck it again. We see that water gushed out, and the community and their livestock drank.

But the Lord said to Moses and Aaron, *"Because you did not trust in Me enough to honor Me as holy in the sight of the Israelites, you will not bring this community into the land I give them"* (Num. 20:12 NIV).

Moses did not cause the Lord to appear as holy in the eyes of Israel. Forty years before, he struck the rock because he was told to strike it. But now he was told to speak to the rock. What changed over those 40 years?

We read in Ezekiel that when Israel came out of Egypt, she was like a newborn baby. The Lord cleaned her of her blood and carried her to safety, like a nurturing parent. Then He says, *"When I saw that you had matured and were ready for love, I covered your nakedness"* (see Ezek. 16:6-8).

They should have grown to maturity during this generation of trials and lessons, and they were ready to hear their leader speak to the rock. They did not need the great drama of the rock being struck and split apart by force. They needed to be mature enough to know that the gentle spoken word of God produces the miracle, and that living water will flow in obedience to the word spoken with authority. To be qualified to enter the Promised Land, God's people needed to know that the Word carries more authority than great physical force or dramatic exhibitions.

The Holy Spirit is a river of living water flowing from the innermost being of those who abide in Him (see John 7:38). We don't need to pound on the Lord's door with a staff; we need to speak to the Rock. Israel was ready for this lesson at that moment, and the eyes of all Israel were upon what

Moses would do. And the friend of God, the one who knew Him face to face, indulged his anger before the congregation.

The Lord's rebuke to Moses was: "*You didn't cause Me to be seen as holy when you struck the rock.*" I did not understand what the Lord was saying in this rebuke. I could understand if He had said, "You disobeyed Me." But why did God say, "*You didn't make Me appear holy*"?

When the Lord Yeshua taught us to pray, He said, "*Our Father in heaven, hallowed be Your name.*" The word *hallowed* means "let Your name be kept holy, revered, and set apart in the sight of the people."[1] Somehow, Moses had not done this in his moment of disobedience. But I still could not understand why this act caused God's name not to be seen as holy.

Then the Lord led me to Deuteronomy 32, which depicts Moses' last moments on earth. Moses was about to die on the eastern side of the Jordan. His punishment for this act of disobedience was not being permitted to enter the Promised Land, despite all he had done to bring Israel to her point of crossing over. He pronounced a beautiful blessing over Israel before being gathered to his fathers.

Then this faithful 120-year-old man climbed up Mount Nebo and looked across at the entire land of Canaan. And then the Lord reiterated why it was that he should not be granted to take possession of the land with his people.

> Because you **trespassed** against Me among the children of Israel at the waters of Meribah Kadesh, in the wilderness of Zin, because **you did not hallow Me** in the midst of the children of Israel (Deuteronomy 32:51).

I noticed that the Hebrew word for "trespassed" means "*You went over Me in the presence of the Israelites.*" This gave me a clue about what it meant to *not* make the Lord holy. There is a difference between a private transgression and one that is committed in the congregation. How do we show reverence and sanctify God's name in the presence of His people, whose eyes are riveted on the leader who knows God better than they do?

In a flash of insight, the Lord showed me how He felt on that day, and I felt great pain as I finally understood. He showed me two different sample scenes from my own life as a parent. In one scene, one of my children spoke to me disrespectfully and disobediently in a private situation. This was upsetting to me, and I explained to her that it is unacceptable to talk to her parent this way. If I needed to punish her, I could do so within the privacy of our own home.

But the other scene the Lord showed me was when my child said something angry and disrespectful to me in front of her friends; I could feel the eyes of her friends watching me to see how I would respond to this nasty challenge. They knew I was a particularly kind and gentle mother, not given to anger or yelling. I felt trapped and humiliated. I hated the way my daughter was speaking to me; everything in me wanted to haul her off to her room and give her a severe "talking-to," complete with consequences, but she was not a baby anymore. She, like Israel, had grown up beyond childhood, and it was simply not possible to take her to her room or punish her as one would punish a young child. I felt incredibly dishonored and demeaned in front of her friends. But to act on what she deserved at that moment would have created layers of other problems, which I was not willing to subject her or her friends to. And so, these incidents passed, and I absorbed the dishonor. Later, I would tell her how her attitude had made me feel.

What the Lord showed me from this personal example broke my heart. It helped me understand that when Moses went above God, he trespassed over His honor and holiness. As the Lord took me back to that moment in time, I got it. The passage tells us, *"Water gushed out, and the community and their livestock drank"* (Num. 20:11 NIV).

The Lord did not have to honor that act of disobedience; in fact, He shouldn't have. He did not have to produce torrents of water when Moses struck the rock. A rock doesn't automatically gush forth hundreds of gallons of water just because someone hits it with a stick. When it had split open 40 years earlier, Israel was seeing a totally supernatural act.

The Lord did not wish to reward this act of anger and disrespect. But if He didn't provide the miracle, His people, whom He had redeemed from slavery at such cost, would have died of thirst. The Lord showed me that His parental heart was so kind and gentle that although He was humiliated by Moses in front of the people, He could not respond the way His righteousness demanded. The Lord put the welfare of the people above His righteous anger. I felt the Lord's humility, in that *He could not bear to bring about the consequences of Moses' disobedience.* But He was demeaned and diminished in the eyes of Israel by that action. This is what He meant by, *"You did not make Me holy in the eyes of Israel."*

I saw the Father's humility reflected in His Son, Yeshua, who did good to those who hurt Him, humiliated Him, stripped Him, beat Him, spit on Him, and cursed at Him. The Lord could have responded to them according to their disrespect, but His gentle character would not let Him respond in holiness and righteousness, but rather in mercy and humility. This shows us that the Lord Yeshua is the exact representation of His Father's character (see Heb. 1:3).

EXAMPLES FOR THE CHURCH

Moses' walk with God was among the greatest walks of any man on earth, except for the Lord Yeshua. And yet his penalty for this one act of disobedience was huge. I wondered why the Lord was so severe and unrelenting in His punishment of Moses, even though Moses pleaded to be allowed to cross over into the Promised Land. I said, "Lord, You were very strict with Moses."

In response, the Lord showed me that if He had not punished Moses severely, it would have sent this message to His last-days' Church: *"There is no lasting consequence for disobedience. If you disobey, just say you're sorry, and all will be well."*

He needed to make Moses an example to His Church, who foolishly takes His grace for granted in many instances. Likewise, Paul warned the Church to carefully study and heed Israel's history because every severe punishment that fell upon them was an example and a warning to us. Here are some of the punishments that fell upon that generation:

In one day, 23,000 fell to plague; some were killed by the sword of their fellow Levites; some were killed by serpents; some were swallowed up alive into the earth; some were burned alive with fire from heaven; and some were destroyed by the destroyer. Furthermore, we know that even Moses could not enter the Promised Land due to disobedience.

> *Moreover, brethren, I do not want you to be unaware that all our fathers were under the cloud, all passed through the sea, all were baptized into Moses in the cloud and in the sea, all ate the same spiritual food, and all drank the same spiritual drink. For they drank of that spiritual Rock that followed them, and that Rock was Christ. But with most of them God was not well pleased, for their bodies were scattered in the wilderness....***Now all these things happened to them as examples, and they were written for our admonition, upon whom the ends of the ages have come. Therefore let him who thinks he stands take heed lest he fall*** (1 Corinthians 10:1-5; 11-12).

If we apply this warning to the Church, we see a similar pattern. We are all baptized into Yeshua, partaking of His body and blood, which is our spiritual food and drink. We are all worshiping, singing, and meeting in His presence. We all believe we are following our Rock, who is Messiah. We are all sojourning to our Promised Land, while enjoying the infilling of His Holy Spirit.

Taking a hard look at Paul's warning, we see that even if the glory cloud itself were to come into our meetings, it would not mean that we would make it to the Promised Land. The Israelite's bodies fell in the desert, despite partaking of all this glory. They experienced food from heaven and water from a rock. Their clothes and sandals never wore out, and they received supernatural healings. The visible glory of the Lord hovered over them and led them for 40 years, and they saw their enemies supernaturally destroyed by God. And yet, they died in obscurity, *without being found pleasing to God.*

What were their sins, according to Paul? They lusted after evil things, they committed sexual immorality, they were idolatrous, they tested the Lord, and they grumbled and complained against their hard circumstances. We also know that they refused to enter the land when it was time to cross over, due to hearing reports about how large and warlike the inhabitants were; thus, they were fearful and unbelieving. They looked back toward Egypt as if it had been better there. The Lord Yeshua warned us, *"Remember Lot's wife!"* (see Luke 17:32 NIV). She had looked back toward Sodom and became a pillar of salt, which still stands in the Dead Sea region to this day.[2]

Only two men of that generation were found pleasing to the Lord and were granted permission to enter in. Interestingly, these two men were comprised of one Jew and one Gentile. Although Caleb's lineage is listed as part of the tribe of Judah (see Num. 13:6), he was "grafted" into Judah by Moses. His actual ancestry was through Esau's marriage to a Canaanite woman (see Josh. 14:6, depicting his heritage as a Kenizzite). Caleb was not biologically from Jacob or his son, Judah. But the Lord found his heart pleasing, and he inherited his allotted portion with Judah in the good land that he fought so hard to conquer.

Paul's warning shows us that we could attend the most anointed meetings, but we could miss God's best destinies and callings on our lives. We must be *"of a different spirit,"* as were Joshua and Caleb. They were uncomplaining, despite the same lack of water, the same scorching sun, the same 40 years of wandering, and the same merciless barbarians they would have to face upon crossing the river. They knew God was sovereign and powerful and that complaining would not bring His approval. They were active in pursuing their destiny and inheritance, rather than sitting back and "waiting" for God to make it all happen around them. They fought in many wars and risked their lives many times to receive their inheritance. What will we do in these perilous times and onslaughts of evil?

ACCOUNTABILITY OF LEADERSHIP

Through the painful example of Moses, we learn about the high accountability of leadership. Rather than being exempt from punishment, leaders are chastised at least as severely as the people under them. Leaders and teachers are held to a high standard of holiness. This is why James cautions us not to seek such positions, for it is a fearful thing.

Likewise, the congregation must not treat the Lord with contempt, whether in our private lives or in the worship we offer to Him. Church is not an entertainment center, and we must not come to hear great music or even to listen to great sermons. We are offering worship to the Lord, and He is searching our hearts to see what we are bringing Him.

How do we conduct ourselves in church? What kind of conversations do we have before the worship, and are we completely reverent and focused on the Lord during the worship? We need to behave as if we see the Lord standing in our midst visibly, searching out each heart and receiving our worship.

We need to make Him holy in the eyes of the congregation. A church service is not the same as our normal social and business activities. It is not a place for chit-chat. His house shall be called a house of prayer for all nations. It must be set apart from the ordinary, in all that we say and do in the house of the Lord.

If we understood what His holiness would do to us, we would not act and speak the way we do before, during, and after church. I have overheard people discussing a bloodthirsty movie they had "enjoyed" the previous night, while waiting for worship to begin. Is this how they would speak before the throne of God?

The Lord will hold His leaders accountable for the atmosphere of their services. If the people are casual and disrespectful, the leader must exhort them strongly, whether they are offended or not. If our leaders seek to make church a place that rivals the high-impact entertainment of this world, they will be held accountable. If they neither warn their flocks of the severe troubles coming to our nation, nor lead their flocks into weeping and repentance for our personal and national sins, they will answer before the Lord for this. Moses warned the people of the Lord's judgments and also interceded to spare their lives with fasting and prayer.

If the Lord were to visit us with His holiness at this time, many would die needlessly in this fearsome presence, due to practicing secret sins. The Lord's holiness is the most fearful part of God. It was His holiness that killed Aaron's sons; His holiness killed Uzzah when he touched the ark; His holiness killed Ananias and Sapphira when they lied to the Holy Spirit; His holiness killed a great number of Israelites in the desert. He changes not!

Presumptuous Fire

In Leviticus 9, we see that the glory of the Lord had appeared, and His fire had come down from heaven and consumed the burnt offering on the altar. The people shouted for joy and fell facedown. Shortly after this visitation, we read this:

> *Then Nadab and Abihu, the sons of Aaron, each took his censer and put fire in it, put incense on it, and offered profane fire before the Lord, which He had not commanded them. So fire went out from the Lord and devoured them, and they died before the Lord. And Moses said to Aaron, "This is what the Lord spoke, saying: 'By those who come near Me, **I must be regarded as***

*holy; and **before all the people I must be glorified.***" So Aaron
held his peace (Leviticus 10:1-3).

The Hebrew word for "profane fire" can also be translated "unauthorized fire, strange fire, or foreign fire." As high priests, Nadab and Abihu were under the strictest accountability for making the Lord's name holy before Israel. By presumptuously burning incense outside of the Lord's exact prescriptions, they demeaned Him before the people. For this, they were burned alive by a fire not lit by human hands.

After just having seen the glory of the Lord, Aaron now stood staring in horror at the smoldering remains of his sons with their censors still in their hands. In God's mercy, Aaron was in too much shock to speak or cry out. Moses then quickly counseled him that the Lord must be regarded as holy before all the people. Thus, Aaron was not allowed to further dishonor God by wailing and mourning for his renegade sons. *If Aaron mourned publicly before the eyes of Israel, he would have died too, because it would have made God look cruel and unreasonable in front of the people* (see Lev. 10:6).

STRANGE FIRE TODAY

Sometimes church leaders or worship leaders feel that things aren't exciting enough, and the people aren't pumped enough. It is at these dry moments, that we are tempted to light strange fire in our meetings. If the Lord does not seem to be consuming our worship with *His fire*, or we do not feel the desired level of His presence, we try to stir up something in the room with our human energy.

I have seen this happen in a number of services. When it happens, I feel very uncomfortable, because it seems like a modern version of strange fire. I feel grieved and embarrassed for the leaders who are stirring up the crowd with their own antics, games, and lively spiritual "exercises."

When Moses descended the mountain, carrying the tablets of the law, he and Joshua heard a tumult in the camp below. Joshua said to Moses, "*There is a noise of war in the camp.*"

But Moses said, "*It is not the noise of the shout of victory, nor the noise of the cry of defeat, but the sound of singing I hear*" (Exod. 32:17-18).

Moses did not hear a rousing, victorious shout of praise; nor did he hear a weak and humble cry of desperation for the Lord's servant to return from the mountain. Rather, he just heard the people making noise and stirring up mindless, sensual, wild activity. Does this sound a bit familiar? We don't want to be like Aaron's sons and work something up in our flesh, just because the meeting feels boring or unanointed. There was one particular Coffee Talk when the Lord said to me, "*No fire is better than strange fire.*"

It is better to pray diligently in an unanointed meeting than to produce dramatic results in the flesh. The Lord is very displeased with this practice and looks at it as "stinking flesh." We will look at this in more depth in the chapter on true and false revival. Strange fire is a big factor in false revival meetings.

Touching the Glory

There are things that the Lord has tolerated in the past that He will no longer accept, and there will be consequences. We are moving into a season where holiness is not optional. When His glory comes, how will we steward this? King David learned a terrible lesson about presumption in the presence of God's glory. David's motivations and decisions were righteous, but he didn't handle God's glory reverently, and a man was needlessly killed.

David loved God with all his heart, and he desired to bring the Ark of the Covenant back from Kiriath Jearim to the City of David on Mount Zion.

> *Then David consulted with the captains…and with every leader. And David said to all the assembly of Israel, "If it seems good to you, and if it is of the Lord our God…let us bring*

> *the ark of our God back to us, for we have not inquired at it*
> *since the days of Saul." Then all the assembly said that they*
> *would do so, for the thing was right in the eyes of all the people*
> (1 Chronicles 13:1-2a;3-4).

At that time, the Ark of the Covenant was the physical dwelling place of the Manifest Presence of God. The leaders of Israel needed to consult the Mercy Seat for guidance, where the Lord's *Sh'chinah* glory hovered between the wings of the cherubim.[3]

After the Lord Jesus was born and took on human flesh, He became the permanent dwelling place of the fullness of the Lord's glory. Yeshua the Messiah became the living Ark of the Covenant, and His Spirit resides in the temple of our bodies. Therefore, we have continual access to the Lord's presence and His guidance, even though we cannot always see, hear, or feel this reality. We must act by what we know to be true, not by what we feel or do not feel.

During the reign of Saul, God's glory was not in Jerusalem, and no one could consult the ark for guidance. Even if Saul had been able to consult the ark, it would not have helped him, because Saul was a fleshly and unholy king. He was disobedient to the words of Samuel, the prophet whom God had given him for guidance. Saul was demonized and had to be soothed regularly by David's harp. But his deliverance was never permanent, due to the condition of his heart. That is why Saul said to Samuel, "I tried to do what the Lord *your* God told me to do." He did not say, "the Lord *my* God" (see 1 Sam. 15:15).

And so, under David's righteous leadership, the whole assembly of Israel agreed to bring the ark back, because it truly was the right thing to do. The action and the motivation were indeed pleasing to the Lord.

> *David and all the Israelites with him went up to Baalah of*
> *Judah (Kiriath Jearim) to bring up from there the ark of God*
> *the Lord, who is enthroned between the cherubim—the ark that*

is called by the Name. They moved the ark of God from Abi-
nadab's house on a new cart, with Uzzah and Ahio guiding it.
David and all the Israelites were celebrating with all their might
before God, with songs and with harps, lyres, tambourines, cym-
bals and trumpets (1 Chronicles 13:6-8 NIV).

Twenty years earlier, the Philistines had placed the ark of God on a cart and sent it with guilt offerings to Beth Shemesh. After capturing the ark, they had suffered tumors, rats, and death, and were eager to send it back to its rightful owners. However, the men of Beth Shemesh presumptuously lifted the lid and looked inside the ark. The Lord struck down 50,070 of them for not treating Him with fear and reverence (see 1 Sam. 6:13-20).[4]

In shock and fear, the residents of Beth Shemesh quickly sent the ark to Kiriath Jearim, where it remained until the time that David determined to bring it up to Jerusalem. Like the Philistines before him, David placed the ark on a new cart, driven by oxen. Although he had inquired of all Israel's leaders as to this move, he had not inquired of the priests as to *how* the ark should be transported, according to the Law of Moses.

It was a joyful and worshipful procession. David and all the Israelites were celebrating with all their might before God with songs and instruments. And then the oxen stumbled, and the ark tottered on the new cart. In a moment of impetuous helpfulness, Abinadab's son Uzzah reached out his hand to steady the ark, and the Lord's anger broke out against him and struck him dead.

Do you remember the chilling scene of Aaron gaping at the smoldering bodies of his sons? David had just been dancing a moment before, when he was suddenly confronted with the death of one of the young men who was guiding the cart. David's worship celebration stopped in mid-song. This was the day the music died, and David was angry. And suddenly, he was afraid of the Lord. He decided he could not bring the ark up to Jerusalem if this was how severely the Lord was going to deal with those who transported it.

It was too dangerous to touch God's glory. If God could do such a thing, David needed to leave the ark somewhere else. He chose the nearest Levitical family, the house of Obed-Edom, and the ark was left in his care. The ark rested there for three months, and the Lord did nothing but *bless* that household. It is not God's will to harm people who steward His glory. It is His will to bless them. However, Uzzah had not been instructed in the fear of the Lord and was presumptuous in how he handled the glory of God, and he died for it. David felt responsible for his death because he had not sought the Book of the Law before moving the ark.

The Lord's people must know His *ways*, so that they will handle the glory according to His holy requirements. It was written in the Law of Moses that only the Levites may touch the ark. They were to place the poles through rings on the four corners of the ark, and then lay the poles on their shoulders to carry the ark from place to place. This is the way the Lord required His glory to be handled.

How can we know God's ways? By understanding His character, as displayed throughout the Scriptures. Paul said, *"I would not even have known what sin was, apart from the law"* (see Rom. 7:7). David forgot to consult God's Word.

David had three months to think about the terrible punishment that befell them in the middle of a celebration. He needed time to process the severity of God and to reconcile this with His kindness, which David had experienced in the past. Paul warned the Church to learn from Israel's difficult punishments and not to presume on His goodness.

> *Therefore consider the goodness and severity of God: on those who fell, severity; but toward you, goodness, if you continue in His goodness. Otherwise, you also will be cut off* (Romans 11:22).

When David learned that Obed-Edom's house was greatly blessed during those three months, he realized that if he would handle the Lord's glory with fear and reverence, he would also be blessed, for it is not the Lord's will to harm anyone. The Lord has a right to set the terms for how He desires to be worshiped. We cannot just do whatever we please. Some Christians assume that because we are operating in the New Covenant, "anything goes." No, once again, anything *doesn't* go.

As the leader, David was responsible to consult God's Word and learn how the ark was to be transported. He was no longer afraid of the Lord, because he realized that God's glory brings a blessing, not a curse. Uzzah did not premeditate that fateful transgression. He was careless and acted impulsively.

I have done such heedless things as Uzzah many times. It is against my nature to think before I speak. I have always said or done whatever pops into my head at that moment. Like Peter, who jumped into the water with all his clothes on, I am overly spontaneous and impulsive. This has a good side, in the sense that I can be quick to obey a prompting of the Holy Spirit. But it has a bad side as well. I have gotten myself in more trouble with my heedless words than poor Peter! And then it's too late, and I find myself on my face weeping before the Lord because I can't undo it. I have not been punished, because the Lord has seen my tears and has dealt graciously with me countless times, but I do not presume on His grace. I am finally learning to be careful and prayerful about what I say and do.

REPENTANCE AND OBEDIENCE

Three months later, David handled the ark with obedience and reverence, and the Lord blessed his second attempt to bring in the ark.

> *Then David said, "No one may carry the ark of God but the Levites, for the Lord has chosen them to carry the ark of God and to minister before Him forever."…And David called for Zadok and Abiathar the priests, and for the Levites…He said to them, "You are the heads of the fathers' houses of the Levites; **sanctify yourselves**, you and your brethren, that you may bring*

up the ark of the Lord God of Israel to the place I have prepared for it. **For because you did not do it the first time, the Lord our God broke out against us,** *because we did not consult Him about the proper order"* (1 Chronicles 15:2,11a, 12-13).

David and the Levites sanctified themselves. And although he was a king, David wore a linen robe as well as a linen ephod, the holy garments of a priest. He understood that he was functioning more as a priest than as a king during that holiest of processions.

We also read that after he had progressed six paces, David sacrificed oxen and fatted sheep. And David danced before the Lord with all his might, leaping and whirling at the head of the company (see 2 Sam. 6:13-16). The Lord was honored as holy on that day, and He shined His favor on David's reign.

"I Am Undone!"

In the year of King Uzziah died, I saw the Lord sitting on a throne, high and lifted up, and the train of His robe filled the temple. **Above it stood seraphim;** *each one had six wings: with two he covered his face, with two he covered his feet, and with two he flew. And one cried to another and said: "Holy, holy, holy is the Lord of hosts; the whole earth is full of His glory!" And the posts of the door were shaken by the voice of him who cried out, and the house was filled with smoke. So I said:* **"Woe is me, for I am undone! Because I am a man of unclean lips, and I dwell in the midst of a people of unclean lips;** *for my eyes have seen the King, the Lord of hosts"* (Isaiah 6:1-5).

If we could be taken into the throne room of Heaven as Isaiah was, we too would cringe in our inescapable uncleanness. If we could remember this throne room scene, we would be much more careful with our words.

In Hebrew, the word *seraphim* means "burning ones."[5] These high-ranking angelic beings seem to be made of fire, and they carry the fierce burning of the Lord's holiness. Even one of these burning ones did not dare to touch the live coal from the altar, but used tongs to bring it near to Isaiah's mouth. And he touched him with the live coal and said, *"Behold, this has touched your lips; your iniquity is taken away, and your sin purged"* (Isa. 6:7).

Prophetic teacher and writer Neville Johnson has been shown by the Lord that the *seraphim* are coming to the earth to purge His people in these days.[6] Their very presence in a meeting will bring to us a spirit of repentance, due to the fiery holiness of God that they carry fresh from His throne. We cannot be made holy without this purging fire, which brings a holy fear of God and compels us to deep repentance. Our sins are atoned for by Yeshua's blood, but we are purged by His fire.

We see many references to this purging fire in both the Old and New Testaments.

> *I came to send fire on the earth, and how I wish it were already kindled!* (Luke 12:49)

Some commentators believe that Yeshua was expressing His longing for fiery judgments, but this is not what the Lord was saying. I believe that the fire He yearns to see kindled is the fire of zeal, purity, holiness, and lovesick desire for God. *The Lord wishes to kindle a burning flame of jealous love in the hearts of His people, just as His Father called Himself* **"a jealous God and a consuming fire"** (see Deut. 4:24). Are we burning as hot for Him as He burns for us?

The Lord is looking for passionate lovers who are completely holy and set apart for the Master's use. Holiness is a jealous flame of love. It consumes the life and passions of the worshiper. We become obsessed with knowing and pleasing the Lord Yeshua. We are ruined for the things of this world because His flame burns away the taste of the world, the enticements of the evil one, and our own complacency.

After His resurrection, the Lord told John that He needed His people to be either hot or cold, but that He would spew the lukewarm out of His mouth (see Rev. 3:16). Yeshua lived out what was written of Him: *"Zeal for Your house will consume Me"* (see John 2:17). It is this consuming zeal that the *seraphim* will bring to the Lord's Bride when they come to us. The fire of holiness must do its purging work, for *without holiness no one will see the Lord* (see Heb. 12:14).

A Higher Priesthood

Peter speaks of the holiness of our conduct, our sacrifices, and of every word we speak:

> *As obedient children, not conforming yourselves to the former lusts, as in your ignorance; but as He who called you is holy,* **you also be holy in all your conduct,** *because it is written, "Be holy, for I am holy."...You also, as living stones, are being built up a spiritual house,* **a holy priesthood, to offer up spiritual sacrifices** *acceptable to God through Jesus Christ....**If anyone speaks, let him speak as the oracles of God.**...For the time has come for judgment to begin at the house of God; and if it begins with us first, what will be the end of those who do not obey the gospel of God?* (1 Peter 1:14-16; 2:5; 4:11,17)

Do you remember how holy the high priest had to be on the Day of Atonement, as he offered the sacrifices critical for Israel's atonement that year? We have a higher accountability than the Levites because *"we have an altar from which those who serve the tabernacle have no right to eat"* (Heb. 13:10). Our holy priesthood is higher than that of Aaron's sons because we are the offspring of a greater High Priest, Yeshua, who is of the order of Melchizedek.

JEALOUS LOVE

Hear, O Israel: The Lord our God, the Lord is one! You shall love the Lord your God with all your heart, with all your soul, and with all your strength (Deuteronomy 6:4-5).

Our Lord Yeshua said that this was the most important commandment in the entire Bible. Somehow, if we could attain and obey this one command, everything else in our walk with the Lord would fall into place. What does it mean to love Him with all our heart, soul, and strength?

The Lord is jealous for our hearts toward Him, more jealous than we could ever realize. He will not share you with anything that you love more than Him. This even includes family members. If you force the Lord to share you with your other loves, you will be driving Him away, for He is yearning for what you have given to other things. It is an honor to be loved this fiercely by Someone so good.

Throughout the Bible, we find the Lord portraying His relationship with His people as a husband with his wife. It seems that the Lord instituted human marriage in order to paint a picture of the intimate relationship He desired to enjoy with us.

Everything the Lord created on earth is a reflection of those things that are in Heaven (see Heb. 8:5; Gen. 2:10; Rev. 2:7b). In Heaven we see a tabernacle, an altar, a rainbow, and a river. There is a garden called Eden, or Paradise, and a tree of life in Heaven. There are many types of living and intelligent beings enjoying the Lord and His surroundings. We hear music in Heaven and behold beauty and grandeur, trees and mountains. We see government and order, authority and spheres of influence. We see worship, love, generosity, and sacrifice.

All of these things are found on earth as well, although in a lesser degree of splendor. The Lord created earth in the image of Heaven. He created man in the image of God. *And He created earthly marriage in the image of heavenly marriage between the Lord and His people.* The Lord has prepared, planned, and yearned for this heavenly union before the worlds were formed.

In this higher version of marriage, the Creator becomes a Husband to a corporate Bride, composed of millions of worshipers. These people retain their individual characteristics, and yet they form a unified expression of devotion and adoration, a composite Bride.

HIS NAME IS JEALOUS

One of the characteristics of God that is difficult for many Christians to embrace is His jealousy. Some compare His jealousy to the controlling and insecure version that they have experienced in a human relationship. There is definitely a twisted, demonic version of jealousy that some of us have seen in a spouse or friend, who was angry or violent, distrustful, controlling, and a frightening person to endure.

But when this trait is seen in the Father's heart, it becomes something intimate and sacred between an adoring husband and his beloved wife. The jealousy of God has become precious to me. It makes me feel passionately loved by the kindest and most worthy of men. Why would I ever arouse His jealousy?

> *Do not worship any other god, for the Lord, whose name is Jealous, is a jealous God* (Exodus 34:14 NIV).

We were made for love! We were created for the purpose of being united with our God in an intimate relationship, which is like a husband and wife. Therefore, our Lover feels grieved, rejected, and angered when His Bride prostitutes herself with the world and its counterfeit delights and idolatrous systems. We see throughout both the Old and New Testaments that the Lord suffers terrible rejection at the hands of His own people, both Israel and the Church, when they provoke Him to jealousy by their unfaithfulness (see Hos. 2:1-5; Ezek. 16:15-19; James 4:4-5; 1 Cor. 10:22).

The Lord deserves our unadulterated devotion. I wouldn't want to be married to a God who didn't care if I flirted with other lovers who consumed my time, thoughts, or affection.

> *Hear, O Israel: The Lord our God, the Lord is one. Love the Lord your God with all your heart and with all your soul and with all your strength* (Deuteronomy 6:4-5 NIV).

We know that this verse is the Lord Yeshua's highest priority for our lives. It takes effort and much mental and emotional discipline to love the Lord with all our hearts, souls, and strength. It does not happen automatically to all who are born again.

Likewise, Paul and James have warned us in many passages that God is jealous for our love, and our friendship with the world makes us His enemy! Is the Lord coming back for a harlot or a Bride?

> *Adulterers and adulteresses! Do you not know that friendship with the world is enmity with God?...Or do you think that the Scripture says in vain, "The Spirit who dwells in us yearns jealously"?* (James 4:4a,5)

> *You cannot partake of the Lord's table and of the table of demons. Or do we provoke the Lord to jealousy?* (1 Corinthians 10:21b-22a)

> *Come out from among them and be separate, says the Lord. Do not touch what is unclean, and I will receive you....Let us cleanse ourselves from all filthiness of the flesh and spirit, perfecting holiness in the fear of God* (2 Corinthians 6:17; 7:1).

The Lord is jealous of the hours we give to the television instead of giving those hundreds, even thousands of hours to Him in intimate communion. The price for seeing God and knowing His destiny for our lives is holiness.

Worldly entertainment is a distraction of the flesh that will not profit us on that day that we account for every hour we have had on this earth since we received salvation.

I wasted untold hours in front of the television. I will never get those hours back, but I know the Lord will help me redeem the time I have left, since I have repented and forsaken all worldly entertainment. When we are so tired or bored that we choose to entertain ourselves instead of drawing apart with the Lord, *those hours will be played before our eyes when we stand before the throne.* We will feel bitter remorse for that priceless commodity of our time. The Lord is far more fascinating than entertainment, anyway.

If we are addicted to any form of worldly entertainment, we should go before the Lord and ask Him to help us get free, so that we do not suffer regret or shame when we stand before the Judgment. *The Lord is so kind and merciful if we will do the cleansing work now, rather than facing Him when it is too late to do anything about it.* Be accountable to another believer if this area is a stronghold in your life, as it is for millions of believers.

Just so there is no misunderstanding, there are many Christian movies (and certain Jewish ones, as well) that present powerful biblical messages and are wonderfully edifying. The Lord loves these filmmakers, blesses these family times, and does not consider these to be worldly entertainment. I have been greatly blessed to watch Christian movies with my family, even to this day. *Of course, even these should not replace our personal intimate time with our Lord.*

As the professing Church, we have enjoyed a long period of grace, when our Father has been patiently waiting for us to mature, and to correct ourselves in matters of purity and righteousness. As you know, the Bible makes it clear that He cannot wait indefinitely for us to examine our hearts, cleanse our motives, humble ourselves, and ask Him to purify our thought life.

It is time to cross the Jordan, but only those who have sanctified themselves and had their hearts circumcised by the Lord will qualify to cross over. You must ask the Lord to circumcise your heart; He will not do it against your will. *People have mistaken the Lord's goodness for His approval of our lives.* The fact that the Lord is so patient and gentle does not mean He approves of all that we do. In the end, we will most assuredly hear the Lord's assessment of how we used our time.

> *All Scripture is given by inspiration of God, and is profitable for doctrine, for reproof, for correction, for instruction in righteousness,* **that the man of God may be complete, thoroughly equipped for every good work** *(2 Timothy 3:16-17).*

> *Therefore, leaving the discussion of the elementary principles of Christ,* **let us go on to perfection** *(Hebrews 6:1a).*

> **Blessed are the pure in heart, for they shall see God** *(Matthew 5:8).*

OUR ADULTERY!

The Lord's Church has dealt Him an unbearable wound. She has committed adultery before Him, even as my people Israel grieved Him with their adulteries. We might think that the laments and whoredoms found in Hosea apply only to ancient Israel. I wish it were so! But the truth is, we are no better than Israel and have also broken our Husband's heart with our adulteries.

Since the Lord is too good to leave us as we are, He will make our way difficult. He did this with Israel, not for the purpose of destruction, but for the purpose of waking us up to our first love. His cry to the Church is equally heartbreaking: *"I have this against you, that you have left your first love. Remember, therefore the height from which you have fallen and repent!"* (see Rev. 2:4-5).

He will cause us to become holy unto Him by way of hardships because we were not willing to become holy under pleasant circumstances.

*Therefore, behold, I will hedge up your way with thorns, and wall her in, so that she cannot find her paths. She will chase her lovers, but not overtake them; yes, she will seek them, but not find them. Then she will say, "**I will go and return to my first husband, for then it was better for me than now.**" For she did not know that I gave her grain, new wine, and oil, and multiplied her silver and gold. "And it shall be, in that day," says the Lord, "that you will call Me 'My Husband,' and no longer call Me 'My Master'"* (Hosea 2:6-8a, 16).

The Lord will not leave us like this. He will clean up His church and bring her back to unadulterated devotion. He will allure us into the wilderness and comfort us. He will raise us up that we may know Him and live in His sight. He must and will remove the defilement from His Church.

The Garbage Pit

I had a terrible dream about the level of defilement in the Church, which I need to share. In this dream, I was living in a large community, where we all lived in a huge house and property. I saw the outside walls of the house near the ground level.

Immediately next to the house was a vast, cavernous, rectangular pit set deep into the ground and extending for a great distance outward and downward. Lining this massive pit was a plastic garbage liner, which covered the bottom and sides of this pit. The pit was filled to overflowing with garbage, and the underground sides of the pit were putting pressure on the house's foundations.

I knew that the pit kept enlarging itself to make room for the ever-increasing amounts of garbage that were being added to it daily. Later, I remembered the verse that says, "*Hell has enlarged itself and opened its mouth beyond measure*" (see Isa. 5:14). The weight of the garbage within the pit was impossible to calculate, perhaps many thousands of tons. The pressure was so great that it had already begun to split the asphalt pavement around the base of the house.

I knew that "the garbage men" were coming soon, but I wondered how anyone could lift out the liner containing this amount of garbage. I felt very motivated to remove it myself because I didn't want to wait for the garbage men to come. I tried to pull on one edge of the liner, but obviously, it was too heavy for me to move. I knew that when the men came, the act of removing the entire liner and its contents would severely split the asphalt pavement, as well as break open the very foundations of the house. In fact, it would destroy the house.

Then the scene changed, and the gigantic pit was now a garden plot of the same size and shape as the pit had been. I saw a "leader" in the community punishing a family of parents and their children, who had displeased her in some way. She was publicly burying this family alive in this vast "garden." The whole community watched as she covered them with earth and then left them there to "teach them a lesson." Somehow, it was assumed that they would stay under there for a while and would not actually die, but would be retrieved at a later time. Everyone watching seemed to think it was amusing to observe this punishment, and that the family would be "fine" later on.

I was very concerned that they would die under there, but everyone thought it was no problem. I felt I couldn't interfere while the leader was watching, and I was afraid of her. I waited all day until it was dark and crept back to this plot of earth. It was now cold, and an ice and snow storm had covered the roads and the ground. I searched for this burial plot, hoping that someone had remembered them and let them out by now.

Instead of a garden plot, the pit had now become a deep freezer, vast, almost endless in its dimensions. The freezer was covered by a heavy lid. I lay with my face on the freezing ground, banging on the lid, and crying out, "Hello? Can you hear me?" Since I heard nothing, I hoped that someone had taken them out.

Then I lifted up the lid and called out, "Hello?" into the black, frozen, cavernous depths. It was dreadful and eerily silent. I knew that they must be dead. A rat scurried out of the hole past my face, and I woke up in horror.

When I awoke, the first part of the dream seemed to have an obvious interpretation. The Church is defiled with ever-increasing impurity and filth. We have polluted the earth, our churches, our homes and families, our institutions and ministries with unholy words, activities, television and movies, music, books, magazines, computer games, and other material. Who is strong enough to clean up the massive defilement in our temples, both personally and corporately? The weight of our sin is so excessively burdensome! I was reminded of a passage in Isaiah:

> *The earth is broken up, **the earth is split asunder**, the earth is thoroughly shaken. The earth reels like a drunkard, it sways like a hut in the wind; **so heavy upon it is the guilt of its rebellion** that it falls—never to rise again* (Isaiah 24:19-20 NIV).

If we wait until the Lord's "garbage collectors" come to remove the Church's defilements, the weight of our filth will crush us and destroy our structures. *Only that which is holy will remain when "**the Son of Man will send out His angels to weed out of His kingdom everything that causes sin and all who do evil**"* (see Matt. 13:41 NIV). These angels are "the garbage men" in this dream. Woe to us, if His holiness should expose us as we are currently!

I can't be certain about the meaning of the cruel leader who buried the church family alive in a grave that became a deep freezer. It may be a warning to some leaders who "punish" or marginalize people who are not fully compliant with church programs or organizational structures that the church considers vitally important. Perhaps these leaders are not allowing their people to obey urgent promptings from the Holy Spirit because it seems threatening to the power structures, the comfortable programs, and the status quo. Therefore, these "different ones" are kept locked away in a cold and dismal space, where there is no life support. Do we isolate these people or emotionally "freeze them out"? Do we subtly identify certain ones as "scape-goats," who are blamed for the dysfunctions and lack of dynamic growth in the church? May the Lord grant us wisdom in this matter, if this dream is indeed relevant to the reader.

If we cleanse our temples now, the Lord will show us mercy and will heal us. He will revive us and bind up our wounds. For those who have sanctified themselves and asked the Lord to circumcise their hearts, He will transform them into His likeness, even as Yeshua was transformed into His glory on the Mount of Transfiguration. Amen.

ENDNOTES

1. *Zondervan NIV Study Bible* (Grand Rapids, MI: Zondervan, 2002); commentary on Matthew 6:9. The definition of "hallowed" is the author's understanding of the Hebrew text of the Lord's prayer, combined with the NIV commentary.

2. Israeli tour guides, while taking visitors through the Dead Sea region, pointed out one particular salt formation. As we looked out the window of our bus, we saw a white formation that is about the size and shape of a woman. The tour guides told us that traditionally, this pillar is Lot's wife, a permanent reminder of the Bible's reality.

3. The word Christians commonly use for this Presence is the *Shekinah* glory. This word comes from the Hebrew verb, *shochen*, which means "to dwell." The noun is *sh'chinah*. This refers to the Lord's tangible, manifest presence.

4. If you read this verse in the NIV, it says that the Lord struck down 70 men. In the NKJV, it says He struck down 50,070 men. The Hebrew construction is slightly ambiguous, but it does contain the words "fifty-thousand men," so I am choosing the NKJV as the better translation.

5. See http://www.studylight.org/lex/heb/view.cgi?number=08313; http://www.studylight.org/lex/heb/view.cgi?number=08314.

6. Neville has seen these beings in Heaven and has described them as "a blow torch." To read Neville Johnson's writings or to purchase his extraordinary prophetic teaching material, go to www.lwf.org.au.

Chapter 11

Balaam's Seduction

THERE is a very unusual character found in the Book of Numbers, who is one of the few Gentile prophets found in the Bible. Of course, there were pre-Hebraic prophets, such as Enoch, Methuselah, Noah, Abram, and possibly Job. However, Balaam was a contemporary of Joshua or Moses, and as such, could accurately be called "a Gentile prophet."

Moses considered Balaam a serious enemy of Israel. When the Lord commanded him to take vengeance on the Midianites, the Israelites made a point of executing Balaam, apart from those slain on the battlefield (see Num. 31:8, 15-18; Josh. 13:22). Moreover, Moses was so angry at the seduction of Israel's men, that he insisted that his army also execute the Midianite women whom Balaam had trained to seduce them. *The seduction of Israel took place just before they were to cross over into their Promised Land.* The Church might wish to make a note of this warning from Israel's history.

Balaam is also mentioned three times in the New Testament, including one warning from the Lord Yeshua Himself. Clearly, there is something about Balaam's continuing influence into the New Covenant church, which caused the Lord to issue these latter-day warnings to His people.

BALAAM'S ERROR

In his warning letter to the Church, Jude speaks of certain ungodly men who have crept in among the believers. These men had turned the graciousness of God into a license for sexual sin, and they denied the Lordship of Yeshua. He then adds this:

> *But these speak evil of whatever they do not know; and whatever they know naturally, like brute beasts, in these things they corrupt themselves. Woe to them! For they have gone in the way of Cain, have* **run greedily in the error of Balaam for profit,** *and perished in the rebellion of Korah* (Jude 10-11).

Jude cites three characters from biblical history who were infamous to the early believers: Cain, Balaam, and Korah. Cain offered a displeasing sacrifice and then nurtured anger and jealousy in his heart toward his brother; he then yielded to his sinful hatred and killed his innocent brother.

Korah also indulged in demonic jealousy and rebellion because Aaron and his sons were granted higher priestly authority than his clan was given. After publicly leading a rebellion against Moses and Aaron, the earth opened up and swallowed him alive. His followers were then burned alive by fire that fell from heaven.

But what did Balaam do? Jude mentions the word *profit*, and so we see that money changed hands. Peter also refers to these *"false teachers who bring in destructive heresies,"* causing many believers to blaspheme the ways of truth (see 2 Pet. 2:1). And Peter also compares their covetousness to that of Balaam:

> *By covetousness they will exploit you with deceptive words.... They are spots and blemishes, carousing in their own deceptions while they feast with you, having eyes full of adultery and that cannot cease from sin,* **enticing unstable souls.** *They have a heart trained in covetous practices, and are accursed children.*

*They have forsaken the right way and gone astray, following the
way of Balaam the son of Beor, who loved the wages of unrighteousness* (2 Peter 2:3a, 13b-15).

Our Lord Yeshua warned us that in the days preceding His return, there
would be false prophets. As author Rick Joyner points out, if there would be
no true prophets in the last days, the Lord could have simply said, "All prophets in the last days will be false." However, He was warning us that among the
true prophets, there would be false ones as well.[1]

In order for us to understand the distinction between true and false
prophets in the New Covenant, we need to understand the dangers of
Balaam's example. We have seen the warnings of Peter and Jude. Our third
witness is the Lord Yeshua Himself, who warned the Church in Pergamos,
where satan's throne was found (see Rev. 2:13). Pergamos was the center of
satan worship, idol worship, and Roman emperor worship.

After commending this church for holding fast, including the steadfast
faith of Antipas, the first martyr of Asia, the Lord says,

*But I have a few things against you, because you have there
those who hold the doctrine of Balaam, who taught Balak to
put a stumbling block before the children of Israel, to eat things
sacrificed to idols, and to commit sexual immorality* (Revelation 2:14).

In His New Covenant church, the Lord sees Christians following the
way of Balaam. We would do well to know what this sin looks like, since
it exists in the professing Church today. Since we have three witnesses in
the New Testament that Balaam's sin is a warning to the Church, we must
understand his story, found in the Book of Numbers.

THE TIME TO CROSS OVER

In Numbers 22, we find the children of Israel very close to crossing the Jordan and coming into their Promised Land. The Lord took His people through 40 years of wandering in the desert, and they had already suffered both plagues and punishments for their grumbling. When they complained about the manna, the Lord sent venomous snakes to bite them, killing many people. When they repented, the Lord stopped the plague by directing Moses to lift up a bronze snake on a pole. If they looked up at the snake, they were healed. If they would not look at the snake, the poison killed them.

We remember that the Lord Jesus referred to this incident, saying, *"Just as Moses lifted up the snake in the desert, so the Son of Man must be lifted up, that everyone who believes in Him may have eternal life"* (John 3:14-15 NIV). It may seem strange that the Lord compared Himself to a bronze serpent on a pole, but He was speaking of faith and healing. Like the Israelites, those who look at the Man lifted up on the cross will be saved.

Israel had defeated a number of Canaanite peoples, and the dread of the Lord had fallen on those living on the eastern side of the Jordan River. Israel was about to cross into Jericho and was camped in the plains of Moab on the eastern side.

Although Moses had made it clear he had no intention of killing Moabites, the Moabite king was terrified of what Israel would do to them. The Scripture teaches that the Israelites did not randomly slaughter people groups, but only attacked those who attacked them as they journeyed, such as the Amalekites and the Amorites. But in his irrational fear, King Balak of Moab hired a popular sorcerer to curse Israel. This man was financially successful in his prophetic ministry because those whom he blessed were blessed, and those whom he cursed were cursed. The Law of Moses refers to his practices as "divination," a forbidden pagan art. His name was Balaam, son of Beor, from the area that would now be northern Iraq, near the Syrian border.

*So Balak son of Zippor, who was king of Moab at that time, sent messengers to summon Balaam, son of Beor...and said, "A people has come out of Egypt; they cover the face of the land, and have settled next to me. **Now come and put a curse on these people,** because they are too powerful for me. Perhaps then I will be able to defeat them and drive them out of the country. For I know that those you bless are blessed, and those you curse are cursed"* (Numbers 22:4b-6 NIV).

Balaam had a genuine prophetic gift, but he allowed his gift to be bought by the highest bidder. Thus, he was serving customers who worshiped false gods, and was willing to tell them what they wanted to hear and to put curses on their enemies. His words had real power. However, as we will see in this strange story, God can choose to override a false prophet's intentions and put His own words in his mouth.

BUYING THE ANOINTING

The elders of Moab and Midian departed to bring back Balaam, taking with them the payment for his divination. *Divination is trying to get information, guidance, or revelation from an occult source.* We find some ancient methods of divination described in Ezekiel 21:21 and Deuteronomy 18. In modern times, an example of divination would be using a Ouija board, Tarot cards, or palm-reading. In ancient times, one method was casting lots with arrows. They would write different choices on several arrows and would reach into the quiver; whichever arrow they pulled out would determine what "the gods" were telling them to do. Another method was killing a sheep and examining the color or condition of its liver. On other occasions, the pagan peoples consulted their idols; since little wooden statues cannot speak, we can only assume that they received demonic directions when they consulted these household "gods."

When these elders reached Balaam with the king's request, he said, *"Spend the night here, and I will bring you back the answer the Lord gives me"* (see Num. 22:8). Interestingly, we see in the Hebrew text that he used the true covenant name of the Lord, which is "*Yehovah.*" This leads some to believe that Balaam was a worshiper of the same God that Israel worshiped. In addition to this, Balaam's response sounds like a prophet who was obedient to the Lord.

He believed in the one true God to some degree and wanted to be obedient to Him. However, Balaam was accustomed to receiving payments for his prophetic gift and had compromised the exclusiveness of Israel's God. He already had a sense that cursing Israel could be a dangerous thing to do because he could feel in his spirit the Lord's protection over them.

That night, the Lord told Balaam he must not go with these men or curse the people of Israel, for they are blessed. Indeed, this man could hear the Lord's voice! He refused Balak's offer and sent his nobles back to their own country. When the king learned that Balaam refused to come, he sent other nobles, more numerous and high-ranking than the first group. They offered him more money and tried to entice him to change his mind. Balaam's answer was righteous. He said, "*Even if Balak gave me his palace filled with silver and gold, I could not do anything great or small to go beyond the command of the Lord my God*" (Num. 22:18 NIV).

This shows us that many believers start out saying and doing godly things, but end up in a collision course with God's will and His covenants. If it had ended there, Balaam would not have become a hated enemy of Israel, whom they would shortly execute. But he was tempted by Balak's higher offer, and I believe this is where he made his mistake. Instead of sending them away, he said, "*Spend the night here and I will see what else the Lord will tell me*" (Num. 22:19).

It seems that Balaam was hoping that God would change His mind, or else he would have simply dismissed them. We know that he was wealthy, for Peter tells us that he loved the wages of unrighteousness. Money is a huge snare to many people, and it causes us to compromise what we know is right. Those who prophesy with a motive of financial gain are false prophets, even if they speak many things that come true. Paul writes to Timothy, *"For the love of money is a root of all kinds of evil"* (1 Tim. 6:10 NIV).

So that there is no misunderstanding, let me add the following clarification: when a godly prophet travels from place to place to minister in a church or conference, it is expensive to do so. Therefore, it is absolutely right and fitting that he or she should receive an offering that, at the very least, covers his or her expenses. It is wonderful if the amount exceeds expenses, since this prophet is ministering to God's flock, rather than working a "normal" job with a paycheck. The Lord's view of this financial arrangement will totally depend on the prophet's inner heart motivations, whether to encourage or warn the people, or to gain fame and finance. Only the Lord can see the heart's motives.

At this point, the Lord gave Balaam a different answer than He did the first time, which is very confusing to people. This time, the Lord told him, *"Since these men have come to summon you, go with them, but only do what I tell you"* (Num. 22:20 NIV).

Sometimes the Lord gives us what we ask for, but if our request does not please Him, we wind up on a deadly collision course with Him.

> *So Balaam rose in the morning, saddled his donkey, and went with the princes of Moab. Then God's anger was aroused because he went, and the Angel of the Lord took His stand in the way as an adversary against him* (Numbers 22:21-22a).

When Balaam's donkey saw the Angel of the Lord standing in the road with a drawn sword in his hand, she turned off the road into a field, but Balaam beat her to get her back on the road. Then the Angel of the Lord stood in a narrow path between two vineyards, with walls on both sides. The donkey then pressed close to the wall, crushing her master's foot against it, so he beat her again. Then the Angel of the Lord moved on ahead and stood in a narrow place, and the poor donkey had nowhere to turn, so she lay down under Balaam, who beat her in a fury. Then the Lord opened the donkey's mouth, and she said to him, "*What have I done to you to make you beat me these three times?*"

Balaam answered the donkey, "*You have made a fool of me. If I had a sword in my hand, I would kill you right now.*"

The donkey replied, "*Am I not your own donkey, which you have always ridden, to this day? Have I been in the habit of doing this to you?*" (see Num. 22:28-30 NIV).

"No," he said.

> *Then the Lord opened Balaam's eyes, and he saw the Angel of the Lord standing in the road with his sword drawn. So he bowed low and fell facedown. The Angel of the Lord asked him, "Why have you beaten your donkey these three times? I have come here to oppose you, because your path is a reckless one before me. The donkey saw me and turned away from me these three times. If she had not turned away, I would certainly have killed you by now, but I would have spared her"* (Numbers 22:31-33 NIV).

His donkey had higher spiritual discernment than this prophet! Finally, Balaam saw into the spirit realm and repented of his cruelty and folly. When an individual or a nation goes against the Lord's will and curses Israel, the Lord opposes us with a drawn sword, but we are too blind and reckless to see what we are walking into. *Our nation would do well to heed this warning.* If we come against Israel, we will find ourselves opposing God Himself, and we will walk into destruction.

The Angel of the Lord told the frightened prophet, "*Go with the men, but speak only what I tell you*" (Num. 22:35).

When Balak heard that Balaam had finally arrived after so much wasted time, he impatiently demanded that they hasten their business of cursing

Israel. Balaam warned him, *"Can I say just anything? I must speak only what God puts in my mouth"* (Num. 22:38).

Balak should have realized that this didn't bode well for his scheme, but he was too busy planning his occult ceremony to notice.

A BLESSING INSTEAD OF A CURSE!

The king and the prophet went up to a high place, sacrificed animals to the gods, and ate the food as part of the idolatrous ceremony. Even so, this pagan feast would not stop the Lord from inserting His words into the prophet's mouth.

The next morning, Balak took Balaam up to a mountain, and from there, the prophet looked down on the Israelite tents spread below him in the valley. After another series of pagan sacrifices, Balaam withdrew to a barren place to hear from the Lord what he should speak over this unsuspecting and peaceful people below them.

When he returned from his prayer time, Balaam spoke his first prophecy in the presence of all the princes of Moab. Instead of the curse that he was paid to utter, Balaam blessed Israel, saying, *"How can I curse those whom God has not cursed? How can I denounce those whom the Lord has not denounced?"* (Num. 23:8). He finished his blessing with, *"Let me die the death of the righteous and may my end be like theirs!"* (Num. 23:10)

When Balak protested this blessing, Balaam answered, *"Must I not speak what the Lord puts in my mouth?"* (Num. 23:12)

This cycle of pagan sacrifices, followed by "involuntary" blessings upon Israel, was repeated three more times. With each progressive prophecy, the blessings grow more anointed. In the second prophecy, Balaam proclaimed,

> *God is not a man, that He should lie, nor the son of man, that*
> *He should change His mind. Does He speak and then not act?*
> *Does He promise and not fulfill? I have received a command to*

bless; He has blessed, and I cannot change it. No misfortune is seen in Jacob, no misery observed in Israel. The Lord their God is with them; the shout of the King is among them (Numbers 23:19-21 NIV).

This is the first place in the Old Testament where God's kingship was declared—out of the mouth of a Gentile sorcerer prophet. He declared that there is *"no sorcery against Jacob, no divination against Israel."* There are no magic formulas that will stand against a people whom God has blessed, who are under His divine covering.

In the beginning of chapter 24, we read,

> *Now when Balaam saw that it pleased the Lord to bless Israel, he did not resort to sorcery as at other times, but turned his face toward the desert* (Numbers 24:1 NIV).

As he looked out and saw Israel encamped, tribe by tribe, it says, *"the Spirit of God came upon him"* (Num. 22:2 NIV). This expression is only used in the rest of the Bible for true prophets. He completed this prophecy by using the same words that were spoken to Abraham. *"May those who bless you be blessed and those who curse you be cursed"* (Num. 24:9 NIV).

Balaam's third prophecy is chanted in the synagogues to this very day by the Jewish people. It goes, *"How beautiful are your tents, O Jacob, your dwelling places, O Israel!"* (Num. 24:5 NIV) I wrote a song to this blessing, called "Ma Tovu."

In his fourth oracle, Balaam actually predicted the coming of the Jewish Messiah out of the loins of Jacob. Finally, the exasperated Balak cried out, *"If you can't say something bad about them, don't say anything at all!"* (see Num. 24:10).

Balaam Returns to Wickedness

Sadly, after yielding himself to the Spirit of God and arousing the fury of the king who would have paid him handsomely, Balaam returned to his home in the eastern mountains. He was unable to complete his assignment to curse Israel. If this were a fairy tale, this born-again pagan sorcerer would have lived happily ever after, since he spoke godly prophecies over the Lord's people. However, his heart was not pure, and thus, his character and future motives were inconsistent with this righteous "fever." He recovered from this temporary godliness and went back to his old ways. He was a spring of both sweet and bitter water, a mixture. His deeper motivations of heart were shown to be false.

In a few short weeks or months after failing to curse Israel, Balaam came up with another way of destroying them. Since the Lord would not allow him to destroy Israel by cursing them, Balaam taught Balak a strategy of seduction into sexual immorality and idolatrous worship.

Balaam realized that Israel's pure devotion to *Yehovah* was the basis of His divine covering and blessing over them. He knew enough about the Lord's character and His relationship with this unusually favored people to know that *if he could lure them into spiritual and physical adultery, God would remove His blessing from them.* They would fall easily under the weight of their own immorality and corruption, without the supernatural protection of their God. Later in history, we would also see that the Roman Empire did not fall because of attacks from a stronger military power, but because of moral decay from within the society.

Balak sent the Midianite women to Israel's camp to seduce the men and entice them to attend their pagan worship festivals. This would include sexual sin as well as eating *"at the table of demons"* (see 1 Cor. 10:21). Because the Israelites were enticed into idolatry, the Lord executed many and killed 24,000 with plague. In fact, God Himself became their enemy. The Israelite men had no idea they were stepping into a deadly snare when they lustfully followed their Midianite seducers into satan's festival.

All at once he followed her like an ox going to the slaughter, like a deer stepping into a noose till an arrow pierces his liver, like a bird darting into a snare, little knowing it will cost him his life (Proverbs 7:22-23 NIV).

THE SEDUCTION OF CHRISTIANITY

Notice the moment in Israel's journey when this incident occurred. They were in the fortieth year of wandering in the desert. Aaron had recently died, as a punishment for his part in the striking of the rock, which dishonored the Lord. He died just before the people were to go into the Promised Land. Moses would also die without crossing the Jordan. Israel had gone through 40 years in the desert, which was the punishment for their unwillingness to cross over and fight the giant Canaanites. And now they were camped opposite Jericho. This was their staging ground for the conquest of the land.

Israel had seen the Lord's kindness: Manna fell from heaven six days a week for 40 years; water gushed out of a rock; their clothes and sandals never wore out; none of them got sick, nor did they miscarry.

They had also seen the wrath of God: They had been afflicted with plague disease and venomous snake bites; they saw the earth swallow up the rebels alive and fire consume others; the Lord had even threatened to destroy them all. And Moses had pleaded, fasted, and interceded for them, and the Lord had shown mercy.

Now in the last phase of their journey, Israel was camped among the Moabites and the Midianites, whom they had no intention of harming. It was at this moment that the king of Moab hired a pagan prophet to curse Israel. When that didn't work, he successfully enticed them into sexual sin and idolatry. Satan was afraid of the Lord's people entering their Promised Land and driving out his demon-worshiping, child-sacrificing slaves of wickedness. He knew his time was short, and he would try anything to keep them from walking into the fullness of their inheritance. Does this remind us of the Church's current moment in history?

When Balaam saw that he could not curse God's covenant people, he seduced them, and through their own sin, separated them from the Lord. If satan is not permitted to afflict, kill, or curse us because the Lord has placed a hedge of fire around His praying people, then he will try to corrupt, entice, and defile us from within our own weaknesses. *The enemy studies us and targets the very areas where we are most likely to fall.* He devises strategies that are crafted according to our weakest areas. Then he goes before the throne of God and demands to tempt us or sift us.

If we succumb to these clever traps, we shame the Lord before His angels. This gives the enemy satisfaction because it ruins us, it shames God, and it causes the Lord to remove the protective hedge of fire from around us; thus, we become prey for every swarming hornet and ravenous beast. In addition, satan knows that the Lord will execute judgments on His own people for this harlotry. This is exactly what the enemy brought upon Israel through Balaam's seduction.

This is also what satan is about to unleash on the Church. **He is bringing such strong and deceptive enticements that even the elect could be enticed, unless extremely alert and prayerful.**

GLORY AND TESTING

I know this is the truth, because of the tests that have come upon me personally. They always come just at a moment when the Lord is taking me to a new depth of consecration and union with Messiah. *A test comes just when I am about to cross over into the next allotment of my inheritance, which is the fully crucified life.* The personal two-part test I'm about to share is terrible, and I have absolutely no desire to share it publicly. However, it will save many of the Lord's people from ruin, and for the sake of the Lord's flock, He desires me to be transparent with you.

Part 1 — The Stranger's Kiss

I have previously written about what I call "power dreams." These are unusual dreams that are accompanied by a high level of the power of God. This power disturbs my sleep and impacts my body with the discomfort of the Lord's glory. It causes me to tremble as I am dreaming, and I often curl up tightly on my side, so as to "minimize" the impact of the glory.

In 2007 I had such a dream, which lasted more than four hours. It came during the season when my first book was being published, and in fact, I could see a banner over this lengthy dream scene, which read *Coffee Talks With Messiah*. It began at around midnight, and I saw the Lord Yeshua facing a crowd of people. I was standing next to the Lord and slightly behind Him. I watched and listened intently as the Lord taught and imparted truths to His flock. His back was turned toward me as He faced the crowd. At the same time, He was also teaching me how to bring His people into deeper intimacy with Him. Somehow, the entire dream was about this book and how it would bring people closer to the Lord.

At times, the Lord and I were ministering together, like a team. Sometimes, I would simply watch the Lord Yeshua teaching. At other times, He would instruct me what to do to bless the people, and I would obey. At still other times, I somehow *became* the Lord and was doing the very things He would have done, but these impartations were entrusted to me. I did not see the Lord's face.

One theme was that we were covering the people with the Lord's prayer shawl (called a *tallit* in Hebrew). You may remember that when Ruth crept down to the threshing floor and lay at Boaz's feet, she said to him, *"Spread the corner of your garment over me, for you are my kinsman redeemer"* (see Ruth 3:9). When the Redeemer covers His Bride-to-be with the corner of His garment, it is a loving gesture of protection and betrothal. It was exactly this gesture that the Lord desired me to impart to His flock. At one point, He told me to grasp the edge of His large *tallit*, slowly lift it up, and spread it across the heads of the crowd, from left to right. As I obeyed in the dream, I felt my left arm raise up in bed, and I completed the spreading motion in the air. The *tallit* formed a canopy over His people. The Lord had me repeat this gesture two more times.

At this point, the Lord suddenly turned around to face me. The face I saw surprised me, for it was not what I expected the Lord should look like. He seemed different from the back view I had been observing, although He was wearing the same white garments. He had short, jet-black hair, and His eyes were black and narrow. He grabbed my shoulders and suddenly kissed me hard. He wanted us to leave the crowd and said, "C'mon. It's just you and me."

I felt strange about the way His face looked and the way He grabbed me; it did not seem loving, but felt forceful. I wondered why the Lord would want to be alone with me when we were ministering to His people so lovingly. The flock needed us, and there was still work to do!

I was confused because it seemed to be the same person with whom I had been ministering all that time, who had simply turned around to face me. And yet something felt wrong. I quickly tried to calculate if the Lord would feel insulted if I rebuked Him, thinking it might be satan. I decided that it was safer to rebuke this person, and if it turned out to be the Lord, He would understand that I was trying to protect myself from deception. I said, "The Lord rebuke you!"

Instantly, the "stranger" was gone, and the dream resumed with the Lord's back toward me again, continuing our ministry as if there had been no interruption. This continued until I woke up at 4:50 A.M. I looked at the clock and went back to sleep for one more hour. This time, I found myself in the middle of the worst seduction dream I have ever experienced, and one which eventually morphed into a virtual reality.

While the description of the dream below is not at all graphic, I would encourage the reader to pray before reading it, that the Holy One would cover your mind and heart from any defiling images.

Part 2—The Test of Balaam

I was in a western rodeo bar and lounge, and my attention was focused on a sweet young woman who was hanging out there. She had black, shoulder-length hair, pale skin, and dark eyes, and was wearing a classic, cream-colored sleeveless dress with a high neckline, which fell just below her knees. She seemed innocent and naïve as I looked at her, and I felt concerned when I observed a stranger watching her, unnoticed. I felt like I was "on her side," and didn't want him to get to her.

He had short black hair and narrow black eyes. At that moment, I knew he looked familiar and unpleasant, but I hadn't retained a memory of the previous dream. In this scene, he wore modern clothes you might see in a rodeo bar. He was muscular, with bulky chest and arms, and I knew he was planning to seduce her. At times, I was merely observing this girl, but at other times, I could feel all that she was feeling. There was some type of identification I felt with her, which was unclear until the last second of this dream. She did not know that he was watching her or that he was a predator, and I felt worried about her falling into his trap. I could not communicate with her, for some reason, being merely an observer. He watched her for a long time, and I knew his intentions were to get her into a back room of the lounge and seduce her.

In the next scene, I *was* the woman, and I was standing in a narrow passageway, leading to some back rooms. The man started to come through the passage and squeezed past me, as if he was trying to get by me to go toward the back. However, he acted like there was not enough room for him to get by me, and he was actually trying to push me backward along the long hallway with his large body. I pushed myself back against the wall as flat as possible and said, "Just go past me!" He knew I was not going anywhere. He pushed by me, pretending to continue, but soon stopped when he realized I wasn't going with him.

The scene changed. I was still the woman. I found myself in another passageway, where there was a mechanical bull with very long, curvy, sharp horns. This evil bull had a muscular chest and the face of a man, and it was mechanically bucking, like at a rodeo. But its head was moving in a deliberate way as to try to gore me with those sharp horns. It kept turning its head this way and that, trying to gore me, but I kept deftly pushing against the wall, barely avoiding those horns.

In the final scene, I was no longer the woman but was observing her again as an outsider. However, I could feel everything she was feeling. She was seated in a chair in a passageway. The man knelt at her feet, and began to kiss her feet. He then continued, kissing her legs. She protested, "You're going too far."

He stopped, looking up at her as if she had hurt his feelings. In a moment of misplaced sympathy, she then uttered the equivocal statement that would determine the outcome of this seduction. She said, "I love it, but you're going too far."

The moment she uttered those words, the dream no longer existed, and I was instantly aware of a sexual assault that was occurring to me as I still slept. My mind tried to wake up as I suddenly felt this unthinkable assault in its initial stage. Looking back on this terrible moment, I now realize that this was not actually impacting my physical body. However, the Scriptures teach that we have a "spirit body" that feels exactly like our earthly body during encounters of a spiritual nature, whether from the Lord or the enemy (see 2 Cor. 12:2-4; Matt. 4:5-11; Rev. 4:1-2; Ezek. 8:3; 11:24; 1 Kings 18:12; 2 Kings 5:26). What was happening to me felt absolutely physical.

We see this same confusion when Paul wrote, "*I know a man in Christ who was caught up to the third heaven, **whether in the body or the spirit, I do not know**" (see 2 Cor. 12:2-3). Paul could not tell if he was caught up to Heaven in his earthly or spirit body, because they felt identical. Likewise, Peter had a bodily experience with an angel, which he thought was only happening in his spirit in a vision (see Acts 12:9).

My mind flew into a panic, trying to grasp what was happening. I knew I had to rebuke this thing immediately, or this vile act would continue to its completion. Still partially asleep, I heard myself say aloud, "I renounce you! I rebuke you!" And at that moment, it was gone. The whole assault may have lasted three seconds, the time it took me to wake up enough to rebuke it.

The dream had suddenly been replaced with what felt like physical reality, at the speed of thought. I was stunned and horrified as I got up to spend my early morning time with the Lord.

I remembered that almost two years earlier, the Lord had warned me that the next time I would face a test of seduction, it would be far more powerful than the first test. The earlier test took place in a dream that is recorded in my first book.[2] The Lord had also warned me that the consequences for failing the coming test would be far more deadly, even a matter of life or death. I'm not sure what He meant by that, but I certainly did not want to find out.

We are in a real battle, and the stakes are very high. There are real casualties and consequences of failure to overcome the onslaughts of the evil one. Whether the Church is ready or not, these terribly devised strategies are coming and even now are upon the Lord's chosen ones to destroy them. Just as Balaam found the perfect strategy of seduction to destroy Israel before they crossed over into their inheritance, so the enemy is looking to defile the Lord's army before they can reap the final harvest.

I realized that this terrible test took place after an awesome four-hour power dream, where I was learning to minister to the Lord's people as He ministered to them through me. This ministry is a type of the "Promised Land," in which we will move with the very words, feelings, healings, and impartations that the Lord desires to impart to His people.

But instead of waking up excited and happy about all that the Lord had taught me in the heavenly dream, I was disgusted by what the enemy was permitted to do to me at the ending of the second dream. Apparently, he was granted this permission because "the woman" was too concerned with not hurting the stranger's feelings and was too weak in protesting his strong enticements. Even so, the enemy's permission to assault me was limited, while I was granted a few seconds to wake up and use my only weapon before it was too late.

I realized when I awoke that the woman must have been a thinly disguised "me," since I was the one under attack, the moment she failed her test. *The dream ended at the very same moment that my nightmarish reality began.*

This taught me that at least in some cases, we are held responsible for what we do in dreams. The enemy can be granted permission to assault us based on how we respond to tests in our dreams, if these tests and assaults are permitted by the Lord. I do think that there may be some dreams where we do weird and uncharacteristic things that the Lord does not hold us responsible for. I am adding this so that the reader does not fall into unnecessary guilt over various behaviors in dreams.

It happens that the night I finished writing this section, I dreamed that I did recreational drugs with my brother. I have no idea why I did that, since I have not used any substances for over 30 years, nor have I ever dreamed about doing drugs. But just after writing that we are responsible for our behavior in dreams, this dream occurred. When I woke up, I repented for having used drugs in my dream, just in case the Lord held me responsible. In the case of the seduction test, however, I was indeed held responsible.

As I discussed this awful incident with the Lord, I knew that He did not want me to take offense at what He had permitted to happen to me. *I would have previously said that the Lord would never let something like that happen to a believer who was not sinning or opening any unclean doors in her life or thoughts.* But the fact of the matter is that He did permit it.

Therefore, we need to know how terrible the onslaughts will be in these last days against those who strive to walk at the highest and holiest levels of intimacy with the Lord Jesus.

As It Was in the Days of Noah

This incident caused me to think very hard about a strange and controversial passage found in Genesis:

> *Now it came to pass, when men began to multiply on the face of the earth, and daughters were born to them, that the sons of God saw the daughters of men, that they were beautiful; and they took wives for themselves of all whom they chose....There were giants on the earth in those days, and also afterward, when the sons of God came in to the daughters of men and they bore children to them* (Genesis 6:1-2, 4a).

Having read this passage in the original Hebrew, it is not easy to twist it into a meaning outside of the obvious meaning. I realize that some Christian scholars have concluded that it cannot possibly mean what it says. They would say, "How could fallen angelic beings have sexual relations with mortal women and impregnate them?" I can certainly understand why they would feel this way. However, this is what the biblical text says quite plainly.

The Hebrew expression for "sons of God" is *b'nei haElohim*; this phrase is used in other Scriptures to refer to angels (see Job 1;6, 2:1, Ps. 29:1). We see further support for this in Jude 6-7. Although I don't fully understand how procreation could take place between fallen angels and mortal women, I simply believe that this is exactly what the Scriptures tell us. There are certainly a number of biblical cases where angelic beings take on human flesh and form.

For example, Jacob was visited by a strong angel who came in the flesh; he wrestled with this angel all night long in his fleshly body. The angel was physically able to overpower him and put his hip out of joint. If the Angel of the Lord could come in the flesh and permanently affect Jacob's body, why couldn't a high-ranking fallen angelic being come in the flesh and permanently affect a woman's body?

According to Genesis, these women gave birth to a hybrid seed of men, who were larger than normal men. They corrupted the lineage of mankind, through whom the Lord planned to send a Savior, who would crush the serpent's head (see Gen. 3:15). Satan needed to thwart God's plan of salvation, which would come from a particular human descent. And so the human genealogy was polluted, and the Lord destroyed all flesh but eight people in the flood.

In the NKJV, the verse reads, *"This is the genealogy of Noah. Noah was a just man, perfect in his generations"* (Gen. 6:9). The Hebrew text literally says, *"This is the genealogy of Noah. Noah was a righteous man, **his generations were pure.**"* Since all men are sinful, we know that the phrase "pure generations" cannot mean utterly sinless. Thus, it must mean "uncorrupted" with bad seed, which was sown into the human genome.

Noah had three sons, and the son who would produce the Messianic lineage was Shem. From his loins came Abraham, Isaac, and Jacob, and from Jacob came the tribe of Judah. From Judah came King David, who was the ancestor of both Joseph and Miriam (Mary), the earthly parents of Jesus the Messiah. Although Joseph was not Jesus' biological father, he was His legal and ancestral father, and God the Father needed both parents to be descended from the lineage of King David.

Thus, the Lord thwarted satan's plan to prevent a pure, royal, Jewish seed from giving the world a Savior. This Savior would come to destroy the works of the devil, and the devil would do anything to prevent His arrival on the earth. Glory to God in the highest, for He was born from the *pure generations* that sprang from Noah's son, Shem.

For those interested in an in-depth study on this topic and its last-days' implications, I recommend an outstanding teaching series offered by author and speaker Paul Keith Davis.[3] This teaching explores the Lord Yeshua's warning, *"As it was in the days of Noah, so it will be at the coming of the Son of Man"* (Matt. 24:37 NIV).

In these messages, we learn that the terrible and demonic evils that abounded in Noah's day will also be present in these final years leading up to the Lord's return. Paul Keith explains, *"What overcame Noah's generation must be overcome by our generation."*

The enemy also desires to corrupt the perfect seeds of life-giving food that the Father created. Most grains, vegetables, and fruits we now eat have been tampered with genetically—something the Lord never intended, since He created all the seeds of life with their perfect DNA. Genetically engineered wheat and other crops cannot reproduce effectively in the following growing season. Therefore, farmers in poor nations who have received our engineered seeds will starve to death the next year, as these crops do not come up.

As it was in the days of Noah, when the enemy tampered with the human seed, so today his evil scheme to destroy life has come full circuit. Once again, he tampers with the seeds of life, including the human genome, with human cooperation.

A Lawless Church

The Lord Yeshua rebukes the church in Pergamos this way:

> You have people there who hold to the teaching of Balaam, who taught Balak to entice the Israelites to sin by eating food sacrificed to idols and by committing sexual immorality (Revelation 2:14b).

The blunt truth is that sexual immorality in the Church today is a snare of epic proportions. The Church, across *all* of its various streams, movements, and denominations, is impure and corrupted with sexual sin. They are committing acts of immorality at the foot of the cross, while the Lord looks down with shame and agony, knowing that His suffering and death was offered to save them from the curse of sin. Hebrews tells us that when they do this, they are crucifying Him again and putting Him to open shame (see Heb. 6:4-6). When Christians deliberately sin, thinking they will repent later, it is like breathing in poison gas and thinking they can exhale it later.

There are currently a very great number of Christians and leaders who are committing sexual immorality on an ongoing basis, without being disciplined by those to whom they are accountable. In fact, some of those in leadership are not accountable to anyone, and they continue in this activity for years, while retaining their positions of control and leadership. Somehow, these Christian leaders do not realize what the cost will be to their eternal souls when they stand before the Lord.

The Lord Yeshua warned us that those who have done miracles in His Name, but who are "lawless" and do not do the will of the Father, will not enter the Kingdom of Heaven. The Lord will tell them, *"I never knew you"* (see Matt. 7:22-23). In Greek, the word for *lawless* is *anomia*, which literally means "without the Law."[4] To be "lawless" in this verse means to show careless contempt for God's righteous standards of behavior that He expects of His people.

Not only have I heard many reports and news stories of this type of sin in church leadership, but a number of people I know personally have been damaged and have experienced church divisions over this very issue. The following story is true and is representative of many cases of spiritual and sexual abuse of naïve believers by pastors or other spiritual leaders.

Since there is nothing new under the sun, we see that in ancient Israel, the sons of Eli the priest committed the same kind of abuse as what is happening in the church today. We also see the same warnings in the New Testament, particularly in the letters of Jude and Peter, and in the Book of Revelation.

> *Now Eli, who was very old, heard about everything his sons were doing to all Israel and how they slept with the women who served at the entrance to the Tent of Meeting* (1 Samuel 2:22 NIV).

With eyes full of adultery, they never stop sinning; they seduce the unstable (2 Peter 2:14a NIV).

Because this book is holy, the following story will only provide a general description of the sinful behavior that this particular pastor committed in an ongoing way. He did this while preaching the Word mightily every week, praying for healings, seeing signs and wonders in his church, and spending hours studying the Bible. This took place in a charismatic church, although this story is in no way meant to accuse charismatic churches in particular.

Almost every good work that the Lord Jesus desires to do among His people can be counterfeited by the enemy. We cannot throw out the baby with the bathwater, but must exercise discernment. We must test the *fruit* of a church and its leaders, and not merely judge by the spiritual gifts that are in operation. Sadly, there is sin across the camps of the Lord's Church: the mainline, the evangelical, and the charismatic. For obvious reasons, all names and identities have been replaced with fictional names.

MINDY'S STORY

Mindy was 20 when she was invited to attend DayStar Church. She was hungry for a church where she could be spiritually fed, and so she began attending. When she first saw Pastor Jim and his wife Gloria, she was surprised that they dressed like "bikers from the '80s." She found that refreshing and different.

When Mindy arrived, her heart was judgmental toward her father's church, where he was the pastor. She held resentment toward him, believing his church was dead. In addition, her father's cultural background caused him to be unaffectionate as Mindy grew up, leaving her vulnerable and insecure, always looking for affirmations and fatherly love.

On her first visit to DayStar, during the worship, Mindy stood in the back with her face to the wall and began to worship freely, as she was desperate to find the Lord's presence and purposes for her life. As she worshiped, she sensed someone staring at her. She turned, and it was Pastor Jim. She felt a little intimidated, wondering if she was a distraction, but kept worshiping.

During Pastor Jim's teaching, Mindy took thorough notes, believing that some day she would attain to the level where she could understand the deep revelations he was teaching. Afterward, she met Jim and Gloria. She told them she believed the Lord had sent her there to help her father's church come back to the Lord. She made it very clear to them that she had deep issues with her parents. Jim then prayed for her, and she sensed a strong presence, which she assumed was an impartation of the Holy Spirit. For the next two days, she felt like there was a blanket of glory around her.

The next week, Jim told Mindy that he had been praying for her concerning her dad. This greatly boosted her, to know that she had made such an impression on him. She began to sense that her destiny was unfolding, as the vision of this church embodied everything that was in her heart. She believed that she was going to be a part of a true New Testament church that would impact the coming revival to her region. Mindy had found her spiritual home.

Jim began to "disciple" Mindy and spoke about being a spiritual father to her. Her parents were not happy about her attending this church and did not trust Jim. He and Gloria advised her not to listen to her parents' advice, as it was given from "a religious spirit."

Soon, Pastor Jim told Mindy that she had a great call on her life, and that she would be traveling with him to many nations, seeing revival, healing, and deliverances. He even talked about her moving in with them, saying that she would be a daughter to him.

Since Mindy was very insecure, vulnerable, and had a low self-image, she gladly absorbed his praise, affirmations, and affection. She began to wish that Jim were her father, instead of her own. She found a place of such acceptance with Jim that it met her need to be loved, admired, favored, and accepted by her own father. During church each week, he would spend so much time with Mindy that people started to notice and comment on it.

Jim began to spend more and more time alone with her. He explained to her the importance of his ministry and how elevated his role in the Spirit was over the region. She felt flattered that a man of such caliber found her worthy of such special attention. Gradually, he increased the gestures of physical comfort and affection that he expressed to her. This began with holding her hand and continued with long, private hugs, back rubs, and similar gestures. She was also invited to homeschool their children and spent much time at Jim and Gloria's home. Perhaps Gloria needed and appreciated the help with the children and the housework and was therefore not concerned about Mindy's extended time in their home. An important factor in Mindy's vulnerability is that she had been molested over a number of years as a child by a young male babysitter. He was the son of one of their church elders. She shared with me that whenever she felt mistrustful or uncomfortable with Pastor Jim's advances, she concluded that her fear was because of her past abuse, rather than because Jim was violating the pastoral relationship. She believed that by accepting his long, fatherly hugs, she was letting down a wall of fear from her past.

The relationship progressed over many months, including daily phone calls, text messages, secrecy, and as much time alone together as possible. They became obsessive in their need for contact.

The rest of this terrible story can be summarized briefly. Pastor Jim gradually increased the physical and sexual nature of his contacts with Mindy. Gloria seemed to be conveniently away on many occasions, or Jim and Mindy were somehow alone in many contrived trips and situations. She was obsessed with his love, attention, and flattery about her spiritual depths and destiny. Whenever she protested that what they were doing seemed inappropriate and obviously sexual, he perpetually insisted that nothing they were doing was sexual, but was rather a deep spiritual bond between a father and his most favored daughter. Mindy had no prior sexual experience, and I believe this contributed to her naïveté. The Holy Spirit repeatedly gave Mindy conscience "checks," but because of the gradual escalation, her neediness, and Jim's superior spiritual status, she allowed herself to be deceived over a long period of time.

On one occasion, an intercessor at the church actually called Jim when she learned about a "sleepover" Mindy and Jim were having, but Jim politely thanked her and hung up. He justified everything as perfectly fine.

Incredibly, Pastor Jim quoted Song of Solomon verses and even prayed aloud for God to send revival to their region, while engaging in sexual behavior. I found this level of hypocrisy and deception almost impossible to believe. However, this is a true account. Originally, the idea was that he would "disciple" Mindy and that they would study the Bible together. However, this never happened.

Mindy became more confused, depressed, and guilty over time, and yet she was afraid to confide in anyone. Even so, she was also addicted to Jim's love and affection. She went to Jim about her emotional turmoil, but he treated it as "not a big deal." She began to have breakdowns at church, as her soul was confused and disturbed, but no one knew why she was so distraught. It felt so wrong in her spirit, yet she wanted it. Jim still insisted that it was the Father's heart that was bringing healing to her. I do believe that Jim actually believed this deceptive justification until the situation had become glaringly sexual.

After a long and progressive decline into blatant sin, when lust had finally grown to a point where the obvious nature of this thing couldn't be denied, Jim had a moment of conviction. He stepped back, knowing that this act was wrong. One might wonder why he didn't realize this long before, but at least the man must have had some thin residue of his God-given conscience. Although Jim felt convicted with regard to the sexual sin, he did not realize what emotional, physical, and spiritual damage he had wrought on this young woman. He did not understand that he had not merely sinned against God, but against Mindy as well.

From this point on, Jim pushed Mindy away and avoided her, viewing her as needy and unappealing. His intense favor and obsession suddenly turned to utter rejection! This reminded me of the biblical story when King David's son Amnon raped his half-sister Tamar, thinking he was lovesick for her. But the moment the rape was over, he despised her more than he had loved her (see 2 Samuel 13:1-16). Jim's sudden rejection, not only of the physical relationship, but also of Mindy as a dear friend, caused this unstable girl to exhibit obsessive anger and to pursue legitimate closure and repentance. But Jim and Gloria closed ranks around this sinful interlude to minimize and contain the damage. And Mindy was left out in the cold, with no one she was allowed to tell.

Jim quickly found a new teenage girl to "disciple," and Mindy's torment, rejection, and mental instability grew alarmingly. She felt she was reliving the abuse of her past, but because the abuse was at the hands of her pastor, she had no one she could consult.

She then submitted to counseling and "deliverance" ministry at this same church, although the counselors did not know about her relationship with the pastor. She was hoping to be "delivered" of her past issues concerning abuse. However, the counseling they practiced on her was very dangerous and irresponsible, and I'll share a bit more about this particular practice in a moment.

Jim "helpfully" suggested antidepressants for Mindy's chemical imbalance. He was very afraid of her mental instability and that she would tell someone what had happened. It would have been convenient for him if he could stabilize her with a chemical, instead of entering true weeping and repentance on her behalf. Later, Jim and Gloria urged Mindy never to tell anyone what had happened, as if this advice was in her best interests. They warned her that her future husband would not want her if he knew she was not pure. She was told to delete all e-mails and evidence that this affair took place, which she did.

Since then, the Lord has restored Mindy's relationship with her family. She repented to her father for rejecting him and placing Jim as her father. She repented for rejecting her parents' counsel. The pain and damage she experienced from Jim was far worse than any unintentional rejection she had felt from her dad.

The biggest factors in Mindy being deceived and seduced were these:

1. She was wounded because of past sexual abuse.

2. Mindy was rebellious against her parents, who were not perfect, but who loved her.

3. Mindy repeatedly ignored the "check" she felt in her spirit, concerning Jim's physical advances.

4. Insecurity and desire for fatherly love and a man's approval left Mindy open to misplaced affection.

5. She believed that if a church has "good" worship, miracles, or healings, the Lord must approve of it, and the pastor must be an upright man.

6. Mindy was so afraid of "judging" Jim that she threw away her God-given discernment.

I will conclude this shameful narrative here, except to issue one final warning to the Lord's Bride. The counterfeit church discussed in this story employed a particular counseling method on their members that was dangerous and destabilizing.

It is not the purpose of this book to detail this form of spiritual/psychological abuse practiced by some churches, but it is a counseling method that opens the door to demonic deception and oppression in those who submit to it. I have a master's degree in counseling, and I'm going to exploit my degree for one minute to warn you and your loved ones.

If you encounter a "biblical" counselor who tells you that you have multiple personalities inside yourself and encourages you to "talk to" and "listen to" the various voices or "parts" inside your own soul, run for your life! *It is a recipe for mental illness and demonic invasion.* Go to a true biblical counselor!

A true counselor will teach you the biblical principles of repentance and how to appropriate the truths about who you are in God's eyes. He or she will help you to receive healing from Jesus in all the broken places in your soul. This healing is often gradual, but can also come in a huge download of healing and freedom from the Spirit of the Lord. It is different for each unique child of God, but He will always use *His truth* to heal and cleanse your heart.

I understand that this is a big topic, and I should not be simplifying years of psychiatric theories. I also understand that some forms of child abuse are so hideous and satanic that the victim does indeed fragment inside as a protective mechanism. Nevertheless, this method of counseling at the hands of unqualified church counselors *leads to false revelations of the past.* Sometimes the truth is quite simple: Jesus can and *must* heal the fragmented, wounded soul, rather than engaging the "voices" in our soul in a dialogue. The enemy's minions would just love to play the role of your inner voices! They can tell you any lie about your past, and you will believe it because you think it is your own voice.

The Lord God created us with one spirit, one soul, and one body. The only voice you should ever listen for "inside," is the voice of the crucified, resurrected, and glorified Jesus the Messiah, who speaks to us through His Holy Spirit. He will never manifest as multiple personalities or parts of your soul. The enemy will, though. And the only one you should talk to in your innermost heart is this same Jesus. If you are a sincere, repentant follower of Yeshua the Messiah, He lives in you, and He is the only "other" personality allowed to reside there. Amen!

MARTHA'S STORY

I will now provide one more example of secret sin in a pastor's life as it affected a church member, rather than the woman he seduced. As before, this woman's name and details have been changed.

Martha rededicated her life to the Lord later in life, after being raised in a denominational church. She joined a contemporary, nondenominational church, and was immediately impressed by the love, joy, and sense of community of the people there. It was unlike any church she had attended, and Martha found it refreshing, authentic, and grounded on biblical principles. She soon became involved in an outreach ministry and started taking classes offered by the leadership. Within a year, she was baptized by immersion and became a member of the church.

The pastor was very charismatic and taught from the Scriptures; people were accepting the Lord Jesus each week. Martha was exhilarated to find a church that welcomed *all* people and followed the teachings of Jesus. A few weeks after she began attending, she asked the pastor to come and pray for a family member who was dying. Although he did not know the family, he came and ministered to the woman in a gentle and nurturing way, praying for her and reading Scripture. Martha was growing spiritually, and she loved using her gifts to help out at the church.

After she had belonged to this dedicated church family for a year and a half, it came to light that the pastor was having a sinful relationship with a woman in the church. This had been going on for some years. Suddenly, the man who had been revered for his dedication to the Lord, the church, and his family, was exposed in blatant and continual sin. This secret sin destroyed the pastor's own family, the other woman's family, and the flock he had been leading for over three years. The far-reaching devastation of this ongoing deception was unbelievable. Martha wondered how he could stand up each week and exhort the flock not to go after worldly things for comfort, when in fact he was doing exactly this.

The pastor was dismissed, and there appeared to be no repentance on his part. The other leaders of the church began to pick up the pieces and start again. As the people came together in the aftermath, the Lord's presence brought them a sense of joy and unity that Martha hadn't experienced up to that point.

There was a feeling of being set free as she suddenly realized how much they had been under the influence of this man, his ego, and his grand scheme for this church. He had made it more about him and his vision for this church than about the Lord. Many realized that they had been unduly influenced by this pastor and had followed him more than following Jesus. Whenever a leader in the church falls into sin, *it is vital that the people turn their eyes on the Lord Yeshua* and follow hard after Him, rather than wallowing in the betrayal and hypocrisy of their leader.

In hindsight, Martha realized there were some red flags. First, there was a lack of accountability over this pastor. He had orchestrated the leadership structure so that he was in total control. They trusted him, but realized later that not requiring accountability was a big mistake.

Second, the pastor was unnecessarily spending church funds that they could not afford, more to impress others than to further the Kingdom.

Third, the pastor and the woman were meeting privately, but no one wanted to question the situation. It was awkward to suspect impropriety in a man who is beloved and trusted.

Last, it came to light that the younger leaders whom he was mentoring felt more held back and suppressed than nourished and encouraged. It turned out that the pastor's way of keeping control was to subtly tear others down and make them feel unworthy, and to pit people against each other.

Any of us could potentially fall into momentary sin. But the moment we are made aware that we have fallen, whether in thought or deed, we must humbly go before the Lord in repentance. We must never presume on the Lord's grace by continuing in the sin deliberately. How far His Bride has fallen! She has played the harlot, as did Israel before her. She has fallen into Balaam's snare and has been seduced by immorality. As satan knows and exploited so skillfully in the days of Balaam, this will cause the Lord to send judgments upon His own people.

> *If we deliberately keep on sinning after we have received the knowledge of the truth,* **no sacrifice for sins is left,** *but only a fearful expectation of judgment and of raging fire that will consume the enemies of God* (Hebrews 10:26-27 NIV).

> **For it is time for judgment to begin with the family of God;** *and if it begins with us, what will the outcome be for those who do not obey the gospel of God? And, "If it is hard for the righteous to be saved, what will become of the ungodly and sinner?"* (1 Peter 4:17-18 NIV)

A word that the Lord is speaking to His leaders and to all His people in these last days is *"Hypocrites will be judged."* When I hear this warning, it puts the fear of the Lord in me, and I ask the Lord to search my heart once again to make sure there is no wicked way in me (see Ps. 139:23-24).

BALAAM: TRUE OR FALSE PROPHET?

As we study the fruits of this complex man who had a genuine prophetic gift, we remain perplexed by the inconsistencies we find. On the one hand, Balaam was known to resort to sorcery, sacrificial feasts offered to idols, and payment by powerful rulers to bring either good fortune or curses upon various people groups.

On the other hand, he called God by His Hebraic covenant name and proclaimed his loyalty and obedience to His word, even at the risk of angering a wealthy king. He was privileged to see into the spirit realm and was obedient to prophesy only what the Lord showed him. Toward the end of his unsuccessful employment by Balak, Balaam was moved in his heart with affection toward the simple beauty of Israel's tribal encampments in the desert. God's love for Israel touched something in him, and for a brief moment, he aligned himself with the tender emotions of the God of Israel toward His covenant people.

On the third hand, after his seeming conversion and "revival" into the true prophetic ministry, Balaam devised a wicked scheme of seduction and trained the Midianites to corrupt this same people that he had recently blessed. In the end, Moses insisted that this man be executed as part of the vengeance inflicted on Midian, who led Israel into adultery just before attaining the long-awaited inheritance of the good land.

Although Balaam had prophesied, *"May my end be as theirs,"* indeed, it was not so. The end of his life was violent and without mercy, at the hands of those he enticed with crafty intent. Isaiah tells us that the end of those who practice divination is the sword:

> *But as for you who forsake the Lord and forget My holy mountain, who spread a table for Fortune and fill bowls of mixed wine for Destiny, I will destine you for the sword* (Isaiah 65:11-12a NIV).

As the fortune tellers prepared bowls of mixed wine for divination, so Balaam's heart was a bowl of mixed wine, a mixture of truth and falsehood.

Balaam was used to dealing with many gods from the nations. Every ethnic group had its own version of a false god, which Paul tells us were actually demons (see 1 Cor. 10:20). The people knew how to appease the demons, who demanded sacrifice, self-mutilation, sorcery, and divination. At first, Balaam thought that Israel was just one of the nations and that the Lord *Yehovah* was like the other gods. If Balaam performed the right sacrifices and the right incantations, Israel's god could be influenced or outbid.

But Balaam began to realize that he was dealing with the one true God. In his first oracle, he said, *"I see a people who live apart and do not consider* themselves one of the nations" (Num. 23:9 NIV). Having met a deity who was stronger than magic tricks, he proclaimed, "*There is no sorcery against Jacob, no divination against Israel*" (Num. 23:23).

He believed in the one true God in his mind, and yet his heart was not walking in a lifelong commitment to this personal God. He felt that his options were still open when the Lord was finished chastising him over the Balak debacle. *Balaam did not love the Lord from a heart of devotion, although he respected His supernatural abilities.*

In the end, the Lord would say to Balaam,

> *Yes, you prophesied in My name. Yes, you were privileged to see the Angel of the Lord. Yes, you even had supernatural communication with a donkey. Yes, you obeyed Me and blessed My people before the raging nations. But I never knew you! You do not love and revere Me as your creator. You are not a son after My own heart! Depart from Me, you lawless one!*

Does this not remind you of Matthew 7:22-23? As it was in the days of Balaam, so it is in the end-times Church. Even a false prophet can speak a true word when compelled by the Spirit of God to do so. *The Lord is teaching His people that false prophets can say true things.*

If false prophets only told lies, no one would believe them or be deceived. The Lord Yeshua warned us that in the last days there will be many false prophets, so deceptive that even the elect could be deceived if it were possible (see Matt. 24:23-25). For something to be this subtle and deceptive, the false prophet must be saying truth mingled with falsehood. Or, he will begin by teaching true doctrine, and then, when the people trust him, he will gradually mingle in strange and heretical teachings. But the Church will be seduced and deceived and will assume it must be true, since his earlier teachings were true.

We must expect doctrines to appear on the scene which will be a mixture of true and false, and our discernment must be more finely tuned than it is now.

This is one of the things that the Lord wants to cultivate in us. The Lord wants His people to listen carefully to all that a prophet or teacher says. Even if there is genuine truth spoken, we must not assume that the whole package is true. We must know the whole counsel of Scripture, or we too could be deceived in this perilous generation!

The Bride of Yeshua is about to cross over into her Promised Land, and the enemy will unleash many forms of deception. As we move into discerning true and false prophecy, as well as true and false revival, the Lord wants His people to be very aware of the kinds of deceptions that will come against us. These will be difficult tests for us; if it were easy, the Lord Yeshua would not have said, *"Even the elect would be deceived if possible"* (see Matt. 24:24).

In the next chapter, we will look more carefully at distinguishing the true from the false—in the charismatic church in particular. We will look at true and false prophecies and revivals. May the Lord grant us the wisdom to know the difference, that we might be wise virgins.

Paul wrote to the Corinthians that all the judgments that befell Israel during the desert wanderings were written as an example to the Church. These warnings were given so that we do not fall into the same traps and suffer the same wrath that Israel suffered. The fact that Balaam is used as a warning three times in the New Testament lets us know that **there will be truth mingled with falsehood in the last-days' Church**, as well as powerful enticements coming against us.

May we have the spiritual eyes of the donkey, that we would see the Angel of the Lord standing before us with drawn sword in hand. May our eyes be opened that we would discern the true from the false, which will be subtle and deceptive. *May we not compromise our moral standards by turning a blind eye to warning signs of immorality in our flocks or our leaders.* May we speak only blessings over Israel and the Jewish people that the Lord may bless us. Amen.

Endnotes

1. Rick Joyner, *The Prophetic Ministry* (Charlotte, NC: MorningStar Publications, 1997).

2. *Coffee Talks With Messiah*. This dream is recorded in Chapter 4, in the section appropriately entitled, "The Warning of Balaam."

3. To browse the extensive books and teachings of Paul Keith Davis, as well as many other anointed ministers of the present and past generations, go to www.whitedoveministries.org. The series on the Days of Noah is an mp3 downloadable teaching series. I have greatly benefited from Paul Keith's bold and prophetic presentation of the unique challenges facing this last generation before the Lord's return.

4. See http://www.studylight.org/lex/grk/view.cgi?number=458.

Chapter 12

True and False Revival

THE Lord Jesus and the apostles warned us that there will be false prophets, counterfeit signs, and lying wonders, false messiahs and strong delusion in the last days. The Lord's people must be given clear guidelines to distinguish between true revival that is a work of the Holy Spirit, and a false revival that looks spectacular, but that is "strange fire" in the Lord's eyes. How will we know, and by what shall we be warned? *The fruit and character of professing Christians will be the proof of their authenticity, whether for good or for evil.* Just as the Lord told us that we will know people by their fruits, so we will know whether a movement or revival is true or false by its fruits.

Before we examine these distinctions, let us be clear about one thing. It is a fact that there will be false doctrines and false revivals. Even so, this doesn't mean that there will not also be true apostles and prophets, and a true revival that will produce a great harvest of redeemed, healed, and sanctified souls for the Kingdom.

Before we look at revival meetings, let us examine what an individual Christian would display after experiencing *personal revival*. This would always include having a genuine encounter with the Spirit of the Lord and with His Word. Merely knowing God's written Word does not produce heart transformation. There is a response of the heart that must embrace the Person and work of the Lord Jesus, as well as God's Word as a living, transforming reality in our innermost being. Personal revival is when the Holy Spirit breathes power and life into biblical truths, causing our hearts to be transformed into the likeness of Yeshua's heart, thoughts, and motivations (see Eph. 4:11-13).

WHAT DOES PERSONAL REVIVAL LOOK LIKE?

There are themes already covered in the previous chapters that are the signposts of a truly consecrated believer:

+ Humility and meekness of heart;

+ Loving the Lord with all our heart, all our soul, and all our strength;

+ Asking the Lord to circumcise from our hearts carnal strongholds and sinful thought patterns;

+ Consecrating our lifestyles by being separate from the values and whoredom of the world's systems;

+ Being holy and set apart in our speech, thoughts, and behaviors;

+ Having the lowly heart of a servant toward others rather than a superior or haughty attitude;

+ Not desiring human admiration and recognition;

+ Having a broken and contrite heart, which is quick to repent when sin is found;

+ Entering into repentance and weeping on behalf of those who are oppressed, enslaved, starved, and sexually abused,

and for the innocent blood of the unborn, shed in our
nation to this very day.

At some point, a believer who has encountered the Lord will begin to walk in a new level of supernatural power, such as tongues, words of knowledge, dreams, visions, healings, and miracles. However, you can have a deep and genuine encounter with the Lord for a long time, without receiving miraculous gifts at that moment. *Fruits are more important than gifts when it comes to testing authenticity.*

This last generation is marked by a terrible trend of self-centeredness, pride, rebellion, greed, and sexual immorality, which is not limited to unchurched atheists. In fact, when Paul wrote to Timothy about this godless trend, he was warning him more about false believers than outright unbelievers!

> *But mark this: There will be terrible times in the last days. People will be lovers of themselves, lovers of money, boastful, proud, abusive, disobedient to their parents, ungrateful, unholy, without love, unforgiving, slanderous, without self-control, brutal, not lovers of the good, treacherous, rash, conceited, lovers of pleasure rather than lovers of God—**having a form of godliness** but denying its power* (2 Timothy 3:1-5a NIV).

All of these ugly traits described by Paul are the opposite of those traits listed before, which bear the mark of true personal sanctification. And so, before the Church clamors for a great end-time revival, in which we draw many souls into the Lord's Kingdom, we must each take a hard look at our own hearts privately and in the presence of the Lord.

As we have seen in the parable of the wheat and the tares, the bad seed, which is the sons of the evil one, are permitted to grow to maturity, alongside the sons of the Kingdom. The Lord tells us that at the end of the age, the harvesting angels will gather all stumbling blocks and those who commit lawlessness, and will remove them before bringing in the good crop (see Matt. 13:24-30; 37-43).

In his outstanding book, *Angels That Gather*, Paul Keith Davis explains that not only will these angels gather and remove evil people from the harvest fields, but they are also assigned to gather out the tares within our hearts.[1] The tares or weeds in the hearts of believers represent soulish strongholds, besetting habits, unclean obsessions, and deeply held false patterns of thinking and behaving that separate us from our holy Lord. As He uproots our tares with our permission, His Spirit also is faithful to heal the broken and wounded places in our hearts that were open doors to unrighteousness.

The Lord Jesus told us, *"Blessed are the pure in heart, for they shall see God"* (Matt. 5:8). The Lord desires to uproot every area of our soul that is not fully yielded to His Lordship and righteous requirements. This deliberate cleansing and purification of our hearts is a prerequisite to experience the full measure of Messiah's character and maturity in our lives. Paul writes about building up the Body of Messiah, so that we may *"come to the unity of the faith and of the knowledge of the Son of God, to a perfect man, to the measure of the stature of the fullness of Christ"* (Eph. 4:12-13).

This cleansing will not happen to us automatically. If we do not ask the Lord to search us, circumcise our hearts, and uproot the tares He reveals to us, He will very politely leave us in our present condition. This, in turn, will disqualify us from participating in the coming revival and the great harvest. The Lord of the harvest must trust His harvesters. Would you hire harvesters who would misappropriate the grain they were gathering from your field?

We must grow up into the full stature of Messiah as individuals. Then, when even a small group of such dedicated soldiers come together, we see the small flames that will ignite into corporate revival. It would be like building a house with bricks that had been strengthened and tempered in a kiln. If the individual bricks are faulty, the structure will be unsound. The Lord is building a Body of living stones. The corporate revival is a reflection of the quality of each individual stone who is crying out for revival.

We must ask the Lord to look deep into our hearts and show us what His holy eyes see there. Otherwise, how can we save and disciple unbelievers who come to our revival meetings? Can we disciple others above the level to which we ourselves have attained?

ARE WE READY FOR GOD'S GLORY?

We will all stand before the judgment throne of the Messiah. If we have deliberate, ongoing, hidden sins in our hearts, surely it will be too late to repent of them when we stand before the Judge! On that day, our eternal destiny will be sealed, and hypocrites will have their place in the lake of fire. We must repent now, while there is still time. He is still a sacrificed Lamb, full of grace and compassion, but when the Lord Yeshua comes back, He will appear as a dreadful, righteous Judge. Before His wrath, even the earth and sky will flee away (see Rev. 6:16-17). And what will *we* do on that day?

Yes, the day of judgment is still a future event. But do we understand that when the glory of God enters a room, it is like the Righteous Judge is already standing before us? His holy presence can be dangerous to casual, carnal, and disobedient Christians. It would be as if the day of reckoning has just come down to earth *now*, instead of waiting until we face the Judge later in heaven. Although we all say that we want revival, do you know what would happen if the glory of God would come into a meeting where some professing Christians are living in secret sin or compromised lifestyles?

It has been the Lord's mercy not to come down as He did in the days of the tabernacle and Solomon's temple. The Lord knows that if He were to visit us with His holiness at this time, many of His people would die needlessly in this fearsome presence, due to hypocrisy and evil attitudes.

He is the same God whose holiness killed Aaron's sons, when they offered strange and unauthorized worship. His holiness killed Uzzah, who presumed to casually touch the Lord's manifest presence. His holiness killed Ananias and Sapphira, Christians who lied to the Holy Spirit, in order to appear more generous than they really were. His holiness killed Korah and his followers, who were jealous of Moses and accused him of self-appointed authority.

Before corporate revival, we must experience personal revival, on an individual basis. Otherwise, we will be:

- easy prey for the enemy's counterfeit revivals, signs, and lying wonders which will deceive those who have not consecrated their lives privately before the Lord;

- in danger of being harmed by the holiness of the Lord when He enters the room;

- in danger of being swept away by the coming calamities and plagues, for which the lukewarm will not have supernatural protection;

- unable to exercise the needed authority over sickness, crippling afflictions, and demonic activity that will be brought to our revival meetings;

- unable to quickly deliver, equip, and disciple the demonized generation who will be saved in their thousands in our meetings;

- offended by the unseemly people the Lord puts in our midst as new believers.

Think about Mindy's situation in the last chapter: if the tares in her heart had been gathered and uprooted—the tares of insecurity, woundedness, rebellion, and needing human admiration—before she began attending DayStar Church, then she would easily have seen through Pastor Jim's deceptive enticements. **This is a perfect example of a person whose heart has not been cleansed, falling prey to counterfeit leaders and revivals.**

GODLY REVIVALS

We can look at the great revivals in recent history to see what character-istics accompanied a great harvest of souls coming to salvation. Some examples of past revivals include the evangelistic ministries of Charles Finney, Jonathan Edwards, and John Wesley.

As people sat under the preaching of these uncompromising leaders, they began to experience the fear of the Lord, which brought weeping and repentance for personal sins. Edwards preached on "Sinners in the Hands of an Angry God," and the people saw visions of hell opening up beneath them. Finney asked how this generation of vipers would escape damnation. As he preached, the Spirit of conviction caused people to fall from their seats and onto the floor, crying out for mercy so loudly that his voice could not be heard. [2]

We have seen the unprecedented evangelistic and healing ministry of Mrs. Maria Woodworth-Etter, beginning at the end of the nineteenth century and spanning four decades. And as the twentieth century dawned, we saw the Welsh revival, ignited by Evan Roberts and bringing in 100,000 Welsh souls.

THE LORD'S PURPOSE IN HEALING REVIVALS

In addition to these and other earlier revivalists, the Lord has continued to send powerful ministries into the twentieth century. These included the Pentecost revivals of Charles Parham and William J. Seymour in Los Angeles; the Canadian Latter Rain revival in North Battleford, Saskatchewan, in 1948; and the thousands of documented healings and salvations that occurred through the ministries of John G. Lake, Kathryn Kuhlman, and William Branham, spanning more than the first half of the twentieth century. These are only a sampling of the men and women who pioneered the last-days' outpouring of God's Spirit.

During these and other healing revivals, the Lord performed great numbers of documented healings, similar to those seen in the Gospels and in the Acts of the Apostles. *But was His purpose more than simply to alleviate suffering?*

The Father wanted to show the world that His Son, the Lord Jesus Christ (Yeshua the Messiah), is the same compassionate Man as when He walked the shores of Galilee and the streets of Jerusalem. As He healed then, so He heals now. The Lord's purpose in healing has always been to display His love, power, and willingness to heal, which should lead to *people repenting of their sins and accepting Him as Savior and Lord.* The Lord's predominant Kingdom theme has always been, *"Repent, for the Kingdom of God is at hand."*

Healings and deliverances are to set the captives free, but they are also a demonstration that the Kingdom of God had come. The Lord said,

> *But if I drive out demons by the Spirit of God, then the kingdom of God has come upon you* (Matthew 12:28 NIV).

The miracles He performed when He was on earth were to demonstrate Kingdom reality, as well as to alleviate suffering.

Sadly, although the Lord Yeshua healed so many, the religious leadership in Israel missed the day of their visitation. The majority of the nation did not repent and believe on a large scale, nor did they exhibit the fruit of radically transformed hearts.

In a similar vein, with respect to the great and godly healing revivals of the twentieth century, the fruit of lasting, national repentance did not flourish in the long run, despite the incredible miracles granted to these ministries. It is true that tens of thousands of individuals were saved, as well as healed. Even so, neither America nor Canada embraced the Lordship of Jesus on a national level. Lives were touched and changed, but it was still only in a remnant, as with Israel before us.

Despite huge numbers of documented healings of cancers, deformities, and crippling afflictions, people tended to embrace the signs more than the Person accomplishing the signs. One of the dangers of the human heart is that we can run after the healings without becoming intimate with Healer Himself.

America did not embrace the true and complete revival message of the great healing evangelists whom God sent to her. The crowds came for healings and miracles in their tens of thousands, but America did not produce the lasting fruit of repentance. We could rightly conclude that like Israel before us, we missed the day of our visitation, despite having the Healer in our midst. After giving us more than a decade to repent, the Lord removed the healing revival from our midst when it did not produce the changed hearts and lives for which it was sent.

WHAT DOES CORPORATE REVIVAL LOOK LIKE?

There is indeed a mighty revival coming that will fulfill the words of the Lord Yeshua. It will include the powerful preaching of the Gospel, accompanied by mighty demonstrations of supernatural power to heal, work creative miracles, cast out evil spirits, and raise the dead.

> *I tell you the truth, anyone who has faith in Me will do what I have been doing.* ***He will do even greater things than these,*** *because I am going to the Father* (John 14:12 NIV).

> *And these signs will follow those who believe: In My name they will cast out demons; they will speak with new tongues; they will take up serpents; and if they drink anything deadly, it will by no means hurt them; they will lay hands on the sick, and they will recover* (Mark 16:17-18 NKJV).

Daniel also speaks of the power, authority, and preaching of repentance found in those who know their God in the last days:

> But the people who know their God shall be strong, and carry out **great exploits**....Those who are wise shall shine like the brightness of the firmament, and **those who turn many to righteousness** like the stars forever and ever (Daniel 11:32b; 12:3).

The Lord's coming revival will bring in a great harvest of souls. The first wave of this harvest must be quickly trained in discipline, doctrine, and holiness. This great army will then become harvesters of the second wave: the massive, final, global harvest before the Lord's return.[3]

What will this revival look like? Do we picture a crowd of people shouting, praising, healing and being healed, with many receiving Jesus as their Lord and Savior? Yes, we should certainly expect excitement, praise, healings, miracles, and salvations. And we can also expect weeping, repentance, godly sorrow, and people lying prostrate on the floor before a holy God.

However, the sad reality is that there will be counterfeit revivals going on during the same time period as the true revivals. These two types of revival will be different from each other in character and fruit, but only those who are consecrated to the Lord will be able to discern the difference. There will be a different breed of excitement in the false revival: *strange fire!*

Some examples of strange fire are entertainment-type music and hype; fleshly manifestations and sensuality; worldly dancing that resembles a music video more than biblical worship; showmanship; leaders manipulating people to respond in certain ways, such as pushing them down in their fleshly strength; not allowing times of silence before the Lord; emphasis on dramatic signs, rather than reverent worship; a lack of repentance or tears; a lack of the fear of the Lord; a lack of biblical prayer, biblical preaching and teaching; and a lack of servant-like humility.

Strange fire is presumptuous; holy fire is based on what the Lord desires, and worshipers move prayerfully, not calling attention to themselves. Counterfeit revival is of the feelings and emotions of man; true revival is obedient to the Spirit of the Lord. True revival is careful not to grieve the Holy Spirit's gentle nudgings; false revival does what feels good at the moment. It is often focused on the anointing of one man or woman, or a small, elite group, rather than the Spirit-orchestrated participation of all believers in the room. It is more concerned with signs than works that serve a Kingdom purpose. Strange fire is never concerned with repentance or holiness.

I know an anointed and exceptional Pentecostal pastor who has had a number of angelic visitations, profound visionary experiences, and personal encounters with the Lord Yeshua. However, he shared that when he receives letters inviting him to come and preach, some will ask, "Do you have gold dust at your meetings?"

While this man would certainly welcome supernatural tokens, such as gold dust or gems, he is running hard after something greater. He desires to equip the Bride to walk in the powers of the age to come, as did our spiritual fathers in the Old and New Testaments, the great cloud of witnesses (see Heb. 6:5; 12:1). Enoch was translated to Heaven; Ezekiel was transported to other regions, both in the spirit and in his body; Paul was taken to the third heaven; Philip was bodily transported after leading the Ethiopian eunuch to salvation; Elijah stretched himself out on a dead boy, who then came to life; Jacob saw the angels of God ascending and descending from Heaven to earth; none of Samuel's prophetic words fell to the ground; Elisha's dead bones raised a dead man to life; Peter saw the secrets of Ananias and Sapphira's hearts and pronounced the Lord's judgment of death over them; Moses prophesied to the skies, and they poured forth hail, locusts, and darkness. Not to mention the works of our Lord Yeshua, who told us that we would do greater works than these.

It is always a joyful surprise when the Lord sends special gifts, such as gold dust. Who wouldn't be excited when that happens? But we must not use these rare and unpredictable signs as a standard for measuring the presence or purposes of the Lord in a given meeting. *He can be greatly pleased and intimately present in a meeting without sending any gold dust.* Our hearts must desire the greater purposes of God for this generation and not focus on the dramatic wonders.

Isaiah tells us that the sacrifice most desired by the Lord is *a broken and contrite heart* (see Isa. 57:15; 66:2). And Samuel tells us that *unquestioning obedience* is more valuable to the Lord than any number of sacrifices, no matter how costly (see 1 Sam. 15:22). Therefore, no amount of excellent music, dancing, praising, signs and wonders, or even awesome healings can replace individual repentance and the reverent fear of the Lord. Without repentance, no salvation is possible. And without salvation, what is there to shout about? Even a healing, as awesome as it is, will not help the person eternally, unless the healing is followed by, or preceded by, a heartfelt, lifelong commitment to walk in holiness with the Lord Yeshua the Messiah.

The primary message preached by both John the Baptist and Yeshua the Messiah was *"Repent, for the kingdom of God is at hand"* (see Matt. 3:1-3; Mark 1:14-15). The Lord's message was all about repentance, which meant **turning completely away from one's sinful life and purposing to walk uprightly and in the fear of the Lord for the rest of one's life.** While preaching repentance, the Lord Yeshua continually exercised the mighty healing power of His Father, healing all who came to Him. He did this to show the Father's love and compassion for His afflicted children. He looked at Israel with compassion, as *"harassed and helpless, like sheep without a shepherd"* (see Matt. 9:36).

True revival will include unprecedented miracles of God, but the focus of the people will be the glory of the Lord, not the charisma of leaders, dancers, and musicians. True revival must be accompanied by repentance, weeping, humility, brokenness, and turning from our wicked ways.[4] When the holy cloud of God's presence enters a room, no human pride, flesh, or dignity can stand. Many will be on their faces, as were our forefathers, when the holiness of God covered the Tent of Meeting.

ARE WE READY FOR THIS GENERATION?

What kind of people will come to our meetings, and how will they respond to the preaching of the Word with power? Do you remember how violent and demonic it was on the earth just before the Lord sent the flood to destroy everyone? The Lord Jesus told us that as it was in the days of Noah, so it will be in the days preceding the coming of the Son of Man. This is going to be a messy revival. We are not prepared!

As Neville Johnson and Paul Keith Davis have taught, church leaders conducting services or revival meetings in the coming days will be facing a demonized generation, who will be brought into our meetings by desperate family members, or will come in out of their own desperation. Deformed and crippled people will be carried in on gurneys, and they will expect that someone has the authority to heal these "impossible" cases. What will we do if we are not prepared?

And some will come down the aisle, cursing and spitting, even violent with elders trying to contain them. They will be terribly strong, due to the powerful demons living in them. These people will not be politely, quietly walking up to the altar to receive Jesus as their Lord and Savior. Someone in leadership needs to be prepared to deal with these people, as demonic behaviors that we thought were only seen in third-world countries begin to manifest in the dignified western churches (see Rev. 12:12).

We have already received a report from a pastor in another nation whose church experienced a mighty visitation of the Lord within the last few months. He was overjoyed at the healings, salvations, and deliverances that the people experienced that night. He reported that at the end of the service, they carried away three large trash bags of vomit and wet tissues. People who are being delivered of demons often vomit. It can really ruin a church meeting, unless you care more about their eternal souls than your clothes. To whom will the Lord trust such authority, and who will be able to deal fearlessly with these cases?

*Then some of the itinerant Jewish exorcists took it upon them-
selves to call the name of the Lord Jesus over those who had evil
spirits, saying, "We exorcise you by the Jesus whom Paul preach-
es." Also there were seven sons of Sceva, a Jewish chief priest,
who did so. **And the evil spirit answered and said, "Jesus I
know, and Paul I know; but who are you?"** Then the man in
whom the evil spirit was leaped on them, overpowered them,
and prevailed against them, so that **they fled out of that house
naked and wounded.** This became known both to all Jews and
Greeks dwelling in Ephesus; and **fear fell on them all, and the
name of the Lord Jesus was magnified*** (Acts 19:13-17).

We can fool people about our level of true spiritual authority, but can
we fool the demons? They know who has the real walk and who does not,
as illustrated by this terrible case of Sceva's sons. Bluff and bluster will not
prevail against evil spirits; only those believers who are walking in obedience,
yieldedness, humility, and holiness, will have the genuine authority to cast
these things out without getting beaten up.

This kind of authority will only be granted to those who have prepared
themselves for this moment in history by walking in the fear of the Lord, in
holiness, intimacy, and the knowledge of His Word as a weapon.

The Lord will bring in the greatest harvest of souls ever seen on the earth
before He returns. It is not acceptable to the Lord for billions of souls who
have never heard the name of Jesus or experienced His love to be eternally
condemned.

He will use his end-time Bride to bring in this massive harvest. However, the Bride must make herself ready by purifying herself for the Bridegroom's soon return (see Rev. 19:7-8). The corporate Bride of Messiah is
a warrior-bride. She is a fierce, resolute army of Special Forces, each one
precisely trained in spiritual warfare. These overcomers will know their spiritual authority. They will train, disciple, clean up, heal, deliver, and send off

these new believers out to the nations, to scoop up more souls for the King's Wedding Banquet, which must be full.

What Does False Revival Look Like?

I'd like to share a true testimony, because it illustrates the dangers of deception facing sincere and open believers who want to experience more of the Lord. This incident occurred to a family I interviewed whose names, as well as the identity of the church and pastor, have been changed. Alex and Bryn are a young couple who are hungry for the manifest presence of the Lord and have sacrificed time and money to attend conferences where respected prophets are speaking in various regions of the United States, as well as in Israel.

Several years ago, a prophetic conference was held by a church called Zion Fellowship, under Pastor Dennis and his wife, Linda. The church had invited three prophetic speakers that Alex and Bryn appreciated, and one in particular was of the highest caliber.

They had visited this church a month earlier to see a more local prophetic speaker. During this meeting, Linda had prayed for Bryn. While praying and prophesying over her, Linda's actions were controlling and manipulative. She pushed on Bryn's forehead as she prayed, trying to push her down. Alex was appalled to see his wife valiantly bracing her legs to resist being pushed over. They both knew this was not the Lord's way, even though Linda's prayers were accurate. Soon after, a friend warned Bryn that this church had problems, but she did not explain exactly what was wrong there.

Sensuality

One month later, Alex and Bryn went to the conference. Although the worship songs were scriptural, the actions of the people in the congregation were contrary to the words being sung. Alex and Bryn sensed a sensual spirit in certain individuals in the church. Some of the women were moving their bodies provocatively, which was confusing and even disgusting to Bryn. She was also very upset to learn that the main prophetic speaker she had come to hear was hospitalized with severe illness and could not attend. There were two other men of God scheduled to speak.

Alex noticed that during the worship, Pastor Dennis seemed to stand apart with a stoic expression. Then, one after another, teenage girls and young women would approach him to receive a very long embrace. Alex saw that the pastor's wife was never with him, and he felt uncomfortable watching these long hugs during worship. This happened in every worship session, and Alex told me that he sensed a spirit of polygamy or lust, as you might find in a cultic church.

One of the guest speakers got up to preach that first night, but he was also very ill and could not remain up on the platform. Pastor Dennis came up and said, "Let's pray for him."

Bryn observed Dennis's public mannerisms, and she later told me, "This pastor had a bizarre demeanor. He was a cool guy, in-control, no worries, and dressed in black leather. And every time I looked at him, he was cradling a teenage girl in his bosom, while his wife was somewhere else."

Bryn continued her story. "Each time we were in worship, it got worse. They were singing holy songs, but there were women who were gyrating their hips, and some were dancing up front. Another woman cried out with high-pitched sighs of pleasure, and I felt very uncomfortable. One girl was wearing a tank top and was dancing the way someone would dance in a bar. I was trying hard not to judge her, and I didn't know if what she was doing was wrong. I kept praying, 'Lord, help me not to judge.'

"She would sachet across the front of the church, thrusting her upper body aggressively forward like a prowling lion. Then she would do karate warfare, jumping with her legs apart and chopping the air in an oriental militant stance. She was the center of attention. How could any man in the room worship the beauty of Jesus while watching this display?"

Bryn shut her eyes and tried not to watch and not to judge. She had never experienced a church with this type of hyper-charismatic activity. She was terribly confused, because she didn't feel it was from the Lord, but was afraid of being judgmental. Since all three of the invited speakers were godly prophetic men, Bryn assumed that this must be a good, solid church.

As the conference progressed, Alex and Bryn would deliberately come in late, hoping to miss the worship. Unfortunately, it went on for up to two hours, and there wasn't much time left for the preaching. At times, they sat in the lobby, waiting for it to end.

The Presence of the Lord Came!

During the Friday night session, one of the prophets gave an excellent, godly message. After he finished, he invited the people to stand up to receive the Lord's presence or to be healed. Bryn was hungry for more of the Lord and stood up. The Spirit of the Lord came upon her heavily, with sensations of weightiness, numbness, tingling, and heat. Unlike her feelings of fear and confusion during the worship, Bryn knew this was the real presence of the Lord. She saw light and glory in the room, and her body trembled. When Bryn looked up, she saw the Lord Jesus in a billowing, white flowing robe over the congregation, and could smell His beautiful fragrance. This was the first time she had smelled a supernatural fragrance or felt the Lord's manifest presence in a room. Although the conference had counterfeit elements, Bryn believes that there was a genuine anointing on this guest speaker. The Lord was vindicating His servant and bringing His glory to those in the room who were sincerely seeking Him.

On the last day, the sensual worship stretched on for so long, that the speaker's time was used up. Bryn walked up and asked the scheduled speaker when he was going to preach.

He answered, "It's up to Dennis. You really have to ask him."

Bryn asked Pastor Dennis if anyone would be preaching that morning. He smiled and said, "Well, he was supposed to, but we're just letting the Spirit lead."

Bryn and Alex left the church.

FALLING AWAY

Although this conference only lasted three days, it had a devastating effect on Bryn's relationship with the Lord. When she returned home the next day and tried to pray, she felt a strange and lost feeling, as if she could fall away from the Lord. She wondered why the two respected prophets did not correct the pastor, and didn't know if she was being judgmental or discerning wrongly.

Bryn was very confused as she tried to sort out the Lord's feelings about the atmosphere of sensual worship. And yet His presence had come strongly. Did He approve of this conference or not? She told me, "If the Lord approved of that, and if that was His manifestation, I wanted nothing to do with Him. I was petrified that I was standing on the brink of falling away from the Lord, losing my salvation, or throwing it away. This event was so horrible, and it was contrary to what I thought I knew of the Lord before this event."

Bryn waited in the Lord's presence and read the Psalms. She sensed that the Lord had allowed her to attend this conference and experience these feelings so that her trust in His character would go deeper than what she felt in a given atmosphere. She knew that a time would come when she would not be able to feel Him, but would have to trust in the Lord's goodness. Despite her prayer time, she felt ill and depressed, though Bryn did not yet realize that she had been defiled.

Later that day, Bryn purposed to spend time with the Lord, worshiping and dancing before Him. Then she made a decision to wait on Him in stillness, although she did not desire to do this. Bryn waited in stillness for 40 minutes, but nothing happened. She had felt close to the Lord prior to this conference and hated feeling so far from Him. Bryn was about to give up and said to herself, "This is stupid."

The Lord answered, "*Don't! You are about to have a breakthrough.*"

She waited another five minutes and began to feel His glory. He told her to kneel and lift her hands to Him. Bryn told me, "My hands started to shake, and then the shaking moved down through my arms, and I kept asking the Lord for more. Then my whole upper body was violently shaking. The Lord knew that I wanted to be sure this was of Him. So He said, "*This is My glory over you, and it causes you to tremble before Me. It is only a little bit of My glory, but it causes you to tremble.*"

She continued, "Then I felt like I was going to fall over, and I did. I just lay on my side on the floor, my whole body trembling in the glory of the Lord's manifest presence. Then it left, and I just lay there. I thought, *I am so glad that no one is at home to see me shaking; they'd think I was crazy.*"

Then the Lord said, "*Does this offend you?*"

She told Him it did offend her, because of how it would look to others.

The Lord said, "*Why shouldn't you shake and tremble in My Presence?*"

Bryn remembered that she had said previously, "Lord, I could never be offended by You."

It is ironic that Bryn's terrible experience at this counterfeit church actually caused the Lord to take her to a new level of His true presence. She continued to feel the physical manifestations of the Lord's presence every day, and yet she remained depressed for the next week and couldn't shake this terrible feeling.

How could that conflicting experience lead to the genuine presence of the Lord coming to her? Why would He show up at a church service full of strange fire? Was this His seal of approval on the whole meeting? Why did the genuine prophetic guests just sit there in the midst of this carnal chaos, even when their speaking time was not guarded or honored?

THE DIFFICULT TRUTH OF THE MATTER

On the following Sunday at Bryn's regular church, she went up for prayer and told her pastor's wife all that had happened. She felt darkness, confusion, and depression, as well as having headaches and sickness. The worship songs from that conference were playing in her head, and they carried her back into bad memories and torment of spirit.

The pastor and his wife were well-acquainted with damaged people who had come out of that church and shared with Bryn that immorality was going on there. It was a counterfeit charismatic church, lacking in godliness, holiness, and righteous leadership. She received prayer for cleansing and healing, which broke her free from all that had damaged her over those three days. The pastor's wife prayed that Bryn would be able to enter into real intimacy again with the Father and Yeshua.

The next morning, Bryn asked the Lord if the heavy glory she had experienced at the conference on the previous Friday night was His manifestation, or if it was the counterfeit. The Lord told her that on that one occasion, He had allowed His genuine presence to come over her. During the remainder of the conference, He had allowed her to feel the confusion. However, the Lord had given her discernment to know that it was not of Him. *It was impure, unholy, and manipulated.*

The next day, Bryn's earnest desire and joy for Yeshua had returned. She knew that after her pastor's wife had shed light on the situation and had prayed for her, the demonic oppression left. She took communion and felt completely free.

Then the Lord Yeshua spoke to her: *"You and Alex have passed the test, and it was a big one."* He had a big smile on His face. *"You have to understand the difference between the counterfeit and demonic activity, and truth."*

Bryn cried and told Him, "That was so scary and so hard."

He became serious, hugged her, and said, *"I know. You have to be able to discern and fight for Me in the midst, not giving up on Me and My goodness."*

The Lord told her that satan is no match for Him or His angelic hosts, but is mighty to us humans, and can defeat us easily if we are not grounded and rooted in Christ.

She told the Lord that she knew what it felt like to almost fall away.

Jesus told her, *"It wasn't that you didn't want more of Me, because what you were experiencing wasn't Me."*

He knew that Bryn had hated the demonic feelings, because she knew what a holy atmosphere felt like. The Lord said that He loved the way she continually cried out for more of Him, and for understanding. The Lord confirmed that it was His presence overtaking her on that Friday night.

He said, *"There can be demonic activity all around, but for those seeking Me, I can show up. I have no boundaries. I can come even into that kind of environment, based on the sincerity and innocence of the worshiper."*

It would be easier to understand if the Lord never showed up in these fleshly churches. What is confusing is the fact that He does make Himself known when some of His children are sincerely worshiping and seeking Him. This might be the only charismatic church they've ever experienced, and they don't yet know that it should not be this way.

Remember Mindy in the previous chapter: DayStar was her first experience in a charismatic church, and she had nothing to compare it to, other than the apparent "dryness" of her father's denomination. That is why both she and Bryn were able to experience the true presence of the Lord, even while being confused by the counterfeit aspects of worship and behavior.

Bryn was only in this church for three days and needed prayer to be cleansed from its destructive effects, which separated her from the Lord. Mindy was at her church for several years, and suffered untold emotional and spiritual damage. However, she now attends a healthy, biblical, and balanced charismatic church and has received much healing.

Bryn needed to understand that although there is a fleshly or demonic manifestation of shaking and dancing, there is also a sanctified expression, where the worshiper might tremble, shout, or dance in a manner pleasing to the Lord. We see examples of this with King David, Isaiah, and with Miriam, the sister of Moses, and the women of Israel.

> On this one I will look: On him who is poor and of a contrite spirit, and **who trembles at My word** (Isaiah 66:2b).

> While he [the mighty angel] was speaking to me, **I stood trembling** (Daniel 10:11b).

> Then Miriam the prophetess, the sister of Aaron, took the timbrel in her hand; and all the women went out after her **with timbrels and with dances** (Exodus 15:20).

> **Then David danced before the Lord** with all his might; and David was wearing a linen ephod. So David and all the house of Israel brought up the ark of the Lord **with shouting and with the sound of the trumpet** (2 Samuel 6:14-15).

The Lord wanted Bryn to understand that satan imitates and counterfeits everything good that He does. That is why He allowed her to experience His power and glory over her, and to tremble before Him. She has seen the counterfeit from satan and is now free to experience the real.

The Lord said, "*This is what I meant when I said, 'test the spirits' in First John 4:1.*"

APPROVAL OR GRACE?

This concept has taken me decades to grasp. We must not mistake the Lord's kindness and grace with His stamp of approval. As we know, the Lord tells us that there will be many who called Him "Lord" and had a miracle-working ministry in His name, but will be cast away from His presence forever.

But if these men were hypocrites, using the Lord's name with great power and yet practicing secret lawlessness, why did the Lord show up at their meetings? Why did He honor their prayers and declarations for healing and miracles, if they were unclean vessels?

The answer is that the Lord was kind and gracious to those of His flock who came to these meetings to receive a touch from Him. He could not bear to stay away, when sincere and innocent believers trusted in this particular healer or revivalist. The Lord loves His people so much that He cannot stay away, even when the leader is far from His heart.

This is why He came to Bryn in the midst of that sensual and counterfeit worship. It was not His seal of approval on the whole meeting; it was His kindness to a sincere worshiper, who did not understand what was happening.

Why do genuine prophetic speakers sit patiently in a service full of carnal chaos? When they do get up to speak, why do they not give the Lord's rebuke to this strange fire?

Genuine prophets of the Lord are humble people, who respect the authority of the pastor who invited them to speak. They would not presume to correct him, since they are guests in his church, over which the Lord has given him authority. This is the primary reason that they sit patiently and endure the terrible worship. But then, when it is time for them to speak, they deliver the true word of the Lord that He placed in their heart for that particular flock. The Lord would want truth spoken into that church, even if they are normally taught falsehood.

There are exceptions to this guest courtesy. There are a few prophetic individuals who are called to be fearless and obedient, to an unusual extent. While they are humble and would not choose to criticize a church where they've been invited, if the Lord specifically tells them to deliver a rebuke, they will do so.

I have heard one of these men of God say, "The Lord Jesus is showing me now that the worship going on here is stinking flesh. It is entertainment and not the beauty of holiness.'" He is not afraid to say this, because he walks in the fear of the Lord and not the fear of man. Then he will deliver exactly what the Lord tells him to say.

If the pastor chooses to repent and change the way they worship, well and good. If he does not, then he has been warned and is without excuse on the Day of Judgment. Someone really needs to warn these leaders that the Lord sees this as strange fire, although they will not wish to hear this. Some of us will never be invited again if we dare to speak the truth!

From my experience, there are many sincere worship teams who truly believe they are offering the Lord a pleasing set of worship songs from a good heart. In my past, I too have led worship or served on a team without entering into the reverent, holy worship that the Lord desires. He came to earth to glorify His Father, and the Father desires to glorify His Son.

It would have shocked me if I had seen the Lord Jesus in a meeting, as one prophet saw Him, with tears running down His bronze cheeks, as He beheld the people's thoughts and attention turned toward the gifted musicians, the pounding rhythms, or the women dancing, *rather than toward His Father.*

True worship is a ministry from the worshiper's heart directly to the Lord, not pleasing entertainment for the audience. The songs should be reverent, and should direct us to the Lord's goodness, His beauty, His sacrifice, and His blood, or they should express how much our hearts yearn for Him. The worshiper should be singing from a passionate heart, and sending up his or her intense adoration straight to the Lord.

BY THEIR FRUIT YOU SHALL KNOW THEM

Just when I was completing the writing of this chapter, the Lord gave me a "power dream." I have not had this unusual type of dream for a long time, and for many months, I have prayed before going to bed that the Lord would visit me in the night in one way or another.

This dream was very simple. It consisted of four different scenes about blueberries. In the first scene, I saw a large cluster of blueberries on several branches from a blueberry bush. These were ripe, normal, attractive blueberries, about 100 berries. They were just clustered on their branches. As I looked at them, I felt the power of the Lord fall on me in my sleep, and I immediately recognized this unique manifestation. I was so happy to feel His strong power again.

The second scene was very similar to the first, except this time, all of the blueberries were very small and hard, green, under ripe, and immature. They were inedible. I felt the power of the Lord even stronger. I heard myself murmur in my sleep, "More." I was telling the Lord I wanted more of His presence, even though it is intense.

In the third scene, I saw similar branches, but they were empty. I saw many green stems attached to the branches, but there was not one berry! Oddly, the branches and empty stems were shaking and vibrating, as if electricity was running through them. I could actually see some kind of energy in the air around these empty branches. I felt a bit uncertain and uneasy as I looked at these vibrating, fruitless branches and saw the aura of energy around them. In my sleep, I felt a very strong power from the Lord cover me again.

Finally, in the fourth scene, I only saw one huge, perfect blueberry. It was not attached to a branch or a stem, nor was it part of a cluster. It was about the size of a cantaloupe, just enormous and desirable, sitting alone. I wanted to eat that beautiful berry so badly! I believe I was still under the Lord's power when I saw that final scene. Then the dream ended.

*Watch out for false prophets. They come to you in sheep's clothing, but inwardly they are ferocious wolves. **By their fruit you will recognize them....**Every good tree bears good fruit, but a bad tree bears bad fruit....Every tree that does not bear good fruit is cut down and thrown into the fire. Thus, by their fruit you will recognize them* (Matthew 7:15-16a, 17, 19-20 NIV).

I believe this dream is about true and false revival, true and false prophets. It is about the quality of the fruit found in various "branches" of the Church, which are experiencing some revival-type manifestations already.

The first branch bore good fruit, 100 berries. This relates to the parable of the sower, where the seed that fell in good soil yielded a crop of 30, 60, or 100 fold. This was a full branch of good fruit, which was pleasing to the Lord (see Matt. 13:18-23).

The second branch was bearing immature, green, inedible fruit. This was bad fruit that couldn't be eaten. It reminded me of a vision given to Jeremiah, where he beheld two baskets of figs.

One basket had very good figs, like those that ripen early; the other basket had very poor figs, so bad they could not be eaten (Jeremiah 24:2 NIV).

The Lord then compared these two baskets of figs to two different groups of His people: those who patiently submitted to His righteous judgments and chastisements, and those who rebelled. This branch that bore bad fruit represents the churches where there is no mature fruit of the Spirit. These churches are full of self-centeredness, human ambition, pride, sensuality, jealousy, competition, and strife.

But the fruit of the Spirit is love, joy, peace, patience, kindness, goodness, faithfulness, gentleness and self-control (Galatians 5:22-23a NIV).

The third branch had no fruit whatsoever. Its naked green stems had nothing to show for themselves. Nevertheless, these branches were lit by strange fire. They were energized by a strange energy that caused them to shake, vibrate, and move to a kind of buzzing in the air. When I saw it vibrating, I felt uneasiness. When Alex and Bryn began to observe the worship in Zion Fellowship, it didn't sit right. They felt uneasy, but were confused as to why this felt so wrong. Churches that offer strange fire will have no fruit, and the Lord tells us that these branches are destined to be burned in the fire if they do not repent.

Finally, I saw a supernaturally large and perfect fruit. It was like a blueberry, and yet no blueberry like this has ever grown on the earth. It reminds me of the "perfect peach," which I wrote about in my last book. This peach produced heavenly ecstasy when I ate it.

The huge blueberry is the taste of the glorious powers of the age to come, which is available on earth to the least believer in this generation. This heavenly fruit is so perfect and desirable that all of the Lord's children will intensely desire to eat of this fruit. This fruit is the Lord's heart for the last generation, that they will experience the full measure of Messiah's character, power, authority, peace, and love. They will have the selfless heart of the Lord, with which to reap the great harvest, for they will have been transformed into His likeness, from glory to glory.

The Lord waited until the end of the chapter to give me this dream. And the final scene was this heavenly fruit, available on earth for the overcomers. He knows that many of His children will experience the fruitless counterfeit movements for a season, with shaking, dancing, and fleshly manifestations in huge meetings, but with no humility, weeping, or repentance from sin; no preaching of the blood of Yeshua; no holiness or fear of the Lord. They will be lit by strange fire, but many will believe this is the true revival we've all been waiting for. The Lord knows that when these hungry believers behold the holy, reverent heavenly fruit He is offering, they will never again be enticed by the fruitless "Woodstock" counterfeit.

It is the fruit of the Tree of Life, which our first parents forfeited. However, our Lord tasted death so that we could taste the fruit of the Tree of Life. He promised it to all those who overcome the deceptions and seductions of Balaam, the presumption of Cain, the prideful rebellion of Korah, and the idolatry of this world's systems. **It is available to us now, to the generation who overcomes the final onslaughts of the evil one. We will pay any price to eat of it.**

> *Remember the height from which you have fallen! ...To him who overcomes, I will give the right to eat from the tree of life, which is in the paradise of God* (Revelation 2:5a,7b NIV).

ENDNOTES

1. Paul Keith Davis, *Angels That Gather* (Foley, AL: Dove Company Publishing, 2007); www.whitedoveministries.org.

2. A teaching on true revival and this summary of past revivals can be heard in an audio teaching by Andrew Strom, entitled, "Repentance in Kansas City"; www.revivalschool.com.

3. This teaching can be found in Paul Keith Davis' book, *Angels That Gather.*

4. Some of these distinctions between true and false revival were inspired by a vision given to Patrick Ersig called "True and False Revival." I am grateful to have read this vision. It can be found at www.mychurch.org and Patrick's ministry can be found at www.jonahproject.org.

Chapter 13

Treading the Winepress

L ET's take a sweeping overview of biblical history and consider this question: What are the three greatest judgments of the Lord we have seen so far on the earth?

The first great judgment was the flood, where all mankind was destroyed, apart from Noah and seven members of his immediate family. Why did the Lord need to bring this terrible judgment on the earth He loved?

> *The Lord saw how great man's wickedness on the earth had become, and that **every inclination of the thoughts of his heart was only evil all the time**. The Lord was grieved that he had made man on the earth, and **His heart was filled with pain**.... Now the earth was corrupt in God's sight and was **full of violence** (Genesis 6:5-6, 11 NIV).*

The evil upon the earth reached such a level that the Lord could no longer bear the pain of watching countless murders, rapes, child sacrifice, sadistic abuse of men and animals, and all manner of demonic perversion that was practiced before His eyes.

The second terrible judgment was executed against Egypt when Pharaoh hardened his heart repeatedly, and refused to free the Hebrew slaves after 400 years of bondage. The Lord raised up His servant Moses to prophetically declare nine limited judgments upon Egypt and its gods. Finally, Moses declared the final judgment over Pharaoh and his nation, a judgment so terrible that he would finally acknowledge the Lord and free the Israelites. Every firstborn in Egypt died by plague in the same hour, and this judgment produced freedom for the Lord's covenant people.

In doing so, the Lord was not only punishing wicked men, but was also executing judgment on the gods of Egypt (see Num. 33:4). *The Lord required Moses to act in agreement and alignment with each judgment He was about to execute.* Moses was in agreement with the Lord, and he prophesied the judgments before they came to pass.

The third great judgment was the Lord Yeshua's work on the cross. In His earthly life, He overcame every sinful temptation that the enemy hurled at Him. He overcame the lust of the flesh, the covetousness of this world's prizes, and the boastful pride of life. He walked in humility and obedience to the Father's will. In going all the way to the cross as a sinless Son of mankind, He overcame death and the power of hell to possess the souls of mankind.

Yeshua told His disciples that after He departed, the Holy Spirit would convict the world of judgment, because the ruler of this world is judged (see John 16:11). You see, if the Lord Yeshua had given in to temptation to use God's power for His own purposes, such as turning stones into bread, although the Father had not told Him to do so, then the Father could not have righteously judged satan. By running His race without sin, all the way to the cross, the Son of Man proved satan guilty.

The first Adam fell, and there was no way for God to forgive mankind without also forgiving satan, since they were both guilty of essentially the same sin. But when the last Adam (the Lord Jesus) overcame, a legal way was provided to redeem the human race. Thus, satan cannot accuse God of having a double standard, since a sinless man paid the full price for humanity's sins legally.

Since satan is judged (and is currently awaiting this certain judgment), those who follow him will also be judged and will share his fate in the lake of fire. The Holy Spirit convicts the world of this judgment; He continually reminds the people on earth that to follow this fallen angel is disastrous, since *he has already received his sentence for eternity.*

MOSES, ELIJAH, AND THE LORD YESHUA

The enemy is judged, and yet he still roams the earth and brings terrible suffering upon the Lord's children. He has been disarmed and sentenced by Yeshua's victory over sin and death. However, the Lord has granted him limited time and power to harm, entice, and plunder the race of men, which he hates with a spiteful and jealous hatred. He carries a particular hatred for the Jewish people, because they must play an integral role in Jesus' soon return to establish His reign on earth, and to imprison satan (see Matt. 23:37-39). The enemy is aware of his dismal future in the abyss for a thousand years, and then in the lake of fire. However, he has not been sent to either of these places of punishment yet (see Rev. 20:1-3, 10).

In his damnable rebellion, he is planning the worst onslaught against the people of God ever seen. He will use a number of evil men, two in particular, to exercise his dominion over the earth and its inhabitants for one last display of his authority over those who are not written in the Lamb's Book of Life (see Rev. 13). His earthly puppets will torment and seek to destroy the Lord's people, both Jews and true Christians.

This demonized potentate and his false prophet will be worse than Pharaoh, Hitler, and Haman combined. Paul tells us plainly that the Day of the Lord will not come until this lawless ruler is revealed. Therefore, the believers will still be here on earth when this evil man is revealed (see 2 Thess. 2:1-4).

How will the sons of the Kingdom respond to the blasphemous reign of antichrist and his false prophet? We need only to look at what Moses and Elijah did, when confronting the early antichrists of their day. How did Moses respond to Pharaoh? How did Elijah respond to Ahab and Jezebel? Moses prophesied the Lord's righteous judgments over Egypt, the gentile empire that defied the will of God. Elijah prophesied the Lord's judgments over Ahab and Jezebel, the leaders of the false prophets of Israel, condemning them for their murder and idolatry.

> *Thus says the Lord: In the place where the dogs licked the blood of Naboth, dogs shall lick your blood, even yours....And concerning Jezebel the Lord also spoke, saying, "The dogs shall eat Jezebel by the wall of Jezreel"* (1 Kings 21:19b, 23).

Aren't these two men the two witnesses who appeared on the Mount of Transfiguration, communing with Yeshua and His sleepy disciples? Aren't these two men the two witnesses who represent the Law and the Prophets, which testified of the first coming of Messiah? Indeed they are, and they will testify one more time during the antichrist's final onslaught against the Lord's faithful people (see Rev. 11:1-12). These two witnesses will judge the earth with some of the identical signs and wonders that they did in their original ministries, which included withholding rain and turning the waters into blood. And they will not be the only ones on earth prophesying judgment over this beast system and its followers.

Judgments Are Always Redemptive

Before we see how the Lord, His angels, and the saints will respond to the lawless one and his followers, let us first grasp a fundamental aspect of God's character: *everything He does is motivated by love.* He cannot think evil thoughts, for God is love. He even loves His enemies, or He would not command us to love our enemies. Therefore, even when the Lord sends judgments on the earth, it is not for the purpose of destroying life, but for the purpose of redeeming and saving lives. Let's look at four Scriptures, two from the Old Testament and two from the New, which prove this point.

> *For when Your judgments are in the earth,* **the inhabitants of the world will learn righteousness** (Isaiah 26:9b).

> *Oh my God, make them like the whirling dust, like the chaff before the wind!...Fill their faces with shame,* **that they may seek Your name, O Lord**...*Yes, let them be put to shame and perish,* **that they may know that You, whose name alone is the Lord, are the Most High over all the earth** (Psalm 83:13,16, 17b-18).

> *Of whom are Hymenaeus and Alexander, whom I delivered to Satan* **that they may learn not to blaspheme** (1 Timothy 1:20).

> *And men were scorched with great heat, and they blasphemed the name of God who has power over these plagues; and* **they did not repent and give Him glory** (Revelation 16:9).

From these four examples, we see that even when people are subjected to judgments, the Lord's intention is that they will *repent, give glory to God, learn righteousness, and cease to blaspheme.* This is the Lord's only motivation, to bring people to Himself. He takes no pleasure in the death of the wicked, and would rather that they turn from their wicked ways and live. The Lord feels great pain in His heart when He has to send disasters (see Ezek. 33:11; Gen. 6:6). Now that this critical point has been proven, let us look at the prophetic role of the saints in the end-times judgments of the Lord.

THE LORD IS JUST IN HIS JUDGMENTS

It is important to the Lord that we do not misunderstand His character when we begin to see ever-increasing judgments poured out upon wicked nations, which, sadly, will include our own. Therefore, in every case where He judges, there are always witnesses in Heaven and on earth declaring that He is righteous to pour out these judgments. This occurs in many places in Scripture, but I will just provide two examples.

> *When He opened the fifth seal, I saw under the altar the souls of those who had been slain for the word of God and for the testimony which they held. And they cried with a loud voice, saying, "How long, O Lord, holy and true, until You judge and avenge our blood on those who dwell on the earth?"* (Revelation 6:9-10)

And the Lord responds to their demand for justice this way:

> *Then a white robe was given to each of them; and it was said to them that they should **rest a little while longer**, until both the number of their fellow servants and their brethren, who would be killed as they were, was completed* (Revelation 6:11).

The Lord does not say that their demand is inappropriate or unloving. Rather, He merely tells them to wait for the cup of the martyrs' blood to be full, and then He will be fully justified in His righteous judgments. As we saw in the parable of the wheat and the tares, and as we also see in Genesis 15:16, regarding the sin of the Amorites, the Lord chooses to let evil rise to its full measure before pronouncing irrevocable judgment.

The final judgments are poured out on the unrepentant in the final chapters of Revelation. As this wrath is poured out, the saints in Heaven, the angels, and a voice from the altar all testify that the Lord is righteous to punish those who hate Him. If Heaven is declaring God's goodness, surely the saints on earth will also be praying in agreement with Heaven, concerning the Lord's justice.

> **Just and true are Your ways,** O King of the saints!...For all nations shall come and worship before You, for Your judgments have been manifested.....**You are righteous,** O Lord...because You have judged these things. For **they have shed the blood of saints** and prophets, and You have given them blood to drink, for **it is their just due**...Even so, Lord God Almighty, true and righteous are Your judgments (Revelation 15:3b,4b; 16:5b-6, 7b).

Isaiah also provides a surprising example of the saints on earth praising the Lord during a time of devastating judgments. The first half of chapter 24 describes desolation, famine, and bloodshed. There are believers on the earth, and they are singing of God's glory in the midst of this wrath. This should give us great hope that the Lord will not sweep away the righteous with the wicked (see also Ps. 91 for this promise of protection).

> They raise their voices, they shout for joy; from the west they acclaim the Lord's majesty. From the ends of the earth we hear singing: "Glory to the Righteous One" (Isaiah 24:14,16 NIV).

THE RETURN OF THE LORD

Later, Isaiah sees a vision of the returning King, marching from Edom and trampling the grapes of His wrath on the way to Jerusalem. Isaiah notices that this glorious One's garments are stained red, and he questions Him.

> Why is Your apparel red, and Your garments like one who treads in the winepress?...I have trodden them in My anger, and trampled them in My fury; their blood is sprinkled upon My garments, and I have stained all My robes. For the **day of**

*vengeance is in My heart, and the **year of My redeemed** has come* (Isaiah 63:2, 3b-4).

Notice that the very day of vengeance is also the year of the redeemed. In other words, the Lord needs to trample the wicked in order to redeem His captive and tormented people from beastly persecutions. As with Moses, the judgment on Egypt produced freedom and redemption for the Lord's beloved children! And as with Elijah, the judgment on the false prophets produced spiritual freedom for Israel.

This passage in Isaiah 63 is a description of the same historical event that is described in Revelation 19:11-21 and in Zechariah 14:2-4. *That event is the return of the Lord Jesus Christ to make war on the beast and to defend Jerusalem.*

> *I saw heaven standing open and there before me was a white horse, whose rider is called Faithful and True. **With justice He judges and makes war....** He is dressed in a robe dipped in blood, and His name is the Word of God. **The armies of heaven were following Him,** riding on white horses and dressed in fine linen, white and clean. Out of His mouth comes a sharp sword with which to strike down the nations. He will rule them with an iron scepter. **He treads the winepress of the fury of the wrath of God Almighty*** (Revelation 19:11, 13-15 NIV).

From this passage, we see that we will participate with the Lord in these judgments. This passage also includes a verse from Psalm 2, where the Father tells His Son that He will inherit the ends of the earth, rule the nations with an iron scepter, and dash them to pieces like a potter's vessel.

Not only will the Son strike down the nations, but the Son promises us that if we overcome, He will grant us this same authority over the nations (see Rev. 2:26-27). *It is amazing that the same nation-breaking authority which the Father gave to the Son in Psalm 2, the Son then gives to His overcoming people in Revelation 2.* This is because the overcoming saints are riding with their Captain as He makes war with His enemies.

On the day of vengeance, the saints will agree and participate with God's judgments on the nations and armies who hate the Lord and His Jewish brethren, and will not repent. This bloodstained march toward Jerusalem from the eastern side of the Jordan, seen in these and other prophetic passages, will physically destroy the forces of antichrist and will rescue the survivors and captives who remain in Israel.

THE END OF THE AGE OF THE GENTILES

I would like to provide some insight as to the mind of the Lord Jesus, concerning the way the nations have treated His Jewish people. This will help us understand His anger, as He finally rides to Jerusalem to make war in defense of His people and His holy city.

My friend David Michael has written an article that is astonishing in its prophetic content and insight, regarding this matter. This article was the result of a personal encounter he had with the Lord Jesus in 1969. Here is a very brief excerpt from this article, and I recommend that you read it in its entirety:[1]

> Why is God growing so impatient with the nations, that the harvest must be speeded up? The answer may shock you, but I saw it expressed visibly by the expression on the face of the Lord Jesus Christ! I saw a look of terrible hurt and utter grief, total disgust and a stern, burning anger with the Gentile nations because of the Holocaust. His lips were not speaking, but He was thinking so loud that it was **frightening** to behold. He was essentially communicating to me the following thoughts and impressions:

How can the nations behave so disgustingly! If they are going to behave like Devils, savagely butchering my brethren whose blessings have been long delayed for the sake of these Gentiles, I will HASTEN the end of the period of grace upon the Gentiles, and turn now to Israel with comfort and favor.

I also saw a frightening, horrified look in His eyes, which, in a slow, deliberate, steady, angered look of resolve, portrayed the following concept:

They will pay for this. They'll pay a price so heavy that they are incapable of bearing it. They will see a side of Me they never knew existed. They will be shocked to see the One they imagined to be a distant, historical figure from the ancient past emerge to violently shake and crush the offending peoples.

The Lord also showed David how He had felt in 1945 to 1948, as the world was realizing the unimaginable scope of the Holocaust, as the Lord's own people were being murdered:

And even then, in the late 1940s He had an intense yearning for His Jewish brethren, and He wanted at that time to rain destructive and fierce punishments on those nations, and simultaneously take the people of Israel to His bosom, and comfort them, and dry every tear, but He couldn't do all that throughout the entire world as it existed during the time of 1945 and shortly beyond. Do you know why? It was because the harvest was not anywhere near completion! Hundreds of millions of souls were not yet reached. Nations were not yet reached. The Church by and large had been neglectful of its duties to get the Gospel to every person on earth. And I actually saw the resolution on the face of the Lord Jesus, which was sufficient to portray these thoughts.

All right. It will have to wait a short period for the ingathering of Gentiles. But, I will make it wind up very shortly. This evil deed of theirs is going to shorten their time of hope.

God is hastening the end because of His anger and grief over the centuries-long and increasingly murderous and insane raging behavior of Gentiles against the Jewish people, who are His own nation.

HE WILL PROVIDE FOR HIS OWN

When we feel fearful about end-times judgments, it is helpful to see how the Lord took care of those who loved Him during past biblical judgments. This boosts our faith and courage that we will not be forsaken during these times, if we have truly loved the Lord more than the things of this world, and have walked humbly and sincerely with Him to the best of our ability.

During Elijah's generation, my people Israel were under severe redemptive judgments for their harlotry, child-sacrifice, and corruption. The prophet Elijah decreed that Israel would receive no rain for three-and-a-half years. Once again, the Lord pronounced His judgments through His servants, the prophets. It is the same today.

But wouldn't the drought and famine affect Elijah, too? Didn't he have to eat and drink, just like everyone else? Why was he not afraid to decree a judgment that would touch his life as well?

Elijah's obedience to the Lord was greater than his concerns for his own life and comforts. But while Israelis were dying of thirst and hunger in their thousands, the Lord hid Elijah by a little brook on the eastern side of the Jordan. This brook should have been dry, but for three years, he drank out of that brook. And the Lord commanded a flock of ravens to bring him meat every morning and every evening and to bring him bread as well!

When the wicked king of Israel saw the drought, he blamed the prophet, since he was the one who had decreed it. Ahab said, "You troubler of Israel, you brought this trouble upon us by speaking it!"

Elijah answered, "*I am not the one who troubled Israel. You brought trouble on Israel by leading them into sinful practices. I just announced the righteous judgments of the Lord*" (see 1 Kings 17–18).

It will be the same with true prophets of the Lord in these last days. They will speak the Lord's judgments upon their wicked nations, and when the disasters come to pass, the people will blame the one who spoke it. They will not realize that the man or woman is simply speaking what the Spirit of God has told him to declare. Don't shoot the messenger!

Somehow, the believers are going to be seen as the scapegoat of society's ills when the Lord's righteous judgments fall. This will resemble the way that Hitler blamed the Jews for Germany's woes, finding it helpful to have a scapegoat. However, those of us who live in a democracy are all responsible for allowing ourselves, our laws, and our elected leaders to carry our society into harlotry, idolatry, and the shedding of innocent blood.

Despite the famine, Elijah had food and water when others were starving. This shows us that the Lord knows how to provide for His own ones. The Lord wants us to lean solely on Him for financial provision. Why will the final test of allegiance be an economic mark, without which no one will be able to buy or sell? This mark is to test our hearts and our loyalties, because most of us are dependent on the financial systems of this world.

DO NOT RECEIVE THE MARK OF THE BEAST!

When the day comes that we can't buy and sell, who will we rely on as our source? Can we be utterly dependent on God, as Elijah was? Will we ask Him to show us the brook with water, and to send us bread from the beaks of birds or the hands of angels? I know a man who was required to evangelize a people group in the remote mountains of Tibet, walking for days at a time without a restaurant or civilization in sight. This man was fed all of his meals supernaturally for many days, until he finally arrived in the next village. This shouldn't surprise us—the Lord is the same God as the God of Elijah, and He never changes! Our theology may change, but the Living God does not change.

The Bible says that we won't be able to buy or sell without this mark (see Rev. 13:15-18). When a person agrees to be marked with this mark, whether by laser, ink, or microchip implant, it will signify that his or her allegiance is to the beast and his economic system. Who will your source be on that day?

Make up your mind now that no matter how terrible the pressure, you and your household will not receive this mark. It is better to suffer on this earth than to be separated from the Lord for all eternity.

> *Then they will deliver you up to tribulation and will kill you, and you will be hated by all nations for My name's sake....For then **there will be great tribulation,** such as has not been since the beginning of the world until this time, no, nor ever shall be. And unless those days were shortened, no flesh would be saved; but **for the elect's sake those days will be shortened....Immediately after the tribulation** of those days...the powers of the heavens will be shaken. Then the sign of the Son of Man will appear in heaven...And **He will send His angels** with a great sound of a trumpet, and **they will gather together His elect** from the four winds, from one end of heaven to the other* (Matthew 24:9; 21-22; 29-30a; 31).

WHEN THE RIGHTEOUS BECOME OUTLAWS

When evil men come to power, the laws of the land are changed, and the righteous become outlaws. As it has happened before, it will happen again in our days.

A wicked pharaoh came to power and made a decree that every Hebrew baby boy that was born must be thrown into the Nile River. It was suddenly open season on Jewish male babies (see Exod. 1:22). The parents of Moses defied this evil law and hid their child, for they knew the Lord had a good purpose for him in the future. In our nation, it is open season on unborn babies. They have no legal protection, like the Hebrew babies in Egypt.

Nebuchadnezzar decided to erect a 90-foot statue, either of himself or of one of his gods. It could be seen for miles on the plains of Dura. And he required all of his officials to fall down and worship this image. Whoever would not worship would immediately be thrown into a blazing furnace (see Dan. 3:6). Daniel's three Hebrew friends refused, and suddenly, they were outlaws and sentenced to die. They declared that the God they serve could rescue them from the flames, but if not, they were prepared to die for their God. May our faith be as theirs!

In the empire that followed Babylon, Darius, king of Persia was tricked into changing the law of the land, such that righteous Daniel suddenly became an outlaw, simply by worshiping the same God he had always worshiped (see Dan. 6). Darius' governors were so jealous of Daniel's authority that they enticed the king to make a new law, without explaining exactly who it would impact. In fact, it was cruelly designed to impact only one man: Daniel, the Hebrew.

Daniel was arrested and thrown into the lions' den. The king was grieved at having passed this irrevocable law, which made his righteous advisor an outlaw. As we know, the Lord sent His angel to shut the mouths of the lions, and Daniel's accusers were then put to death. However, Daniel did not know how it would turn out when he disobeyed the king's "new law."

Another Persian king was tricked into signing a new law, which decreed that all the Jews in the Persian Empire would be slaughtered indiscriminately on a particular day. A wicked minister had risen to power under King Xerxes, whose name was Haman. This man demanded that the citizens show great reverence and fear in his presence. Because one Jewish man refused to do so, Haman devised an evil law, condemning to death all Jews in the Persian Empire. The king signed it into law. Suddenly, the Jewish people were marked for annihilation. Although this evil law was irrevocable, through the fasting and prayers of Mordechai and Esther, it was overcome with a law that would save the lives of the Jews in Persia.

You Will See a Distinction

Although we are entering a time when the laws of our land are being changed before our eyes, it is comforting to know that the Lord makes a distinction between the righteous and those who reject Him. As we have seen in the many biblical examples provided, the Lord can protect His own ones, even in the midst of redemptive judgments falling upon a wicked nation. The prophet Ezekiel was shown an angel, who was assigned to place a mark on the repentant and righteous people in Jerusalem. The rest would be judged.

> *Go through the midst of the city…and put a mark on the foreheads of the men who **sigh and cry over all the abominations** that are done within it* (Ezekiel 9:4).

If we have repented on behalf of our wicked nation, and if we have cried out for mercy and righteousness over our land, then the Lord will place a mark of protection upon us. If we have desired His Kingdom more than our own comforts, then the Lord will not sweep us away indiscriminately with those who do not care about the injustices and bloodshed that break the Lord's heart. The prophet Malachi was told that the Lord would spare those who feared Him, as a man spares his own son:

> *Then those who feared the Lord spoke to one another, and the Lord listened and heard them; so a book of remembrance was written before Him for those who fear the Lord and who meditate on His name. "They shall be Mine," says the Lord of hosts, "on the day that I make them My jewels. **And I will spare***

them as a man spares his own son who serves him." Then *you shall again discern between the righteous and the wicked, between one who serves God and one who does not serve Him* (Malachi 3:16-18).

Surely, the Lord will judge the systems of this world. He will return to set up a new world founded on His righteousness and not the idolatrous systems that the world has perpetuated for 6,000 years. Babylon has fallen! Sadly, so has the Lord's Church. As an institution and as individuals, the Church has committed harlotry with the powers, pleasures, entertainments, immorality, and wealth of this world. She has compromised the Lord's standards for her own comforts, ambitions, and the approval of those in high places.

Where do we want to be found when Babylon is judged? Do we want to be in her or out of her when the Lord destroys her with fire in one hour? I believe that anyone who has taken the trouble to read this book knows that we must come out of her, so that we do not share in her plagues.

> *With a mighty voice he shouted: "Fallen! Fallen is Babylon the Great!...For all the nations have drunk of the maddening wine of her adulteries. The kings of the earth committed adultery with her, and the merchants of the earth grew rich from her excessive luxuries. Then I heard another voice from heaven say:* **"Come out of her, My people, so that you will not share in her sins, so that you will not receive any of her plagues;** *for her sins are piled up to heaven, and God has remembered her crimes"* (Revelation 18:2a, 3-5 NIV).

THE BOTTOM LINE

As the Lord Yeshua has lovingly warned His Church,

Remember the height from which you have fallen! Repent and do the things you did at first. If you do not repent, I will come to you and remove your lampstand from its place (Revelation 2:5 NIV).

We must use every moment we have left, as if we have run out of time. We must make up our minds now to streamline our lifestyle and free ourselves of sinful addictions and worldly distractions, even seemingly innocent ones. The night is far spent, and there is no time to entertain ourselves. The Lord is accelerating everything, because the time is so short. We must spend every spare moment we have as if there is no time left.

Determine fiercely to use your time to worship, pray, fast, read your Bible, or share these warnings with others. Listen to the teachers and prophets who preach this urgent end-time message, whom I have cited in these pages and in my other books. Walk in humility, righteousness, and obedience to all that the Lord has asked of you.

Wait in His presence, even if it feels like nothing is happening. He is there, and you must press in with perseverance to get a breakthrough. There is no more delay possible, and it is for this purpose that this book was written. I am writing this warning out of love and concern for the lukewarm Church. Only the Bride who has made herself ready for her Bridegroom will be found worthy to attend the Wedding Supper of the Lamb.

My love goes out to each reader, and I am speaking as a fellow soldier, who is also seeking to please the Lord Yeshua in every matter I have written about. May the grace of the Lord be upon you in this hour. Even so, come quickly, Lord Jesus. Amen!

Endnote

1. David Michael, "This Is the End of the Age of the Gentiles" (July 2001). This article can be found at: www.worldforjesus.org. Go to "Browse Articles" and then to "Prophetic Articles."

Receiving Eternal Salvation

If you have doubts about where your soul stands with God, or have never made a heartfelt decision to accept the salvation and atonement offered by Yeshua's (Jesus Christ's) sacrifice, then this section of the book is written expressly for you.

The God who created the heavens and the earth, as described in the Book of Genesis, calls Himself by numerous titles and names. His covenant Name is the Hebrew Name *YAHVEH*, best translated, "the God who *is* and *exists*, apart from created things." He also calls Himself our Father and our King. He is the God who is called "The Father" in the writings of the New Testament.

The prophet Isaiah tells us that *"all of us like sheep have gone astray; each has turned to his own way"* (see Isa. 53:6). There is not one who has been born on the earth who has not sinned and fallen short of the righteous standards of a pure and holy God.

When the Lord God saw that mankind would be forever cast away from His presence due to our sinful thoughts, words, and deeds, He sent a part of Himself from Heaven's glory to become flesh and blood, exactly like His earthly children. This part of Himself was always His Son, even before the creation of the universe. King David declared that God has a Son in Psalm

2, which was written one-thousand years before Yeshua was born! This man is the only person who has never sinned in thought, word, or deed, out of all who have ever lived.

When this Holy Son was born of a Jewish virgin in Israel and became a human child, His given name was *Yeshua,* which in Hebrew means "Salvation." We translate His name into many tongues, and in English, it is rendered, "Jesus." He will answer to His Name in *any* language!

In the Bible called "the Old Testament," the blood of animals was a necessary sacrifice to cover the sins of the people of Israel. Only blood can atone for sin, according to Leviticus. However, the blood of animals was not of sufficient value to permanently remove sin from us. Therefore, the Son of God offered Himself as a spotless, sinless offering for the guilt of each and every one of us.

The Lord Jesus gave His life voluntarily. It *seems* that others took His life, but it was the Father's will and the Son's agreement to allow this great suffering and death to take place for our sakes. On the third day, He was raised from death to life, and this physical resurrection opened the gates of eternal life to all who follow Him with all of their hearts.

When we die, or when Yeshua returns to take His people and judge the world, we must face the righteous Judge. He has established the scales of eternal justice such that *no one* will be justified apart from the atoning death of His Son, Yeshua. No matter how "good" one's life is, no matter what religious tradition one lives under, both Jew and Gentile will be cast into hell for his or her personal sins unless they are made righteous and perfect by Yeshua's death and blood. *There is no exception to this heavenly decree, other than the death of babies and children who are under the age of accountability.* Therefore, our only hope is to humble ourselves and accept the resurrected Lord Yeshua the Messiah and His death as our personal covering, righteousness, and entrance to Heaven. (*Messiah* means "Anointed One," as does the title *Christ,* taken from the Greek.)

When we pray to the Father to receive the forgiveness and atonement of His Son, the Holy Spirit of God comes to dwell in our spirits, and He never departs from us after this moment. In Hebrew, the Holy Spirit is called the *Ruach ha Kodesh*. He is the part of God who is able to be everywhere at the same time, who searches and knows our hearts at all times, and who counsels and teaches us God's will in our lives. He always glorifies the crucified and risen Lord Yeshua, and always speaks truth that is in perfect agreement with everything written in the Bible, both Old and New Covenants.

When we pray to receive Yeshua, we are also agreeing to lay down our rights, control, and ownership of our lives. We are not "free" to deliberately indulge ourselves in any sinful word, thought, or lifestyle. If He is not Lord of our lives, we have not understood who He is and what He has done. *To receive Yeshua, the cost is our right to govern our own life and destiny.* He has bought us with the price of His own royal blood, and if we want to hold onto our own rights, we cannot truly accept His purchase of our souls with His blood.

Please count the cost before you pray this prayer, because it is very serious business to make Jesus the Lord of your life. Almost all of the biblical writers were martyred for the Lord's sake; it is common in other nations today. However, the reward we will receive in Heaven and the peace we receive on this earth so far outweigh these hardships that they will not be remembered when we see His face, smiling at us with favor and approval.

If you would like to receive the Lord Jesus now, and be absolutely sure that your soul will be accepted as righteous when you face Him very soon, pray the following prayer (or a similar prayer) from the deepest place in your heart:

> *Dear Lord God, Creator of all things, I humble myself before You as a sinful person. I know I have sinned in my thoughts, words, and deeds, and am not worthy to enter Heaven based on my own righteousness or worthiness.*

I know that You have always loved me, and have sent your Son Yeshua (or "Jesus") to die as a substitute for the punishment I deserve. I accept the sacrifice of His sinless blood which He shed for me on the cross as the atonement for my sins. I believe that You raised Him from the dead on the third day, that He now lives in Heaven, and that I will be raised to life because of His victory over death. I ask for Your Holy Spirit to enter and fill me and change my life from this moment. I voluntarily surrender my rights and control of my life and choose to make You Lord of my life and destiny. I want to be with You forever in Heaven, and I know that Yeshua's death and resurrection is the only way I can enter Your Holy Presence.

Thank You for so great a salvation, and the free gift of eternal life. I love you, Lord. In Yeshua's Name I ask this, amen.

If you have sincerely prayed this prayer, you are now a new person, *reborn* in your spirit into His life of holiness, righteousness, and love. Begin to read the Bible every day, both Old and New Testaments; it is especially important to read the gospels of Matthew, Mark, Luke, and John to learn about Yeshua's ministry on earth. Begin to pray to Him every day. Talk to Him as you would talk to a friend, but with much love, reverence, and respect for who He is. Find a church or Messianic congregation where the people *truly* love Yeshua and live in the power of His Holy Spirit. They will help you to grow in your new faith. The Lord will be with you, now and forever. *Never deny Him*, no matter what wicked men say to you or do to you, and you will receive eternal life.

If you have received the Lord Yeshua after reading this book, please write to me at jill@coffeetalkswithmessiah.com, or go to www.sidroth.org for more information.

About Jill Shannon

Jill Shannon is a Messianic Jewish Bible teacher, author, and singer/songwriter. Growing up in a Reform Jewish home, she accepted the Lord in 1973. In the 1980s, Jill and her husband immigrated to Israel, learned Hebrew, and gave birth to three children. During these years in Israel, she endured hardship and received vital lessons, shared in her first book, *Coffee Talks With Messiah: When Intimacy Meets Revelation* (Gazelle Press, 2007). Jill's second book is *A Prophetic Calendar: The Feasts of Israel*, released in 2009 by Destiny Image Publishers.

Jill currently speaks and writes about experiencing God's glory, holy living, and intimate friendship with the Lord, the biblical Feasts, Israel, and the Church. She is also a singer/songwriter, with four worship projects to date: "A Part of Me"; "Beckon Me"; and her two newest releases, "Remember Me" and "I AM the Broken Piece." She resides outside of Philadelphia, Pennsylvania, with her husband. Jill has a married son and daughter-in-law, and two daughters in ministry school.

For more information about Jill's ministry, please visit www.coffeetalkswithmessiah.com.